Distributive Justice

Distributive Justice

Getting What We Deserve from Our Country

Fred Feldman

OXFORD
UNIVERSITY PRESS

OXFORD
UNIVERSITY PRESS

Great Clarendon Street, Oxford, OX2 6DP,
United Kingdom

Oxford University Press is a department of the University of Oxford.
It furthers the University's objective of excellence in research, scholarship,
and education by publishing worldwide. Oxford is a registered trade mark of
Oxford University Press in the UK and in certain other countries

First Edition published in 2016

Published in the United States of America by Oxford University Press
198 Madison Avenue, New York, NY 10016, United States of America

British Library Cataloguing in Publication Data
Data available

Library of Congress Control Number: 2016936263

ISBN 978–0–19–878298–8

Contents

Acknowledgments

I have been thinking for many years about the theory of justice that I present in this book. Many friends, colleagues, and students have offered helpful criticism and suggestions. Perhaps my greatest debt of gratitude is owed to Owen McLeod. I had the pleasure of working closely with McLeod as he wrote his dissertation on this topic back in 1995. In succeeding years we have talked frequently about desert and distributive justice. As I worked out the views I defend in this book, I made extensive use of McLeod's dissertation as well as of his published work. I believe I have learned more about this topic from McLeod than from any other person. I am tremendously grateful to him not only for his criticism and suggestions, but also for his steady friendship and emotional support.

I am also in debt to Kristian Olsen. He provided important critical and editorial help in connection with the production of a paper from which the book emerged. Pete Graham, Casey Knight, Miles Tucker, and others who participated in a seminar I taught during the Spring of 2012 have also been generous and helpful. Knight sent me a remarkably helpful series of emails in which he raised an important question about my characterization of political economic deserts and bases. He forced me to develop a much more complete version of my view. I am also very grateful to Alex Sarch who gave me a detailed critical commentary on an earlier draft of the book together with a number of very helpful suggestions. Although I have not discussed justice with her in several years, I am also grateful to Serena Olsaretti. Her written work has been a steady source of insight and valuable information.

A paper containing the core of the thesis of this book was presented in December of 2012 at the Princeton Workshop in Normative Philosophy, which was sponsored in part by the Princeton University Center for Human Values. I received valuable comments from several participants at that workshop. I especially want to thank Eden Lin, Daniel Wodak, Chris Heathwood, and Melinda Roberts. Although I have not accepted every last suggestion offered by these friends and colleagues, I have been moved to revise and reconsider quite a lot of what I say here in light of discussions with them. I am grateful to all of them for their suggestions and encouragement.

A group of philosophers at New Mexico State University had heard that I was working on a book about justice. They wanted to use the book in their summer reading group. I was delighted and promptly sent them a copy of the manuscript.

Each week during the summer of 2014 members of the group would read a chapter or two; then they would meet for discussion. One member would work up some sort of presentation; the others would come with questions and comments. As I understand it, their meetings would sometimes carry on for a couple of hours. After each meeting, a member would write up a detailed report summarizing the main points of their discussion. That report would then be sent to me. In many cases I responded to the report and there was further follow up. This same procedure carried on until the end of the summer. I received very helpful detailed comments on nearly every section of the book.

Many of the New Mexican suggestions seemed to me to be perceptive. In light of these suggestions, I made a lot of changes in the manuscript. (One of the members of that group is evidently a stickler for proper spelling, grammar, and word choice. He gave me long lists of blunders that he found in the manuscript. Most of those suggestions were accepted and revisions were made in accord with the suggestions. I learned a lot about the proper placement of commas.) The New Mexican group raised many objections concerning content and made many substantive suggestions for improvement. For all their careful and very helpful attention to the manuscript, I thank the New Mexicans: Jean-Paul Vessel, Mark Walker, and Danny Scoccia.

My friend and former colleague Brad Skow has written extensively on the concept of desert. In several cases he has generously offered to untangle some confused things that I was struggling to say. He has extraordinarily keen insight into the mathematical details of some theories about desert. I am very grateful to him for his friendship, encouragement, and patience. Brad and I co-authored an article on "Desert" that appears in the *Stanford Encyclopedia of Philosophy*. I am grateful to the editors (especially Ed Zalta) for help with respect to that article, and for permission to make use of some material in that article that overlaps with some passages in this book.

In the midst of a discussion of prioritarianism, a friend encouraged me to get in touch with Theron Pummer. I wrote to Pummer and he generously explained some recent work of which I had been unaware. He also allowed me to see some of his own then-unpublished work. All of my interactions with Pummer turned out to be helpful. I am grateful to him.

I am very grateful to the University of Massachusetts at Amherst for awarding me a Samuel I. Conti Faculty Research Fellowship for the academic year of 2013/2014. The fellowship gave me a full year off from teaching to focus my attention on the writing of this book. I knew and respected Sam Conti; it is a great pleasure to have received the fellowship named in his honor. I am grateful to Shelly Kagan, Peter Vallentyne, Roger Crisp, Brad Skow, and Gustaf Arrhenius for the help and encouragement they provided.

Peter Momtchiloff steadily and efficiently shepherded this book through reviews and revisions. I appreciate his encouragement and helpful suggestions. I am also grateful to several anonymous readers for a multitude of interesting comments. I reply to many of these comments at appropriate places in the text.

Throughout all the years during which I have been working on this book, my wife Lois has been a steady source of support and encouragement. Although she never seemed to have much interest in the details of my work, Lois quietly did an extraordinary job of making sure that our home would be a peaceful place in which I could focus on that work without interruption. I fear that I have not said it often enough, or with enough emphasis; so I will say it now: I am tremendously grateful to Lois. Without her and without our daughter Elizabeth, neither this book nor anything else I have ever written would have been possible.

Fred Feldman

Leyden, Massachusetts
October, 2015

Introduction

My central aim in this book is to present and defend a theory of political economic distributive justice based on the idea that justice is fundamentally a matter of receipt in accord with desert. Any such theory is a form of "desertism about justice." I grant that desertism is old and out of style; I believe that the version that is the focus of this book is new. I think my discussion will show that this form of desertism is worthy of serious consideration.

The motto of desertism—in the words of John Hospers—is this: "justice is getting what one deserves. What could be simpler?"[1] But as Hospers goes on to point out, things are not quite so simple. There are many different views about the items we can deserve. There are many different views about the bases on which we can deserve them. For each combination of deserts and desert bases, we get a different form of desertism. Thus, for example, if we say that where justice is concerned what is deserved is always some level of happiness, and the basis for deserving it is always some level of virtue or vice, we get a form of desertism that says that we have perfect justice when each person is precisely as happy as he or she deserves to be on the basis of his or her virtues and vices. On the other hand, if we say that where justice is concerned what is deserved is always some amount of wealth, and that the basis upon which this is deserved is always some degree of contribution to the common good, then we get a completely different form of desertism according to which we have perfect justice when each person has precisely the amount of wealth that he or she deserves to have on the basis of the magnitude of his or her contribution to the common good. There are many other possibilities—some more worthy of consideration than others; some with greater historical precedent than others. In this book, however, I focus on a version of the theory that seems to me to be most promising as a theory of political economic distributive justice. According to this new version, there is an

[1] Hospers (1961: 433). Hospers says that to explore the issues concerning who deserves what and why is "a sticky business." A page later he refers to these issues as "this maze."

important class of what I call "political economic deserts"; we deserve deserts from this class in virtue of our possession of what I call "political economic desert bases"; and we deserve them from our community. The resulting theory is this: there is perfect political economic distributive justice in a society if and only if in every case in which a member deserves a political economic desert in virtue of his or her possession of a political economic desert base, the community ensures that he or she receives that desert.

My statement of the theory makes use of a number of so-far unexplained terms. Obviously I cannot expect that any reader will understand what I am advocating simply on the basis of an introductory sketch. I hope to make the theory clear in the chapters that follow, and to show that it is not refuted by the anti-desertist arguments that can be found in the relevant literature. I also hope to show that my proposed form of desertism yields more attractive results in the hard cases that cause trouble for other theories about distributive justice.

The argument of the book proceeds in a fairly straightforward way. I start, in Chapter 1, by trying to give the reader some sense of the common subject matter of all theories of distributive justice. I call this "locating the target." I do this in part by sketching several of the most familiar theories of distributive justice. In each case, after citing some philosophers who have defended a theory, I proceed to give what I take to be a fair formulation of the theory. Where it is appropriate, I mention some variant forms. I then point out various ways in which the main theories are in conflict with each other. In each case, I do this by describing a certain situation and then showing how one theory implies that there is perfect justice in that situation, while the other theory implies that there is not. One aim in doing this is to introduce some of the main alternatives to my desertist theory; but my main aim is to help the reader to gain a clearer conception of the target of this enquiry—the kind of distributive justice about which philosophers and political theorists debate. It is the thing at which all these theories are aiming.

Since it is a form of desertism, my theory makes essential use of the concept of desert. Unfortunately, there is considerable skepticism about this central concept. In Chapter 2 I try to show how the concept of desert is a slightly more determinate form of a concept that some may find a bit easier to grasp. That is the concept of *requirement*. I cite the work of Roderick Chisholm, who argued for the foundational significance for moral philosophy of the concept of requirement. After discussing a question about the structure of a typical desert claim, I turn to the vexed question about how desert claims can be justified. I first explain my misgivings about the main familiar views about justification; I conclude by admitting that unless the appeal to requirement is sufficient, I may have to be content with accepting something approximating the autonomy of desert—the notion that there is no other more fundamental normative concept to which we can appeal when trying to justify a desert claim.

Chapter 3 starts with the assumption that we understand well enough what is meant by saying that someone deserves something. I go on to sketch several different ways in which we can make use of this concept in the formulation of a desertist theory of distributive justice. One way of doing it yields a form—I call it "cosmic desertism"—that says that we have perfect justice when everyone receives everything he or she deserves. Given a familiar list of all the different sorts of things that can be deserved (for example, apologies, thank you notes, extra miles on your credit card, good luck, high grades, respect, etc.) the resulting conception of justice is extraordinarily broad. Surely when political philosophers debate the merits of a theory of justice, they are not assuming that the theory will demand timely thank-you notes and personal apologies in the just state. A historically important form of desertism can be found in the writings of Leibniz and others. On this view, what is deserved is always a level of happiness; the basis on which it is deserved is always a level of virtue. Leibniz and others have thought that there is justice in the world if God appropriately distributes this desert to us on this basis in the afterlife. Again, however, it is not likely that political philosophers mean to be debating the merits of this desertism about divine moral-based distributive justice.

John Rawls pretty clearly thought of desertism as the view that there is perfect justice in a state if in every case in which a person deserves some level of happiness in virtue of his or her level of moral virtue, the government ensures that he or she gets that level of happiness. This earthly form of moral distributive justice is similar to the Leibnizian form, except that the deserts are to be distributed by governments and during the lifetimes of the recipients rather than by God in the afterlife. Rawls thought (correctly in my view) that this is a pretty outrageous theory of justice.

Near the end of Chapter 3 I introduce my proposed form of desertism about political economic distributive justice. In this view, the deserts are all political economic deserts, and the desert bases are all political economic desert bases, and the distributor is our community. This is the desertist theory of justice that I defend in this book.

In order to understand the proposed form of desertism we must first have a clear understanding of the items that I am characterizing as political economic deserts and political economic desert bases. In Chapter 4 I offer my characterization of these concepts. I claim that because we are all vulnerable to certain sorts of injury, and furthermore because it is only by joining together in a community that we can find protection against these injuries, we deserve to be embedded in a community that will mount a defense against them. I make a similar claim about our need for certain kinds of opportunity that can be supplied only by collective action. Another main desert arises from certain kinds of legitimate entitlement. In this context, I attempt to explain why we deserve certain political rights. All of these deserts—security, opportunity, entitlement, political rights—have a common foundation: as Aristotle said, we are neither gods nor beasts. We need to live in a community that will provide the context in which we may be able to flourish as human beings. This, I claim, is the most fundamental basis for all the political economic deserts. By the end of Chapter 4, my desertist theory has been stated.

In a short digression following Chapter 4, I present my view about desert of wages.

In the first chapter of the book I briefly mention several prominent theories of distributive justice. Among these are various forms of simple egalitarianism, luck egalitarianism, sufficientism, the difference principle, and libertarianism. I engage in a somewhat more extended comparison of my own view with these opposing views in Chapter 5. My procedure in each case is to review some of the main difficulties for the opposing theory and then to go on to try to demonstrate, as might be expected, that my form of desertism is able to deal with these difficulties easily.

The case of prioritarianism is more complex than the cases involving these other theories of justice. It is not easy to make a head-to-head comparison of prioritarianism and desertism. The crux of the problem is that prioritarianism may not be a theory about distributive justice at all. But if we insist, following current practice, to view it as such a theory, it becomes necessary to engage in a fair amount of speculation and hypothesis and reformulation. I try to explain all of this in Chapter 6. After finally constructing what I take to be a reasonable interpretation of what might be the prioritarian idea about distributive justice, I argue that even in its very restricted range of application, this theory seems to generate unacceptable evaluations of the level of distributive justice in a community. I revisit this matter in Appendix B "Two Helpings of Desert" near the end of the book.

It is sometimes suggested that desertism as a theory of justice was pretty well demolished by John Rawls. In fact he did present a collection of objections directed against a view that he took to be desertism. In Chapter 7, I attempt to extract, explain, and evaluate the most interesting of these Rawlsian objections to desertism. The arguments—in their original form—are sketchy and hard to interpret. I admit that I may have misunderstood the points that Rawls was trying to make. Nevertheless, after doing my best to reconstruct arguments based on the text of *A Theory of Justice* and other Rawlsian works, I admit that some of the arguments might have some relevance to an implausible form of desertism that I characterize (in Chapter 3) as Rawlsian earthly moral desertism about distributive justice. Several of the arguments seem to me to be ineffective even against what I take to be their intended target. A more important point from my perspective is that none of the arguments reveals any defect in the form of desertism that I mean to defend.

Some passages in Aristotle suggest that he thought that justice is a matter of "equal treatment for equals; unequal treatment for unequals."[2] Yet other passages suggest that he thought that justice is a matter of receipt in accord with desert.[3] These seem to be two different conceptions of justice, nowadays identified as *comparative justice* and *noncomparative justice*. The distinction became prominent as a result of an important paper by Joel Feinberg.[4] Since I think that justice is a matter of a certain kind of receipt in accord with a certain kind of desert, my theory of justice is a modern variant of the second, or noncomparative, idea. In Chapter 8 I explain the distinction between the two conceptions of justice and discuss the question whether my noncomparative theory of justice needs to be supplemented with a coordinate principle about comparative justice. I claim that there is no need for supplementation.

In the final chapter I summarize what I take to be the most important contributions I have made in this book and I list some of the puzzles about justice that remain unsolved.

There are two Appendices appended at the end of the book. In these I discuss some topics of slightly more personal concern. In Appendix A I discuss philosophical method. I claim that I have been trying to guide the reader into something like reflective equilibrium with my proposed theory of political economic distributive justice. Some advocates of reflective equilibrium apparently think that if you can get yourself into reflective equilibrium with a theory of justice, you will then be epistemically justified in taking the theory to be true. I do not make any such claim. My position is more modest. I present a catalog of other good things that will come your way if you can manage to get yourself into reflective equilibrium with a theory of justice.

[2] I allude here to the passage in *Politics* III, where Aristotle says "justice is... equality, not however, for all, but only for equals. And inequality is thought to be, and is, justice; neither is this for all, but only for unequals."

[3] This seems to be his idea in Book V of the *Nicomachean Ethics* where he says "everyone agrees that a distribution is just if it distributes to each what he deserves, ... "

[4] Joel Feinberg (1974: 297–338).

In earlier work I have defended a theory under the title "Adjusting Utility for Justice." This is a desertist theory in the normative ethics of behavior. It purports to give an account of morally right action as action that maximizes utility *where the value of each bit of utility is adjusted for desert.* In this book I have defended a theory I call "desertism about political economic distributive justice." As the name indicates, it is a desertist theory about justice. Friends have expressed some puzzlement about the ways in which these views are supposed to be related. Is it just the same view in two different guises? Does the new view replace the old? Or are they two different views on two different topics? I take up these questions in Appendix B. I try to explain why the views are distinct; why the new view cannot be intended to replace the old one; and why they are views about different subject matters. After explaining these answers, I turn in conclusion to a discussion of the ways in which theorizing about the normative ethics of behavior can sometimes be confused with theorizing about distributive justice. I point out some passages that suggest that this confusion can be found in *A Theory of Justice*. I raise similar questions about what Derek Parfit was doing in his work on prioritarianism.

1

Locating the Target

1.1 Distributive Justice as a Virtue of States

Everyone agrees that justice is a profoundly important value. People march and protest to demand it; more than a few have died in its pursuit. Yet when we stop to reflect on what makes for justice, or try to state in a clear way what we mean when we speak of justice, we may be perplexed. I am inclined to think that if you are going to die in defense of some value, it is important for you to have a fairly clear conception of what that value is.

At the outset, it is essential that we clarify the target of this enquiry. "Justice" is used in a variety of different ways. Aristotle mentions that there is a conception of justice according to which it is "virtue entire."[1] If we thought of justice in this broad way, we could say that a just person is one who has all the virtues. But we could use the term "justice" more narrowly to refer to just one among these virtues. Aristotle says that this narrower virtue of justice comes in two forms. There is "retributive justice"—the kind of justice that we take to be a virtue of judges in criminal courts. One who has this virtue is motivated to give out sentences that are neither too lenient nor too severe, but in proportion to the seriousness of the crime. The other is "distributive justice." Aristotle says that this sort of justice "is manifested in distributions of honour or money or the other things that fall to be divided among those who have a share in the constitution."[2]

So we have three forms of justice as it applies to individuals:

1. Individual Justice Broadly Conceived—"Justice entire"; the having of all virtues.
2. Individual Justice Narrowly Conceived—specific virtues.

2a. Individual Retributive Justice—being motivated to hand out criminal punishments that are proportionate to the seriousness of the crime.

[1] Bk 5, Ch. 2 in the *Nicomachean Ethics*.

[2] *Nicomachean Ethics*, Bk 5, Ch. 2.

2b. Individual Distributive Justice—being motivated to distribute honors, money, etc. appropriately.

We can conceive of corresponding forms of justice that are not virtues of individuals, but rather of societies or states. Corresponding to the broad conception of justice for individuals, there is a broad conception of justice that applies to states. A just state, under this conception, would be one that has all the virtues appropriate to states. Perhaps such a state would have features analogous to courage, wisdom, and generosity. Perhaps it would play a great role in world history. Perhaps it would nurture great achievements in the arts and sciences. But corresponding to the narrower conceptions of personal justice, there are also narrower conceptions that apply to states. First would be retributive justice. A state would be outstanding with respect to retributive justice if it regularly enforced criminal penalties that were proportionate to the seriousness of crimes. The other narrow conception of justice is again distributive justice, but in this case as a feature of states rather than as a feature of individuals. It is a feature that states have in virtue of the way in which the benefits and burdens that they are called upon to distribute are distributed within them. Thus we have:

3. Statewide Justice Broadly Conceived—"Justice entire"; the having of all virtues appropriate to states.
4. Statewide Justice Narrowly Conceived—specific virtues.

4a. Statewide Retributive Justice—having a judicial system that hands out criminal punishments that are proportionate to the seriousness of the crime.

4b. Statewide Distributive Justice—having political and economic institutions that ensure that honors, money, etc. are distributed appropriately.

My question in this book concerns (4b)—distributive justice as a virtue of states. Given this focus, we can formulate the central question of the book in this way: under what circumstances does statewide distributive justice obtain in a state?[3] What makes for this sort of justice?

Clearly, this narrow form of distributive justice is not to be confused with "justice entire" as it applies to states. Instead of trying to give an account of all the ways in which a state can be excellent, here we focus on only one central virtue of states. Nor is narrow distributive justice to be confused with such valuable features as democracy, or freedom, or the rule of law. While those may be virtues

[3] I sometimes speak of countries, or societies, or communities. This is just loose talk on my part. I vary the terminology mostly just to avoid tedium.

of states, they are different virtues. A simple thought experiment should make it clear that justice and democracy are two different things: a benevolent monarch might be very keen on justice while being very hostile toward democracy. Perhaps he would think that it would be a very bad idea to put the running of the state into the hands of the people. Maybe he thinks that if given political power, the citizens would put the state on a path toward ruin. But on the other hand, he might consistently think that it is very important that wealth, honors, and other benefits should be distributed justly in his kingdom. He might think that increased levels of democracy would lead to decreased levels of justice. Whether the details of the monarch's thought are correct, his fear is at least coherent; distributive justice and democracy are distinct features of states. Another monarch might think that distributive justice is a good thing, while freedom would inevitably lead to chaos and so is to be avoided. Again, the monarch's thought is coherent. Freedom is one thing; distributive justice is another. The same holds in the case of the rule of law. Clearly, we can imagine a state in which the rule of law is firmly in place, but in which there is a very low level of distributive justice. This could happen, for example, if the laws that are so carefully enforced are not very good laws. My focus here is on distributive justice as a virtue of states, not on these other things.[4]

It is often assumed that there is a certain target concept—justice—and that since ancient times philosophers have offered a variety of substantive theories about that concept. Thus, for example, we might naturally assume that in the *Republic*, Plato presented a detailed account of what, as he saw it, makes for justice in a state. And similarly that in the *Politics* Aristotle undertook a similar project, though he gave a different account of the nature of justice. We might go on to assume that in more recent days, philosophers and others have developed and defended a remarkable variety of views about this same target. If we accept this assumption of a single target, we will undoubtedly conclude that utilitarians, egalitarians, sufficientists, prioritarians, libertarians, advocates of the difference principle, Marxists, and others have all been thinking about the same target, but have maintained different views about it.

However, it is not clear to me that this way of viewing the literature is correct. It is not clear to me that Plato's *Republic*—just to pick one important example—is

[4] Of course there are some connections between justice and these other virtues. According to the view I will defend in this book, if there is a very high level of distributive justice in a country, the citizens will enjoy considerable amounts of freedom and the rule of law will be in place. My point here concerns the concept that is the target of this inquiry. That is the concept of political economic distributive justice; it is not the concept of democracy, or the concept of freedom, or the concept of rule of law. My thanks to Jean-Paul Vessel, Danny Scoccia, and Mark Walker for encouraging me to clarify my view here.

exclusively about distributive justice (as I am understanding the concept). It may be more accurate to say that Plato is trying to give an account of something corresponding to "virtue entire" as this would apply to states. Maybe he was trying to identify all the main factors that help to enhance the overall moral and political excellence of a state—and distributive justice is only one of several such factors. Maybe Plato was trying to describe a state that would be outstanding in the arts and sciences as well as in international affairs. If so, he was aiming to give an account of something that goes well beyond the core of distributive justice.

It is important also to distinguish between my intended target and another attractive feature of states. This other feature might be described as "how well things are going for the citizens, all things considered." It should be clear that the concept of justice in a country is different from this concept of aggregate welfare. If the distinction is not already clear, here is a thought experiment that may help to distinguish my intended target from this other important measure. Imagine two countries, S1 and S2. Suppose that these countries have exactly the same laws and policies concerning the distribution of the benefits and burdens that a state is called upon to distribute. Suppose that the laws and policies concerning distribution are enforced in precisely the same way in the two states. As a result, suppose that the pattern of distribution of these benefits and burdens in S1 is exactly the same as the pattern in S2. Suppose that due to fortunate circumstances, the supply of needed resources is large enough in S1 and S2 so that there is in each case plenty to go around. Though I have not given any details about what pattern of distribution is in place in either country, I trust that the reader will share my sense that the level of distributive justice in S1 is the same as the level of distributive justice in S2. If one is perfectly just, so is the other. If one is sadly lacking in distributive justice, so is the other.

But it is consistent with all this to suppose in addition that the population of S1 is ten times the population of S2. In that case, it could turn out that the total amount of utility enjoyed by the citizens of S1 is ten times as great as the total amount of utility enjoyed by the citizens of S2.

I grant that there is a way in which the situation in S1 would be better than the situation in S2. There is more utility going around. The citizenry of S1 has on balance a greater total amount of welfare than the citizenry of S2. In spite of this difference, it still seems to me that the two imagined countries are on a par when it comes to distributive justice. The ways in which these countries distribute benefits and burdens are indiscernible. The difference between them arises simply because there are more benefits to distribute to the larger population in S1.

The thought experiment is intended to highlight a feature of the concept of distributive justice as it applies to states: where this sort of justice is the only factor we are considering, *size does not matter*. Of course, size may very well matter for many other sorts of evaluation. Maybe a perfectly just small country cannot make as large a contribution in science or art as an equally just huge country; maybe a perfectly just small country cannot play as dramatic a role in international affairs as a perfectly just huge country.

My focus in this book is not on what makes for the all-things-considered moral and political excellence of countries; nor is my focus on total welfare of the citizenry.[5] Rather, my focus is on a concept by appeal to which we evaluate states for the ways in which they distribute the benefits and burdens that they are called upon to distribute to their citizens. As I understand this notion of distributive justice, it remains possible for a state to score well with respect to distributive justice, while at the same time failing to score very well on other state-wide virtues. Perhaps the state does a great job of distributing benefits and burdens to its citizens, but it plays no interesting role in science, or art, or international affairs. The failure to have other state-wide virtues might make the state less attractive all things considered.

In this book, when I speak of "justice" or of "distributive justice" or of "political economic distributive justice" I mean to be speaking of this narrowly conceived virtue of states—the virtue that a state has if it does a good job of distributing the benefits and burdens that it is the business of a state to distribute to its citizens. I think that at least a significant part of the historical debate about justice has been a debate about this same target. In any case, the question I propose to answer in this book is a question about this target. As I go along, I will often assume that others who have written on justice were offering answers to this same question. I defend a version of an old—but now largely abandoned—theory, desertism. According to theories of this sort, the fundamental principle about distributive justice as a virtue of a state is that this sort of justice obtains when the state ensures that its citizens receive the benefits and burdens that they deserve to receive from it.

1.2 Some Alternatives to Desertism

Before I present the view I mean to defend, I want to sketch and briefly comment on some of its main competitors. This may help to give a sense of the logical space

[5] Nor do I mean to focus on average welfare of the citizenry. Upon reflection it should be clear that there could be two states that are alike with respect to average welfare, but seriously different with respect to justice. We need only imagine that a fixed total amount of welfare is fairly distributed in the first state, but unfairly distributed in the second. Averages and totals would be the same; but the levels of justice would be different.

into which my theory of justice fits. It will also provide an opportunity for me to introduce some terminology that I will be using, and to make some general comments about how (as I see it) principles of justice are to be formulated. Later, after I have presented and explained my view, I will come back to these and some other theories of justice. I will try to show that the view I defend is more plausible than any of these other views.

1.2.1 Egalitarianism

The concepts of justice and equality are often tightly linked. In some cases it may even seem that the terms are interchangeable. Imagine a crowd of protesters marching in Washington. Suppose some of them are holding up signs saying "We Demand Justice!" and others are holding up signs saying "We Demand Equality!" It may seem that all the protesters are making fundamentally the same demand. Yet in spite of the linkage, the idea of equality is distinct from the idea of justice. Only a fraction of theories of justice maintain that justice is entirely a matter of equality.

Let us assume that at any moment, any person who exists has a "welfare level." A person's welfare level is not intended to be the same as his net worth. It is not an economic matter at all. Rather, it is a matter of how well he is doing—how well things are going for him. A wealthy person could have a low level of welfare (suppose he suffers from a painful and incurable disease that makes his life miserable); a poor person could have a high level of welfare (suppose he is happy, has a delightful family, and enjoys his job in spite of the low pay). There are many different views about what makes for welfare. Some say it is pleasure; others say it is happiness; yet others mention a plurality of items including such things as health, happiness, loving relationships, accomplishments, etc. In the present context there is no need to choose among these different views about welfare. It suffices to say that each person has a level of welfare.

One very simple form of egalitarianism maintains that justice obtains when welfare is uniformly distributed. In other words:

E1: There is perfect distributive justice in a state, S, if and only if every citizen of S has the same welfare level as every other citizen of S.

A different form of egalitarianism would agree that justice requires equality, but would disagree about the item that must be distributed equally. Suppose we think that justice obtains when wealth is equally distributed. Then we accept this form of egalitarianism:

E2: There is perfect distributive justice in a state, S, if and only if every citizen of S has the same amount of wealth as every other citizen of S.

E1 and E2 differ with respect to what has come to be called "the currency of justice." The currency of justice according to a theory of justice is the item whose proper distribution, according to the theory, is what makes for justice. According to E1, the currency of justice is welfare. According to E2, it is wealth.

Yet another form of egalitarianism presupposes a different currency. On this view, there are certain benefits and burdens that a state is called upon to distribute to its citizens. The benefits might include such things as the right to vote, or access to free healthcare; the burdens might include such things as the obligation to give two years of military service and the need to pay taxes on your income. Justice, on this view, obtains when these benefits and burdens are distributed equally.

It appears that something quite like this third form of egalitarianism was defended by Christopher Ake in his paper "Justice as Equality," which was published in *Philosophy and Public Affairs* in 1975:

> Justice in a society as a whole ought to be understood as a complete equality of the overall level of benefits and burdens of each member of that society.

Thus a form of egalitarianism suggested by Ake's remark[6] can be stated in this way:

> E3: There is perfect distributive justice in a state, S, if and only if every citizen of S has the same amount of socially distributable benefits and burdens as every other citizen of S.

Other forms of egalitarianism are straightforward variants of E1, E2, and E3. We get these variants simply by introducing a different currency of justice. One form would say that justice requires the equal distribution of rights; another would say that it requires the equal distribution of opportunities; and yet another would say that it requires the equal distribution of capabilities. What they have in common is the idea that a state has ensured perfect distributive justice if and only if it has ensured perfect equality of the currency of justice.

There are, in addition to these simple forms, many other forms of egalitarianism that are often mentioned. For example, there is "starting gate egalitarianism" according to which justice requires that citizens start out in life with equal opportunities for welfare (or whatever is taken to be the currency of justice). There is also "luck egalitarianism" according to which justice requires that inequalities in the distribution of the currency of justice be removed by improving

[6] I have been writing as if the bearers of justice would be states. Ake writes as if the bearers of justice would be societies.

the share held by the worse-off citizen—except for inequalities that have arisen as a result of the irresponsible taking of needless risks.

1.2.2 Sufficientism

A seemingly contrary view was defended by Harry Frankfurt. In a well-known paper, after describing the popular enthusiasm for equality, he said:

> In my opinion, this is a mistake. Economic equality is not, as such, of particular moral importance. With respect to the distribution of economic assets, what *is* important from the point of view of morality is not that everyone should have *the same* but that each should have *enough*. If everyone had enough, it would be of no moral consequence whether some had more than others. I shall refer to this alternative to egalitarianism – namely, that what is morally important with respect to money is for everyone to have enough – as "the doctrine of sufficiency."[7]

Frankfurt's view is based on the assumption that for any person, there is an amount of money that is "sufficient." If the person has that much money, then he or she has enough. It is reasonable for the person to be content with that much; having more would not reduce whatever unhappiness remains. That level serves as a threshold for the person. Making use of this concept of a threshold, we can state a form of sufficientism in this way:

S1: There is perfect distributive justice in a state, S, at a time, t, if and only if every citizen of S has an amount of money that is at least at the threshold for him or her.[8]

This formulation of sufficientism is based on Frankfurt's idea that what matters is that money (or "economic assets") be properly distributed, rather than on the idea that what matters is how welfare is distributed. This view about the currency of distributive justice seems similar to the view about currency presupposed in E2. If we wanted a sufficientist view that more directly confronts other forms of egalitarianism, we could formulate one version that says that justice requires that each citizen have at least a sufficient amount of welfare; and another version that says that justice requires that each citizen have at least a sufficient share of socially distributable benefits and burdens. It should be obvious that egalitarianism and sufficientism are not equivalent, even when presupposing the same view about the currency of justice. Egalitarianism says that justice requires that people have *the same* amount of the currency of justice; sufficientism requires that each

[7] Frankfurt (1987: 21–2).

[8] The view formulated in S1 explicitly involves states. It takes states to be the fundamental bearers of distributive justice. It is not clear to me that Frankfurt would endorse that idea.

person have *enough* of that currency. It is easy enough to imagine a situation in which everyone has the same amount of money but no one has enough.

One interesting and problematic feature of Frankfurt's remarks is that he does not say that he is offering a theory of justice. Instead, he talks about what is "morally important" and what people "should" have. Perhaps he would insist that S1 is not a fair representation of his view. Maybe he would say that he never intended to advocate any view about justice—just a view about what is morally important. This suggests that we need to distinguish between what Frankfurt actually said, and the sufficientist view that is often attributed to him.

In a passage that will be familiar to all who admire the work of G. E. Moore, Moore said: "It appears to me that in Ethics, as in all other philosophical studies, the difficulties and disagreements, of which its history is full, are mainly due to a very simple cause: namely to the attempt to answer questions, without first discovering precisely *what* question it is which you desire to answer."[9] Moore's warning seems to be relevant here.

I think the central question about distributive justice is this:

> Q1: What makes the situation in some state perfectly distributively just? What makes the situation in one state more distributively just than the situation in some other state?

But many philosophers, in passages widely assumed to be about justice, sometimes write in such a way as to make it unclear whether they really meant to be asking a question specifically about *justice*. I think this point is important since it suggests that at least some of these philosophers might have been trying to answer a question that is different from the one I mean to be discussing. Accordingly, I want to digress for a moment to say a few words about the way in which theories of justice are to be formulated and what this suggests about the aims of those whose work is often taken to be about justice.

a. The "Deontic" Style. Some writers, while seemingly presenting a theory of justice, write in such a way as to suggest that they are hoping to answer a question about what we *should do* when it comes to distributions of benefits and burdens. In an introductory comment in a paper about equality, efficiency, and priority Peter Vallentyne says "Egalitarian theories of justice hold that equality *should be promoted*."[10] Elizabeth Anderson describes luck egalitarianism in this deontic

[9] G. E. Moore, *Principia Ethica*, from the preface to the first (1903) edition. But my citations are to *Principia Ethica: Revised Edition* (1993), ed. and Introd. Thomas Baldwin (Cambridge: Cambridge University Press).

[10] Vallentyne (2001:1). Emphasis added, FF.

style, saying "Luck egalitarianism relies on two moral premises: that *people should be compensated* for undeserved misfortunes and that the compensation *should come* only from that part of others' good fortune that is undeserved."[11] Richard Arneson states what he takes to be the central claim of one form of egalitarianism by saying: "Egalitarian justice here shall be understood as principles that hold that if we are dealing with a fixed population and choosing social arrangements that will not affect the aggregate total of well-being but may affect its distribution across persons, arrangements that would bring about an equal distribution of well-being, if that is obtainable, *should be chosen*."[12] In this context I am not interested in debating the egalitarian doctrines mentioned by these philosophers. I will get to that later. For now, I just want to draw attention to the way in which these philosophers formulate what they take to be the egalitarian principle. They write in such a way as to suggest that they mean to be discussing a question about what people *should do*.

The example involves egalitarianism, but any view about the nature of justice could appear in this deontic style. Thus, for example, taking our cue from Frankfurt, we could state a form of sufficientism by saying that distributors *should behave* in such a way that everyone has at least a sufficient amount of money. We could state something like the Rawlsian difference principle in this deontic style: primary social goods *should be* distributed in such a way as to maximize the amount of such goods held by the worst-off people.[13]

Lots of other philosophers seem to adopt this deontic style as they formulate their theories. They write as if they are aiming to answer this question:

> Q2: What is the morally right way to distribute benefits and burdens to the members of some group? How—morally—ought such benefits and burdens be distributed?

I am uneasy about this. I think that a theory of distributive justice tells us what makes the situation in some state distributively just. It should also tell us what would make the situation in some state more distributively just than the situation in some other state. It should leave out any discussion of what we should do, or how things should be. That is because what we ought to do may

[11] Anderson (1999: 290). Emphasis added, FF.

[12] Arneson (2007: 262). Emphasis added, FF.

[13] Others state principles of justice using a "should" in a different way. For example, Kai Nielsen (1981b: 121) states his idea about justice when he says, "what we should aim at is a structuring of the institutions of society so that each person can, to the fullest extent compatible with all other people doing likewise, satisfy his/her needs." Nielsen apparently thinks that a principle of justice gives an account of what we should aim at giving.

depend upon considerations other than justice. For example, it might depend upon total utilities as well. Suppose two possible distributions are available. Suppose one distribution would make people on the whole much better off, but the other would be more just. I might wonder which I ought to bring about. It is not entirely obvious that I ought to bring about the more just distribution; maybe I ought to aim for the distribution that has the higher utility. But if, when presumably writing on distributive justice, a philosopher formulates the question in the deontic style, he or she seems to be moving away from the question specifically about justice and toward the question about how distributors ought to behave. Does the philosopher mean to be answering a question about justice? Or does he or she mean to be answering a question about what we morally ought to be doing?

b. The "Axiological" Style. Sometimes, when reading works apparently on distributive justice, we find people writing as if principles of justice are to be formulated as principles in axiology—as if they are principles about the intrinsic values of distributions. Parfit sometimes writes in this style in "Equality and Priority." He talks as if egalitarianism is a view about which distribution will be intrinsically best, or which distributions are intrinsically better than others. He says he is talking about "Telic Egalitarianism," and he formulates what he calls "The Principle of Equality" by saying "It is bad in itself if some people are worse off than others."[14]

Many others, including people who are not talking about egalitarianism, state their principles in the same way—as if they were principles about intrinsic value.[15] But this is also a potentially misleading way of talking. It suggests that the philosopher in question is concerned about this question:

> Q3: What way of distributing benefits and burdens to the members of some group would be intrinsically best? What makes one possible way of distributing such benefits and burdens intrinsically better than another possible way of distributing benefits and burdens?

Suppose we are told that there are two possible states, S1 and S2; suppose that we are told that each of these states has citizens receiving various sized allocations of intrinsic good and evil; suppose we are told that S1 is more distributively just than S2.

[14] Parfit (1997: 204). Parfit sometimes presents principles of justice in the deontic style. See, for example *Reasons and Persons* (330) where he says that in one form the Principle of Equality is the view that "no one should be worse off than others through no fault of his own."

[15] See, for example, Rescher (1966: 7), Crisp (2003: 746), Hurley (2001: 52), Casal (2007: 296), Huseby (2010: 180), and Holtug (2007: 127–32).

So far as I can tell, given just this information, we can draw no conclusion about the intrinsic values of S1 and S2. If this is right, then the answer to Q3 could be different from the answer to Q1.

Here is a thought experiment designed to show that there is an important difference between levels of distributive justice and levels of intrinsic value. Suppose every citizen of S3 receives one unit of intrinsic value. Suppose every citizen of S4 receives a hundred units of intrinsic value. Suppose the populations are equal in size. An egalitarian of intrinsic value, noting that within each society the distribution of this sort of value is perfectly equal, might want to say that the situations are equally just; but at the same time she might want to say that the intrinsic value of S4 is much greater—perhaps a hundred times greater—than the intrinsic value of S3.

This suggests that it might be misleading to formulate our theory of justice in the axiological style, as if the amount of justice in a state is the same as the amount of intrinsic value in that state. These are two different sorts of evaluation and they ought to be kept distinct.[16,17]

So some philosophers apparently prefer to formulate principles of justice in the deontic style (viz., "we ought to distribute goods...") and some prefer to formulate these principles in the axiological style (viz., "it is intrinsically good for things to be distributed..."). The former group seems to be focused on question Q2; the latter group seems to be focused on question Q3. I mean to focus on question Q1. In order to avoid the possible misunderstandings I have described, I prefer to formulate these principles simply as principles of distributive justice. As a result, as I formulate the principles, they will not explicitly say that we ought to distribute in some way, or that it would be intrinsically good for things to be distributed in some way. Rather, they will typically start out looking like this: "There is perfect distributive justice in a state if and only if..." Since other contributors to the literature do not always formulate their principles in

[16] Of course, if distributive justice is itself a "value" then greater amounts of distributive justice will invariably have greater amounts of that sort of value. But then we must be careful to distinguish between this new sort of "justice-related value" and the more familiar sorts of value that we typically discuss in axiology. Presumably, the amount of justice in a situation would be determined by something about the way in which some other valuable stuff is distributed to the people in the society. In any case, I am not confident that there is any such special sort of justice-related value.

[17] A reader suggested that we could avoid these problems by saying that the level of justice in a society is equal to the *average* level of intrinsic value enjoyed by citizens. But this suggestion seems to me to be mistaken. Imagine two countries of equal size in which the total and average levels of intrinsic value enjoyed by citizens are the same. But suppose this value is distributed equally and fairly in one country, and wildly unequally and unfairly in the other country. Then, in spite of equal levels of average intrinsic value, there are not equal levels of justice in the two countries. If there is any connection between justice and intrinsic value, it cannot be a straightforward identification.

precisely this form, I sometimes will rephrase what they have said. I acknowledge that in thus rephrasing the principles, I may be departing from the intentions of the original advocates. I admit that some other philosophers may have been trying to provide an answer to some other question. However, when we state the principle in my preferred style—explicitly as a principle about distributive justice—the resulting principle may be interesting and worthy of consideration even if it is a principle different from the one to be found in the literature.

1.2.3 A theory based on the difference principle

In his book *A Theory of Justice* John Rawls says a lot of things about distributive justice. He has a somewhat idiosyncratic way of formulating his view; it does not fit very neatly into the structure I have proposed. The actual theory of justice involves an array of arguments, claims, theories about other topics, etc.[18] But one of Rawls's central ideas is expressed by his so-called "difference principle," which in one place he states in this way:

> [T]he higher expectations of those better situated are just if and only if they work as part of a scheme which improves the expectations of the least advantaged members of society. The intuitive idea is that the social order is not to establish and secure the more attractive prospects of those better off unless doing so is to the advantage of those less fortunate. (1971: 75)

Rawls speaks here of "expectations" and "prospects." Elsewhere, he formulates the difference principle as a principle concerning the distribution of "material benefits." In this form, the principle says that social and economic inequalities are to be of the greatest material benefit of the least advantaged. Rawls imagines a case in which the expectations of the least advantaged are indeed maximized. He says, "No changes in the expectations of those better off can improve the situation of those worst off. The best arrangement obtains, what I shall call a *perfectly just scheme*" (1971: 78. Emphasis added, FF.)

Suppose again that there is a state; suppose that there are economic classes; suppose that there is a "least advantaged class"; suppose there is some actual distribution of material benefits; suppose the actual distribution is not an equal distribution; people in lower classes get smaller allocations of material benefits. But suppose in addition that there is no feasible revised distribution that would make the least advantaged class better off. The difference principle seems to say

[18] In many places Rawls pairs the difference principle with the liberty principle. The liberty principle, which takes priority over the difference principle, is sometimes (1971: 54) stated in this way: "Each person is to have an equal right to the most extensive scheme of equal basic liberties compatible with a similar scheme of liberties for others."

that the situation in this state has the highest possible level of distributive justice—or as Rawls says, it is "a perfectly just scheme."

Although Rawls did not do it this way, we can formulate a version of the difference principle as a stand-alone theory of distributive justice. We will need to assume that in every society there is a "worst off class."[19] Let this be the class of citizens who have the smallest shares of material benefits. Then we can formulate the principle in this way:

> DP: There is perfect distributive justice in a state, S, if and only if there is no feasible way in which material benefits can be redistributed to citizens of S that would yield a larger share of these benefits for the citizens who are in the worst off class.

It should be fairly obvious on reflection that DP is not equivalent to any form of egalitarianism or sufficientism. A somewhat schematic example will illustrate this. Suppose there is a state in which there are several distinct economic groups. Suppose that at the lowest rung of the ladder there are low-skilled, low-paid workers. Suppose their employers cannot feasibly pay the workers higher salaries. Paying them more would price their product out of the market. So there is no feasible way in which the members of the worst off class could get more material benefits. In this case, DP implies that there is perfect distributive justice in the society, but since there are stipulated to be several different economic groups a comparable form of egalitarianism implies that there is not.[20] If we suppose that the low wages put the workers below their thresholds, then the corresponding form of sufficientism implies that there is not perfect justice in this state. If their wages put them above their thresholds, then that form of sufficientism implies that there is perfect justice in our imaginary state.[21]

[19] In fact this seems to me to be a very dicey assumption. I discuss what I take to be the problem later in section 5.4. I also discuss some further things that Rawls says about it in *Justice as Fairness*.

[20] A reader for Oxford University Press suggested that even if DP is not precisely equivalent to any form of egalitarianism, it still has an important egalitarian component. The reader said that a theory of justice has an egalitarian component when it "specifies and sets limits to admissible inequality." DP thus has an egalitarian component, since it says (roughly) that equality would be the default situation; inequalities are admissible only if they are to the advantage of the worst off. But it seems to me that the reader's suggested way of characterizing theories "with an egalitarian component" opens the door a bit too wide. Consider the theory that says that equality is the default situation; inequalities are admissible only if they give greater benefits to lighter-skinned citizens. That theory satisfies the reader's criterion for having an egalitarian component, but it seems to me to be the very paradigm of *anti-egalitarianism*.

[21] I assume, for purposes of the argument, that the wages of the low-paid workers translate directly into levels of primary social goods, or "economic advantage" or whatever is being treated as the currency of justice for purposes of comparison.

1.2.4 Extreme libertarianism

According to one version of this theory, the currency of distributive justice is "holdings." That means "things that are owned." We can say that a person comes to own a holding "fairly from the state of nature" if and only if he takes it from a previously unowned stock in such a way as to leave enough behind so that others will not be adversely affected by his appropriation. A fair acquisition would occur, for example, if someone catches a fish when no one owns that fish, and there are still millions of fish in the sea for others to catch. No one will miss out as a result of that fish's having been caught.

We can say that someone comes to own a holding in a "fair transaction" if and only if he comes to own it as a result of engaging in a free (uncoerced) trade with someone who already owned it. If we were to construct a theory of distributive justice based on these ideas, we might have:

> L: There is perfect distributive justice in a state, S, if and only if every holding owned by a citizen of S is such that either (a) he or she got it fairly from the state of nature, or (b) he or she got it in a fair transaction.

There is a problem here. Suppose everyone has his holdings fairly and no one has any complaint. Imagine that everyone has a nice supply of fish. Suppose then that someone steals some of your fish. That ruins the distributive justice of the situation, since someone has something that he did not get fairly. Suppose next that the police come along and force the thief to give you a new fish equivalent in value to the one that was stolen, thereby restoring perfect justice. L as stated has no clause to cover this case. For in this case you have a fish that you did not catch on your own from the wild stock, and that you did not get in a fair uncoerced trade with someone who already owned it. It makes it look as if once the justice of a distribution has been disrupted, it can never be restored. We need to add something to deal with this problem. Here is a way to add it. First we need to say that when you are entitled to a certain holding, but someone took it away from you without your consent, the state may have the power to rectify the situation by retrieving that holding from its current unfair possessor, and returning it (or something of equivalent value) to you (the rightful possessor). Let us say that when this is done, you come to possess the holding again via a "fair rectification." Now we can say:

> L': There is perfect distributive justice in a state, S, if and only if every holding owned by a citizen of S is such that either (a) he got it fairly from the state of nature, or (b) he got it in a fair transaction, or (c) he got it as a result of a fair rectification.

Libertarianism (in the form of L') differs in an important way from egalitarianism, sufficientism, and the difference principle. We can see this if we reflect on what we would have to know about a distribution in order to tell whether it is just. In the case of egalitarianism, sufficientism, and the difference principle, we would need to know something about the pattern of distribution.[22] If I know that everyone has the same amount of money, then I know all that I need to know in order to determine that this situation is perfectly distributively just according to a simple egalitarianism of wealth, E2; if I know that everyone has an amount of money above his or her threshold, then I know all that I need to know in order to determine that this situation is perfectly distributively just according to our sufficientism of wealth, S1. In the case of these theories, I do not need to know how these distributions came about. Whatever their histories, the theories say that the distributions are just if they have the right pattern.

But merely knowing the pattern of distribution of the currency of justice in this way would not enable me to determine whether a certain distribution is just according to L'. On this libertarian view, a certain distribution might be just, and it might be unjust, depending upon facts about how it came about. Consider an equal distribution of holdings; suppose it came about as a result of a series of fair acquisitions and transfers. Then according to L' it is just. Suppose it came about as a result of theft. (Imagine that those with smaller shares stole some holdings from those with larger shares, thereby bringing about an equal distribution.) Then it is unjust. Nozick describes this by saying that theories like egalitarianism and sufficientism are "patterned" theories, while libertarianism is a "historical" theory.[23]

These reflections on the role of history provide an easy way for us to see that libertarianism is not equivalent to any form of egalitarianism. Imagine a form of egalitarianism that says that justice obtains when citizens have equal sets of holdings. Such a theory would say that even a theft-generated equal distribution of holdings would be just; L' would deny it. A similar line of thought would show that L' is not equivalent to any form of sufficientism.

[22] Each of these theories implies that we would have to have at least one bit of information that goes beyond mere information about patterns. In the case of sufficientism, we would also have to know something about the thresholds; in the case of the difference principle, we would also have to know something about feasible redistributions. But in no case would we have to know anything about how the current distribution came about. History is irrelevant on these theories.

[23] Nozick (1974: 153–60).

1.2.5 Some other theories of distributive justice

One of the most familiar (and historically important) ideas about justice is suggested by the Marxist slogan "From each according to his ability, to each according to his need."[24] This makes use of two new concepts: *need* and *ability*. Assuming that we understand the relevant sort of need, and the relevant sort of ability, and assuming that wealth is the currency of justice, the principle might be this:

> M1: There is perfect distributive justice in a state, S, if and only if every citizen of S makes a contribution to the wealth of S that is appropriate in light of his or her abilities, and every citizen of S receives from S an amount of wealth sufficient to satisfy his or her need.

In spite of the fact that M1 is painfully obscure,[25] it is clear enough so that we can easily see some apparent differences between its implications and the implications of an egalitarianism of wealth. Suppose that different citizens have different needs; some need more wealth than others. Suppose those needs are precisely met. Then M1 could say that the state is perfectly just, while an egalitarianism of wealth (perhaps like E2) would have to say that it is not. For in such a state, people would have different amounts of wealth, though everyone would have an amount of wealth sufficient to satisfy his or her needs.

I leave it to the curious reader to construct a case that shows that the implications of M1 are not equivalent to the implications of a sufficientism of wealth (like S1) or to the implications of the view about justice that I derived from Rawls's difference principle.

In an earlier era, philosophers more or less automatically listed utilitarianism as a theory of justice. Rawls seems to take it to be the most worthy competitor to his own conception of justice. In his work *Distributive Justice* Nicholas Rescher explicitly says—as you might expect given his title—that he is discussing *distributive justice*. But the subtitle of the book is revealing: *A Constructive Critique of the Utilitarian Theory of Distribution*. Apparently Rescher assumed that if you are going to talk about distributive justice, you must start by discussing

[24] Karl Marx, "Critique of the Gotha program," 1875.

[25] Some of the obscurity concerns the idea of contributions "according to ability." We might take this to mean that each citizen is to make the largest contribution he or she is able to make. Alternatively, we might take it to mean that all citizens are to make contributions of the same proportion of the maximum they are able to make. Another possible interpretation concerns the *type* of work that each citizen does, rather than *how much* work he or she does. On this view, the claim amounts to the idea that each citizen is to be engaged in the line of work that is most closely aligned with his or her abilities.

utilitarianism. My view is fundamentally different. As I see it, utilitarianism is a view about the moral rightness of actions, according to which an act is morally right if and only if it maximizes utility (or, perhaps, expected utility). While it might suggest—or naturally be associated with—some theory of justice, it is not such a theory in its own right.[26]

I have here hinted at just a few of the most well-known views about distributive justice. There are many variants of these, and many other views that I have so far not mentioned. But these are some of the most important and well-known views that stand in direct competition with the view that I defend in this book. I mention them here in order to help elicit an intuition about the question I mean to be discussing. My question is: "what makes for political economic distributive justice in a state"? If you can see how each of the theories I have sketched could be taken to be a proposed answer to this question, then perhaps you understand the question well enough to permit us to proceed. You recognize the target at which each of these theories aims.

1.3 Desertism about Distributive Justice

There are passages in the writings of Aristotle, Leibniz, Mill, Sidgwick, Ross, and others in which they state—with varying degrees of approval—the idea that justice is somehow a matter of receipt according to desert.[27] There are many different ways in which this fairly abstract desertist idea may be developed. One of the broadest of these may be called "cosmic desertism about distributive justice." It is the idea that justice obtains when people receive *everything* they deserve on any basis. Although Mill did not accept this conception of distributive justice, he claimed that something quite like it is very widely accepted by "the general mind." Mill said:

> It is universally considered just that each person should obtain that (whether good or evil) which he *deserves*; and unjust that he should obtain a good, or be made to undergo an evil, which he does not deserve. This is, perhaps, the clearest and most emphatic form in which the idea of justice is conceived by the general mind.[28]

[26] I explain my view on this in Appendix B "Two Helpings of Desert."

[27] Aristotle: "all men agree that what is just in distribution must be according to merit (kata axian)..." *NE* V, 3. Sidgwick: "Men ought to be rewarded in proportion to their deserts" *The Methods of Ethics* Bk III, Ch. 5. Ross: "The duty of justice is particularly complicated, and the word is used to cover things which are really very different—things such as the payment of debts, the reparation of injuries done by oneself to another, and the bringing about of a distribution of happiness between other people in proportion to merit. I use the word to denote only the last of these" *The Right and the Good*, pp. 26–7.

[28] This passage occurs in ch. 5, para. 7 of *Utilitarianism*. When stated in this way out of context, the passage is misleading. Mill did not endorse this view; he was just saying that this is what the "general mind" believes.

Perhaps there was a time when "the general mind" conceived of justice in this way. Perhaps because of the enormous influence of Rawls—perhaps for other reasons—the "philosophical mind" nowadays does not take it to be quite so obvious.[29]

Desertism comes in many varieties. If we presuppose different views about the currency of justice, we get different forms of desertism. One version would say that justice obtains when people have the amount of money they deserve. Another version would say that justice obtains when people have the political rights, privileges, and obligations they deserve.

One form of desertism emerges from the view that Mill attributed to "the general mind." On this view, the currency of justice is "things that are good or evil." The view seems to be:

D1: There is perfect distributive justice in a state, S, if and only if in every case in which a citizen of S deserves something good or evil, he or she gets it.

Mill does not mention the basis on which people might deserve good or evil, but Leibniz does. Leibniz says that justice obtains when people have the amount of happiness they deserve, and they have it in virtue of their moral worth. This form of desertism may be seen in this remark from Leibniz:

> There couldn't be a better standard in this matter than the *law of justice,* which lays down that everyone is to participate in the perfection of the universe, and to have personal happiness, in proportion to his own virtue and to the extent that his will has contributed to the common good. This vindicates the charity and love of God, which constitutes the entire force and power of the Christian religion, in the judgment of wise theologians.[30]

In this brief statement of the desert-based "law of justice" Leibniz not only specifies the currency of justice ("happiness and participation in the perfection of the universe"), he also specifies the desert base that would make a person deserve his share of this currency ("virtue and the extent to which his will has contributed to the common good") and he hints that we are to receive our just deserts from God. We can simplify this a bit by assuming that the currency of justice is always a level of happiness or unhappiness to be received from God in the afterlife; furthermore, we can assume that the basis on which this happiness is

[29] Many of the seminal articles concerning desertism about justice can be found in Pojman and McLeod (1999). More recent articles on this topic can be found in Olsaretti (2003), though many of the authors represented in that work are not sympathetic to desertism.

[30] Translation by Jonathan Bennett: http://www.earlymoderntexts.com/authors/leibniz.

deserved is always a level of virtue or vice. With these assumptions in place, we can state a variant of the Leibnizian form of desertism:

D2: There is perfect distributive justice in a possible world if and only if in every case in which a resident of that world deserves to be at a certain level of happiness in virtue of having lived at a certain level of moral virtue, God sees to it that the person comes to be at that level of happiness in the afterlife and in virtue having lived at that level of virtue.

We can formulate a kind of desertism based on the idea that money is the currency of justice, and that people deserve amounts of money depending upon how hard they work. The view would look like this:

D3: There is perfect distributive justice in a state, S, if and only if in every case in which a citizen of S deserves—as a result of the amount of work he or she has done—to have a certain amount of money, he or she has that amount of money.

Desertism is in some respects like the patterned theories of justice. We can see this if we reflect on what we would have to know about a state in order to determine whether it is just. If I know the pattern of distribution of the currency of justice in some state, and I also know the pattern of distribution of desert of that currency in that state, and I also know how these patterns mesh, then I know enough according to desertism to determine the level of justice in the state. Some of the information I would need might turn on things that have happened in the past. In order to determine a citizen's level of desert, I might need information about what he or she has done. So it might be said that there is a historical element here. Clearly, merely knowing the current pattern of distribution of the currency of justice would not be sufficient.

My aim in this book is to present and defend a new form of desertism as a theory of political economic distributive justice. But my view is not equivalent to Leibniz's Law of Justice; neither is it equivalent to the view suggested by Mill. Nor will it be the desertism of money as expressed in D3. Although I briefly discuss some other forms of desertism, the desertist view I defend is intended to be a theory about "political economic distributive justice." I am going to maintain that there is perfect distributive justice in a state if and only if in every case in which a citizen of that state deserves—in virtue of his or her political economic desert bases—to have some political economic desert, he or she gets it. Then later, after I have explained my view, I will compare its implications to the implications of the well-known theories I have sketched here. I will attempt to show that my theory generates more attractive results in some hard cases that make trouble for the well-known theories.[31]

My theory—a form of desertism—makes essential use of the concept of *desert.* I turn next to a more detailed account of this central concept that lies at the heart of my theory of justice.

[31] I should perhaps be a bit more cautious. I am going to compare my theory to slightly revised versions of the well-known theories. In each case, in order to have a head-to-head comparison, it becomes necessary to formulate a version of the well-known theory that is explicitly about the same subject matter as my theory—political economic distributive justice. If the original advocates of these other theories were focusing on some other target, then it is not clear how their views can be compared to mine.

2

Desert Claims and Their Justification

Desertist theories of justice come in many different forms. What binds them together is that every such theory makes essential use of the concept of *desert*. Therefore, it behooves us to take some time to focus on this familiar, but somewhat controversial concept.

2.1 Desert as a Form of Requirement

At the beginning of his remarkable paper "The Ethics of Requirement," Roderick Chisholm says that all the central concepts of ethics can be defined by appeal to the concept of *requirement.*[1] He attempts to establish his claim by offering definitions of "good," "obligatory," "commitment," "prima facie duty," "supererogatory," and others; in each case the definition makes essential use of the concept of requirement. Chisholm's thesis would give the concept of requirement a kind of foundational role in moral philosophy. As I understand it, Chisholm further thought that the concept of requirement could not be defined by appeal to any other concepts of ethics. This would give the concept of requirement a kind of autonomy. Thus, as he saw it, the concept of requirement is both autonomous and foundational within the field of ethics. All other concepts in ethics can be defined by appeal to it, but it cannot be defined by appeal to anything else in ethics.

In the passage at the beginning of "The Ethics of Requirement," Chisholm does not mention justice or desert. He does not say that either of these concepts can be defined by appeal to the concept of requirement. I do not know whether such a definition can be constructed, but I am inclined to think that there is a very

[1] Roderick Chisholm (1964: 147–53). Chisholm discusses this concept in several other places including Chisholm (1974) and Chisholm (1986: 52–3).

intimate connection between desert and requirement. Perhaps cases that are properly described in terms of desert form a subset of cases in which we can speak more generally of requirement. If this suggestion is right, and my central desertist claim about justice is true, then justice can be explained by appeal to desert, and desert can be understood to be a form of requirement.[2]

So then, before we turn to the concept of desert itself, reflection on the somewhat wider concept of requirement might prove to be a helpful introduction.

Chisholm starts by giving some examples of cases in which something requires something else. He says:

> promise-making requires—or calls for—promise-keeping; being virtuous, according to Kant, requires being rewarded; the dominant seventh requires the chord of the tonic; one color in the lower left calls for a complementary color in the upper right.[3]

Note that while the first two examples seem to involve matters of ethics, the second two examples are more properly considered to involve matters of aesthetics.

He goes on to mention some cases involving perception. He says that these were stressed by Gestalt psychologists. He mentions a "curve that demands a certain completion." He also mentions that many words ending in "worthy" or "able" suggest other types of requirement, and gives as examples "praiseworthy," "blameworthy," "valuable," and "despicable." He claims that "requires" could be replaced by "fitting." "In one sense of the term 'fitting,' p could be said to be fitting to q, provided that q requires p; . . . "[4]

There are also examples in epistemology and etiquette. The possession of a certain body of evidence might require the formation of a certain belief. The receipt of a gift might require the sending of a thank-you note.

Chisholm proceeds to discuss some of the formal features of requirement. Obviously, there are cases in which something is required, but it does not happen anyway. Perhaps you received a very nice gift from your grandmother, but you neglected to thank her. So from the fact that something is required, it does not follow that it happens. Another important fact (as Chisholm sees it) is that requirements can conflict. For example, a person who has made two promises may find that the first promise requires him to behave in one way, while the second promise requires him to behave in an incompatible way. He cannot keep

[2] Quite a lot of what I say here about the connection between desert and requirement corresponds closely to things that Diana Abad says about the connection between desert and propriety in her (2007). See especially pp. 47–60.

[3] Chisholm (1964: 147).

[4] Chisholm (1964: 147).

both promises. Not all such cases involve any fault on the part of the person who confronts conflicting requirements: Chisholm imagines someone who can save the life of either of two good people, but cannot save both. He also points out that in cases involving conflicting requirements like these, often one requirement *overrides* the other. Chisholm suggests that reflection on the concept of requirement also may help us to understand the concept of prima facie obligation, and the possibility of moral dilemmas.

There are many cases in which we say that a certain response is required in light of some fact about a person. Thus, for example, we say that the fact that a certain employee has done outstanding work throughout a long career requires that he be given a suitable retirement party. Similarly, we may say that the fact that a certain student has written an excellent term paper requires that she be given a high grade. On the "negative" side, it is commonplace to say, when someone has been found guilty of a particularly atrocious crime, that it would be fitting for the criminal to suffer a severe punishment; such a punishment seems required in light of the viciousness of his crime.

Remarks such as these can readily be expressed using the idiom of desert. We can say that in virtue of his work over a long career, the loyal employee deserves a retirement party; or that in virtue of her submission of an excellent paper, the student deserves a high grade; or that in virtue of the fact that he committed such a vicious crime, the criminal deserves a severe penalty.

The choice of desert-talk seems most appropriate in cases that fall into a certain pattern. In some cases, a person (like the loyal employee) has done something (like doing a good job over a long period); and the fact that he has done this makes it fitting for some other person (perhaps his employer) to respond in some way (for example to hold a retirement party for him when he retires). We can use the idiom of requirement to describe the case of the loyal employee:

1r. The fact that the employee has done a good job over a long period of time requires that he be given a retirement party when he retires.

But we seem to be able to express the same idea by use of the idiom of desert:

1d. In virtue of the fact that he has done a good job over a long period of time, the employee deserves a retirement party when he retires.

I am inclined to think that in many cases in which a certain sort of treatment for a certain person is *required* in light of some fact about what that person has done or suffered, we can express this fact about requirement just as well by saying that the person *deserves* that treatment in virtue of the fact about him.

Not all facts about requirement can so readily be restated as facts about desert. Thus, for example, suppose that a student has this feature: she has parents who would be thrilled if she were to get an A for a term paper. This seems to be a fact about the student; it may seem to require—maybe just a little bit—that the student get an A for the paper, but it does not readily get expressed by the claim that the student deserves an A for the paper. In order for a requirement fact about a person to be expressible as a desert fact, the fact about the person must be more directly about the person—it cannot be a mere "Cambridge fact" about her, like the Cambridge fact that she has parents who would be thrilled. The precise demarcation between suitably intimate facts about a person and mere Cambridge facts is a matter of debate.[5]

Consider the motto of the Bill and Melinda Gates Foundation according to which "Every person *deserves* the chance to live a healthy, productive life." As I understand it, this motto is equivalent to the idea that each person has some feature (perhaps it is just the feature of *being a person*) that requires that he or she have a chance to live a healthy and productive life. When we imagine a situation in which every person actually receives the specified chance, it strikes us as being "correct" in a certain way—it strikes us as "fitting" that people should have such a chance. We might even say that, in a certain way, getting such a chance is somehow "owed" to each person; it is his or her "due." In case the person gets a chance to lead a healthy and productive life, we may naturally think that the person has received what was required. Similar remarks could be made about the loyal employee who deserves a retirement party, or the student who submitted an excellent paper, or the criminal who committed a vicious crime. In each case, some sort of treatment is required by the fact that the subject has some suitably intimate feature; equivalently, we can say that in each case the subject has some feature in virtue of which he or she deserves that treatment.

2.2 Some Examples of Desert

Perhaps further reflection on some examples will help to bring the concept of desert into sharper focus. Suppose a student writes an excellent term paper and hands it in on time; suppose the instructor had announced that she would assign grades in the standard way; then in virtue of the fact that the student wrote an excellent paper and submitted it in accord with the agreed conditions, the student deserves a high grade—perhaps an A—for the work. That would be a clear example of a case in which someone (the student) deserves something (a high

[5] Thanks to Owen McLeod for reminding me of the importance of this point.

grade) in virtue of having done something (he wrote and submitted an excellent term paper). A grade of B or C would seem inappropriate in such a case. Given what the student has done, the most fitting reaction would be to give him an A.

I should digress for a moment to highlight the difference between desert and entitlement. A typical desert claim is a claim to the effect that someone deserves something from someone on some basis. A typical entitlement claim is a claim to the effect that someone is entitled to something from someone on some basis.

There are obvious structural similarities between desert claims and claims about entitlement. As a result, desert claims and entitlement claims can easily be confused. In typical examples of each sort, someone is said to deserve (or be entitled to) something from someone on some basis. However, there is an important difference between the concepts of desert and entitlement. As the terminology is used here, desert is a more purely normative concept, while entitlement is a largely sociological or empirical concept. If some social or legal institution is in place in your social group, and that institution has a rule that specifies some treatment for those who have some feature, and you have the feature, then you are entitled to that treatment. Thus, for example, suppose that when a customer purchased a certain item, he received a legally binding written guarantee from the seller. The guarantee specified that if the item should turn out to be defective, the seller would either replace the item or refund the money that the buyer had spent for the defective item. In such a case, if the buyer satisfies the conditions stated in the guarantee, and the purchased item is indeed defective, the buyer is entitled to the refund or replacement. There is no suggestion here that the conditions stated in the guarantee are the "right" conditions, or that these are the conditions that should have been included in the guarantee. What matters for entitlement is that the conditions are *as a matter of fact* in the guarantee. If those conditions are satisfied, the customer is entitled to his refund.

Typical desert claims have a similar structure, but do not always depend in this way on the existence of laws or contracts or other similar social institutions. A person may deserve some sort of treatment even though there are no rules in place in his society that codify the conditions under which someone deserves that sort of treatment. In such a case, a person may deserve something even though he is not entitled to it. Similarly, a person may be entitled to something by some rules that are in place in his society even though he does not deserve it. Some examples may help to make this distinction clearer.

Let us first consider some cases in which desert and entitlement coincide. The example involving a student who has submitted an excellent paper illustrates this. In virtue of having submitted an excellent paper, the student deserves an A. It would probably also be appropriate to say that the student is entitled to the A.

After all, there are academic rules under which the instructor and her students are supposed to operate, and those rules may imply that certain procedures must be followed when instructors give grades. For example, the rules may specify that grades are to be given in accord with the policies that the instructor set forth in the syllabus for the course. Maybe those policies imply in the case at hand that the student is to receive an A. So the claim of entitlement is consistent with the claim of desert. The student could deserve an A and he could be entitled to it as well.

Let us consider another example. Suppose a neighbor notices that the snow has piled up in my driveway while I have been out of town. Suppose that while he is using his snowblower to clear his own driveway, he generously takes some time to clear my driveway as well. When I get home, I am delighted to find that I will not have to clear the snow before putting my car in the garage. In this case, the neighbor deserves some expression of gratitude from me. Perhaps it would be appropriate for me to send a thank-you note, or to stop by in the morning to tell him that I appreciate his thoughtfulness. We can see that some such reaction would be appropriate, whereas a check for a thousand dollars would be unsuitable, as would an insult or a pile of snow left on the neighbor's driveway. Perhaps there is a rule of etiquette that applies in this case. If so, perhaps my neighbor is entitled by the institution of etiquette to an expression of gratitude from me. Again, this is consistent with the claim that he deserves that expression. Maybe he is entitled to an expression of gratitude by the rules of etiquette, and at the same time also deserves that expression.

In other cases, desert and entitlement do not coincide. Here is a good example involving an inheritance.[6] Suppose there are two grandchildren. One is vicious and rich; the other is virtuous and poor. Suppose their grandfather unaccountably leaves his entire fortune to the vicious grandchild. We have to acknowledge that the vicious grandchild is entitled to the fortune (the rules of the legal system are unambiguous on this point), but at the same time we may say that he certainly does not deserve it (he already has too much money; he is a rotten person who never treated his grandfather respectfully). The same example shows that a person may deserve something to which he is not entitled. The virtuous grandchild deserves at least some of the fortune, but unfortunately he is not entitled to so much as a penny.[7]

Another example illustrates the same point. Suppose that an athlete has her heart set on doing well in a competition. Suppose she has a lot of natural talent

[6] The example is hardly novel. Owen McLeod presented a similar case involving a rich uncle, a vicious nephew, and a virtuous daughter in McLeod (1999a: 189).

[7] I discuss the entitlement/desert distinction in greater detail below in section 2.4.2.

and trains diligently for a long time until she has developed championship-level abilities in her sport. Suppose that the training involves quite a bit of sacrifice on her part. Suppose that at the last minute the competition is cancelled, and the athlete has no opportunity to compete. Then we might say that this was a great misfortune for her; she deserved to have a chance to participate. In this case there is no rule of etiquette that says that she must be given a chance to participate, nor is there any law to that effect. Furthermore, there is no rule in the rulebook of the athlete's sport that says that those who have trained diligently are to get a chance to participate. It seems to me that it would be wrong to say (using the terminology in the way that I have specified) that the athlete is *entitled* to a chance to participate, yet we may still feel that it would have been fitting for her to have gotten that chance. Getting the chance to compete seems the natural and fitting upshot in light of all of her hard preparation. Thus it would be right to say that she *deserved* the chance. This seems to be an example of a case in which someone has completely "non-institutional" desert of something.

I suggested earlier that claims of entitlement are fundamentally sociological or empirical, while claims of desert are more fundamentally normative. Perhaps now we can see why this is so. Suppose the vicious grandchild mentioned a few paragraphs back claims that he is entitled to his grandfather's estate. Suppose this claim of entitlement is challenged. The grandchild could defend his claim by pointing out observable facts about the current laws concerning inheritance, together with observable facts about his own situation and his grandfather's will. He might point out, by appeal to birth certificates or other legal documents that he is in fact the grandson named in the will. He might point out that the relevant clause in the will says that the whole fortune is to go to him. While friends and family might think it is a pity that he would thus come into so much money, they would have to agree (perhaps after some bickering in court) that he is entitled to it.

On the other hand, if someone were to claim that the virtuous grandchild deserves the money, he would not be able to fully justify his claim merely by pointing out observable facts about the inheritance law and the will. The claim of desert involves an irreducibly normative component. Those who make this claim would have to appeal to something about how things "should be," or what would be "best," in a certain way. The details of such a defense are a matter of controversy, but it is agreed that a mere review of the observable facts would not suffice to establish that the virtuous grandson deserves the money.

I assume that desert claims such as the ones described in these examples are familiar. We make claims like these, and seemingly understand them at least in a rough and ready way, every day. However, it may be important to look more closely into the structure of desert facts. This is a topic on which my views are somewhat out of the mainstream.

2.3 On the Adicity of Desert

Several questions are typically of interest when we consider desert claims in ethics or in social and political philosophy.[8] In such contexts, it may be important to know (i) who is the deserver; (ii) what the deserver is said to deserve; (iii) upon what basis the deserver is said to be deserving of that desert; (iv) from whom the deserver is said to deserve to get the desert. We may also want to know (v) the time at which the deserver is deserving of this desert; and (vi) the time at which the deserver deserves to receive this desert.

Some relations are dyadic—they relate pairs of terms. Others are triadic—they relate trios of terms. The "adicity" of a relation is the number of terms that it relates. Many philosophers who discuss desert affirm a familiar view about its adicity. In the introduction to her anthology *Desert and Justice*, Serena Olsaretti says that one of the "few basic points of substantive agreement among desert theorists" is that "desert is a three-place relation between a person, the grounds on which she is said to be deserving (the desert basis), and the treatment or good which she is said to deserve (the deserved good)."[9] Similarly, in his introductory essay "Contemporary Interpretations of Desert"[10] Owen McLeod says "The contemporary literature is agreed that desert . . . is a three-place relation: it binds three sorts of thing: (a) a subject, (b) a thing deserved by the subject, and (c) a basis in virtue of which the subject deserves it" (61–2). Olsaretti and McLeod are right: desert is widely said to be a three-term relation.

However, while questions about the adicity of the desert relation may be of interest to those doing metaphysics or semantics, they are not really relevant to questions in ethics or social and political philosophy. Answers to questions (i) through (vi) above do not depend on the adicity of the desert relation. (Perhaps Olsaretti, McLeod, and others who have claimed that desert is a triadic relation merely meant to emphasize the idea that in almost all cases in which we are considering a desert claim it is especially important to know the deserver, the desert, and the desert base. Maybe this is what they had in mind when they said that desert is a three-place relation.)

Still, in light of the fact that this claim is so often made, and the concept of desert plays an essential role in my theory of justice, perhaps we should briefly

[8] Thanks to Brad Skow for his helpful contributions to this section.
[9] Olsaretti (2003: 4). [10] McLeod (1999b: 61–2).

consider the question whether the desert relation is in fact a three-place relation. A naïve procedure for answering questions like this involves appeal to certain linguistic considerations. We focus on well-formed, grammatically unproblematic sentences in which the relation in question is said to obtain. The sentences we choose must be ones that strike grammatically adept speakers of the language as being "minimally complete"—they do not contain any excess or extraneous information, but they contain enough information to be well-formed and grammatically complete. We then check to see how many arguments are related by the relation according to those sentences. So, for example, since sentences such as "Vermont is near New Hampshire" seem to be minimally complete, we may conclude that nearness is a two-place relation. Since "Massachusetts is between Vermont and Connecticut" is likewise minimally complete, it may appear that betweenness is a three-term relation. Clearly, there is something wrong with the sentence "Massachusetts is between Vermont." It will strike a native speaker as being incomplete; it is missing the third term that is required for the relation of betweenness to obtain.

If we allow linguistic considerations such as these to determine our view about the number of terms that are bound by the desert relation, we immediately run into trouble. Consider these statements:[11]

D1: *You* [1] deserve *a raise* [2].

D2: In virtue of *your hard work* [1], *you* [2] deserve to get *a raise* [3] on *September 1* [4].

D3: In virtue of *your hard work* [1], *you* [2] *now* [3] deserve to get *a raise* [4] from *your boss* [5], on *September 1* [6].

Each of these seems to be grammatically impeccable. None of them is elliptical—each expresses a "complete thought." None of them is so festooned with irrelevant information that we are inclined to say that simply as a matter of linguistic form it must be replaced by several sentences. But D1 suggests that desert is a two-place relation relating a deserver to a desert. D2 suggests that desert is a four-place relation relating a deserver, a desert, a desert base, and the time at which the deserver deserves to receive the desert. D3 suggests that desert is a six-place relation relating a deserver, a desert, two times, a desert base, and a distributor.

Maybe the right response to all this is to say that the desert relation does not have a fixed number of argument places; maybe it is "variably polyadic." Another

[11] In these example sentences, I have italicized the terms that are being used to indicate relata of the desert relation. I have inserted numerals in square brackets to highlight the number of relata in each case.

response would involve saying that there are actually several different desert relations, each with its own adicity. A better response is probably to say that this procedure is too naïve, that to answer questions about the adicity of the desert relation we would need to have a comprehensive and systematic semantic theory for all of English; we would need to determine what this theory says about the semantic value of the verb "to deserve."

It should be clear, however, that we can profitably discuss questions (i) through (vi) without committing ourselves to any view about the adicity of the desert relation. So let us consider the terms that are typically of interest when we speak of desert in social and political, as well as moral, contexts.

a. Desert claims typically involve a *deserver*. This is the person or other thing that is said, in the statement, to be deserving of something or other. In their advertising material, the McDonald's fast food company often repeats their motto: "You deserve a break today." In this example, the deserver is "you." As McLeod points out in his article "Desert" in the *Stanford Encyclopedia of Philosophy*, the deserver is typically a person, but it could be almost anything.[12] An ecosystem might deserve to be preserved, an art work might deserve to be admired—even an old car might deserve to be restored. I am inclined to think that there are cases in which *groups* deserve things—possibly certain pairs of people, or possibly certain ethnic groups. Some of these ideas are controversial. The cases that I will be discussing in this book are all cases in which the deservers are people (or groups of people).

b. Desert claims also typically involve a *desert*. This is the thing that the deserver is said to deserve. In the McDonald's example it is "a break." But there are lots of possibilities. Among the popular examples are such things as grades, wages, prizes, respect, honors and awards, rights, love, benefits . . . Leibniz and Kant would surely insist that we include happiness among the possible deserts; and others would insist that we should mention welfare.

Those deserts may seem at first to be "positive." However, there are "negative" counterparts. Indeed, some of the items on that list are already negative. Thus, some grades are bad grades, as for example, the F a student might deserve for a very weak paper. Other deserts are uniformly negative: burdens, fines, booby prizes, contempt, dishonors, onerous obligations, penalties, condemnation, hate, etc.

Some contributors to the literature on desert and justice write as if they think that every desert is either a plus or a minus. Thus, for example, in the passage quoted in Chapter 1 we see Mill expressing a form of desertism by saying that it is

[12] McLeod (2008). See also McLeod (1999b: 62–3).

the view that justice is a matter of distribution of things "good or evil" according to desert. Others speak of "benefits and burdens," or advantages and disadvantages. However, upon reflection it should be clear that there are cases in which someone deserves something that is neither good nor bad, neither a benefit nor a burden. Suppose someone who has done outstanding academic work deserves to get an A, while someone who has done completely unsatisfactory work deserves to get an F. It is reasonable to suppose that the A is a good grade—something the recipient will be pleased to get. And the F is a bad grade—something that the recipient will be disappointed to get. But suppose a student did mediocre work and deserves a mediocre grade—a C. This is neither good nor bad, neither a benefit nor a burden. Nevertheless, someone might deserve it. This would be a case in which someone deserves something that is neither "positive" nor "negative."

The same could be true of welfare. Someone might deserve happiness and (we may assume) that would be a good thing to get; someone else might deserve unhappiness and (we may assume) that would be a bad thing to get. But another person might deserve to be at welfare level zero, neither happy nor unhappy. And that would be neither good nor bad. This suggests a way in which the situation concerning some group could be outstanding with respect to justice, but not at all outstanding with respect to things of positive value. Imagine the most mediocre of all schoolrooms. Every student deserves a C. Suppose every student gets a C. Since everyone gets precisely what he or she deserves, there is perfect justice according to a possible desertist view about justice in grading; but no student in the room receives anything that is either good or bad. The same thing could happen on a grander scale. We can imagine a country in which every citizen deserves to be at a welfare level of zero.[13] If every citizen in fact is at a welfare level of zero, then there is perfect distributive justice according to a desertism of welfare. But the total value of all the welfare distributed in that country would be zero.

c. In many cases, when we make a desert claim we mention a *distributor*. This is the person or institution that is supposed to distribute the desert to the deserver. In some cases, the identity of the distributor will be clear. In other cases, it is not so clear. In the McDonald's example, no distributor is explicitly mentioned. It just says that you deserve a break. Perhaps when McDonald's makes this statement, they do not have any particular distributor in mind. There

[13] I'm imagining a system for assigning welfare levels that gives a higher positive score for each increasing level of "good" welfare; a lower negative score for each decreasing level of "illfare"; and a zero for the neutral level that is neither good nor bad.

is no person, x, such that McDonald's thinks that x has the responsibility of giving you the break that you deserve. Maybe they just think that you deserve it *from someone*. The same would be true of the Gates Foundation motto. The motto does not mention anyone who has the job of ensuring that everyone gets a chance to live a healthy and productive life. Maybe Bill and Melinda think we all deserve the chance to live a healthy life; but at the same time there is no one such that they believe that he or she is the one from whom we deserve to get this chance. In other cases, there is a distributor and its identity is clear. Consider, for example, the claim that the elderly professor deserves some respect from his unruly students. Here the distributor is explicitly mentioned: it is the unruly students. In the case of the neighbor who cleared the snow from my driveway, the distributor is also clear: it is me. I am the one from whom he deserves an expression of gratitude. In many of the examples that will be of greatest interest in this book, the relevant distributor is the government of the country in which the deserving person lives.

It may seem that we could relocate this reference to the distributor. We could build reference to the distributor into the description of the desert. Thus, instead of saying that the desert in the example involving the elderly professor is *respect*, we could say that the desert is *respect from his students*. For reasons that will emerge a bit later, I prefer to separate the desert from the distributor, though I recognize that it is not utterly essential that it be done in the way I prefer.

d. In some cases a desert statement may also indicate something about the strength of the deserver's desert of the thing deserved. The strength of someone's desert of something might be indicated loosely, as when we say that someone's desert of something is "very strong," or "only slight." In some cases we can use some numbers to represent strengths of desert, though the choice of a numbering system will be to some extent arbitrary. But there are some important facts here: sometimes you deserve both A and B, but you deserve A more than you do B; sometimes two different deservers deserve the same thing and it is not possible for both of them to get it; maybe one of them deserves it more than the other.[14] Sometimes you deserve something, but only to a very slight degree and this desert could easily be overridden by some other consideration.

[14] As I proceed to discuss cases in which someone deserves something, I will generally not include any mention of the degree to which the person deserves the desert. When, in such cases, I say that the person deserves the desert, I mean to indicate that, on balance and all things considered, he deserves it to a pretty high degree. In some cases it will become important to be more explicit. In such cases, I will try to be more explicit.

e. In many cases a desert statement (if fully spelled out) would also indicate some *times*. One of these is the time of the deserving; the other is the time when the receipt of the desert is supposed to take place. Thus, for example, suppose a lot of money has been withheld from a certain person's paycheck each week for a whole year. Suppose in fact the government has withheld more than the person owes in taxes. Then he deserves a refund. Suppose refunds are all given out on April 1. We might want to say this: at every moment in March, the taxpayer deserves to get a refund on April 1. In this example, the time of the deserving is *every moment in March*. The time at which the deserver deserves to receive the desert is April 1.[15]

f. Perhaps the most important and controversial bit of information we typically seek in connection with a claim about desert is the *desert base*. This is the feature in virtue of which the deserver deserves the desert from the distributor. In their advertising material on this topic, McDonald's does not explicitly specify the desert base in virtue of which we deserve a break. Perhaps we could ask them: "what have we done to deserve this break?" Surely there must be some answer to this question. The same is true in the case of the elderly professor. Why does he deserve respect from his unruly students? Maybe it is just because he is so old. Maybe it is because he formerly did such a good job of teaching. In other cases the desert base is made explicit. Thus for example consider this: "In virtue of all his hard work over a period of fifty years, the elderly professor deserves the respect of his students." Or maybe it is just because he is a human being. I think that whenever someone deserves something, there is some desert base upon which he or she deserves it.

In some cases there is little debate about whether a certain property serves as a desert base for a certain sort of treatment. This may be illustrated by the example of the student who produced outstanding work in a course and deserves a high grade. Few would debate the claim that the student deserves the grade in virtue of the high quality of her work. The desert base in that case would be *having produced academic work of high quality*. Similarly consider the case of the cold-blooded criminal who has inflicted great harm on many innocent victims. It is reasonable to suppose that he deserves a harsh penalty in virtue of his evil behavior. In this case, the desert base is something like *having inflicted great harm on many innocent victims*.

[15] For the most part, in the examples I discuss in this book, I will not explicitly mention the times of deserving and the times of receipt. These times will generally be either clear enough from the context or else pretty much irrelevant.

In other cases, however, there would be more controversy about desert bases. A good example involves the desert of wages. Suppose an employee works hard, is productive, is loyal to his employer, and in virtue of some health problems in his family, needs more money. We may agree in such a case that the employee deserves a raise—but we may disagree about the basis on which he deserves that raise.

There is general agreement that properties of certain types cannot serve as desert bases. Consider a case in which punishing an innocent person would have good consequences. The person has this property: *being such that punishing him would have good consequences.* But it would be seriously counterintuitive to say that the person deserves punishment in virtue of his possession of this property.

Certain general principles about desert bases have been introduced in an effort to explain why certain properties seem ineligible to serve as desert bases. Perhaps the least controversial principle is the so-called "Aboutness Principle," mentioned by Joel Feinberg.[16] Understood in one way, this principle says that a person can deserve something in virtue of a certain fact only if that fact is a fact "about the person." The same idea can be expressed by saying that a person can deserve something in virtue of a certain property only if the person actually has the property. The Aboutness Principle does not offer any assistance with respect to the punishment case just mentioned. After all, the innocent person actually does have the property of *being such that punishing him would have good consequences.* The fact that punishing him would have good consequences is a fact about him.

Some have said that if someone deserves something, D, in virtue of having some desert base, DB, then the deserving one must be responsible for having DB. (See, for example, Rawls 1971; Rachels 1978; Sadurski 1985.) This "Responsibility Principle" seems to be satisfied by many of the examples already discussed. The good student, we may suppose, is responsible for having produced good academic work. The cold-blooded criminal, similarly, may seem responsible for his vicious behavior. The hard working employee bears some responsibility for having worked so hard. We may generalize from these cases and conclude that all cases of desert are like this: if someone deserves something, D, on some basis, DB, then he or she is responsible for having DB. Appeal to the Responsibility Principle would explain why the innocent person does not deserve punishment. He is not responsible for having the property of *being such that punishing him would have good consequences.*

[16] The principle is stated in the reprint of "Justice and Personal Desert" that appears in Pojman & McLeod (1999: 72).

Elsewhere I have offered a variety of counterexamples to the Responsibility Principle.[17] Consider, for example, a case in which patrons at a restaurant were served spoiled food. I claimed that the patrons deserved compensation. The desert base here seems to be *having been harmed by the negligent food preparation by the restaurant*—yet the patrons were not responsible for having that desert base. They were innocent victims. A similar thing happens in the case of someone who has been egregiously insulted. She may deserve an apology in virtue of having been insulted, but she is not responsible for the insult. Another case mentioned by McLeod involves a child who, through no fault of his own, comes down with a painful illness. He deserves the care and sympathy of his parents, yet he is not responsible for having become ill.[18]

Others have suggested what may be called "the Temporality Principle": if someone deserves something, D, in virtue of having a certain desert base, DB, then he or she must already have DB at the time he or she begins to deserve D. (See, for example, Rachels 1978; Kleinig 1971; Sadurski 1985.) You cannot deserve something on the basis of a property you will begin to have only later. The Temporality Principle has been invoked in an effort to explain why it is wrong to engage in "pre-punishment." It is said that even if a certain person is going to commit a crime, he does not begin to deserve punishment for that crime until he actually commits it. This line of thought has been debated. One problem is that even before he commits the crime, the future criminal already has this property: *being such that he will later commit a crime*. It might be said that he deserves punishment in virtue of already having this property even before he commits the crime.

2.4 The Justification of Desert Claims

Some philosophers have been skeptical about desert claims. They wonder how—if at all—such claims can be justified. But the question about justification has been understood in several different ways. Some apparently take this to be a question about epistemic justification. (See, for example, McLeod 1995, p. 89.) Assume, for

[17] See, for example, "Desert: Reconsideration of Some Received Wisdom," *Mind* (1995: 63). The paper is reprinted in *What Do We Deserve?*, edited by Louis Pojman and Owen McLeod, Oxford University Press 1999. Also reprinted in my *Utilitarianism, Hedonism, and Desert.*

[18] In section 6 (page 72) of "Desert: Reconsideration of Some Received Wisdom," I engage in some speculation about what could have moved defenders of the Responsibility Condition to accept it. My hunch is that those who believe there is a link between desert and responsibility might be thinking more narrowly of *moral desert* or *merit*. There is some plausibility to the notion that moral desert arises only in cases for which the deserver is responsible. When we reflect on a broader collection of examples, the plausibility of the Responsibility Principle evaporates. My views on this topic were subjected to criticism offered by Saul Smilansky in Smilansky (1996: 157–63).

purposes of discussion, that those who work hard deserve some sort of reward for their efforts. Those who view the question in this way want to know how—if at all—a person can be epistemically justified in believing that hard work is a desert base for reward. Others take the question about justification in a different way. They take it to be a question about explanation.[19] As they see it, the question is: what explains the fact that hard work is a desert base for reward? Others speak in this context of "normative force." (See, for example, Sher 1987: xi.) They seem to be concerned with a question about what explains the fact that when someone deserves something, it is obligatory for others to provide it, or good that it be provided. Still others may phrase the question by appeal to concepts of *grounding* or *foundation*. They may ask what grounds the fact that those who work hard deserve rewards. Still others write a bit more vaguely about the *analysis* of desert claims. (See, for example, Feinberg 1963.)

As I understand the question, it can be explicated in this way: suppose someone claims that in general the possession of some desert base, DB, makes people deserve a certain desert, D. To justify this claim would be to explain how, if challenged, the maker of such a claim could support his claim. If someone were to challenge that claim, how could he argue for his assertion? What facts about DB and D could he cite in order to show that he was right—the possession of DB does make someone deserve D?

So understood, the search for justification is the attempt to give an account of what makes it the case that some feature is in fact a desert base for some alleged desert. If we had such an account, we would not have to appeal directly to bare intuitions about who deserves what as we theorize about justice. We could turn instead to an investigation of facts of the sort that we agree serve as the justifiers of desert claims. This might help to move the debate forward.

The search for justification presupposes that we already have a sufficiently solid grasp of what we mean when we say that someone deserves something on a certain basis. What we then seek is a line of argument that would demonstrate—in a particular case—that the person in the case deserves to receive the desert on the alleged basis. If we knew what makes it be the case that some feature is a desert base for some treatment, we could try to develop a persuasive argument for the conclusion that in fact this alleged desert base really is a desert base for that sort of treatment in the case at hand.

The question may still be obscure. Maybe the point of the question will become clearer if we reflect for a moment on some answers to this question that have been

[19] Brad Skow, in personal correspondence, suggested that in his view this would be the most plausible way of understanding the question.

offered. Many answers have been given; they fall into a relatively small number of fundamentally different families. They are as follows:

a. Consequentialist Views: These try to justify desert claims by saying (roughly) that someone deserves something, G, on the basis of the fact he has feature, F, if and only if giving that person G on the basis of the fact that he has F would lead to the best possible outcome.
b. Institutional Views: These try to justify desert claims by saying (roughly) that someone deserves something, G, on the basis of the fact that he has a feature, F, if and only if there is some social institution, I; the person is governed by I; according to the rules of I, the person is entitled to G in virtue of the fact that he has F.
c. Appraising Attitudes Views: These try to justify desert claims by saying (roughly) that someone deserves something, G, on the basis of some feature, F, if and only if we feel an appraising attitude such as admiration, approval, gratitude, contempt, or condemnation toward those who have F; and we think that giving those people G would be the appropriate way to express our appraising attitude.

There are in addition some mixed views that combine elements from two or more of the categories just mentioned. Thus, for example, someone might combine the consequentialist approach with the institutional approach and claim that someone deserves something, G, on the basis of some feature, F, if and only if some utility maximizing institution has rules that imply that the person is to receive G in virtue of his possession of F.

Suppose we conclude that desert claims cannot be justified in any such way. Suppose we think that desert claims "stand on their own," without the need or possibility of further justification. Then we are committed to a version of "the Autonomy of Desert." According to this thesis, desert claims cannot be justified by appeal to claims about any other normative notion.

2.4.1 Consequentialist justifications

Some popular views about the justification of desert claims are based on the idea that such claims can be justified by appeal to considerations about the values of consequences. Sidgwick seems to be thinking of something quite like this in *The Methods of Ethics*[20] where he mentions "the utilitarian interpretation of Desert." He describes this by saying: "when a man is said to deserve reward for any services to

[20] Sidgwick (1962: 284 fn. 1). It is not clear that Sidgwick personally accepts this view about desert; he seems to be offering it as an account of what a determinist would have to say.

society, the meaning is that it is expedient to reward him, in order that he and others may be induced to render similar services by the expectation of similar rewards."

A similar statement of the utilitarian theory about justification was defended by Austin Duncan-Jones in *Butler's Moral Philosophy*. Duncan-Jones said:

> When we say a man is responsible, and has certain deserts, the whole meaning of our statement can be resolved into two clauses: (1) he has done a good or bad action, or a right or wrong action; (2) it is useful to apply certain sanctions to him—useful, that is, in the way of influencing his habits and other people's.[21]

These statements are open to a variety of interpretations. In the present context I am not particularly interested in trying to figure out precisely what Sidgwick or Duncan-Jones may have meant. I am far more interested in the fundamental idea behind the consequentialist justification of desert statements, which they at least suggest. So let us start by stating a preliminary version of the view:

> CD1: The claim that S deserves G on the basis of S's possession of F can be justified by pointing out that giving G to S on the basis of S's possession of F would maximize utility.

The utility of an act may be taken to be the intrinsic good minus intrinsic evil that would be contained in the consequence of that act, if it were performed. To say that some act, A, maximizes utility is to say that there is some person who has some set of alternatives open to him at some time; one of these alternatives would be A; nothing else open to the agent would lead to a consequence with greater utility than would A. So the immediate implication of CD1 is that in order to justify the claim that S deserves G on the basis of S's possession of F, we need to find some person who has, as a utility-maximizing alternative, the act of giving G to S on the basis of S's possession of F. If there is such a person, then there is nothing else that this person can do instead that would have better consequences.

While there surely are some cases in which giving someone what he deserves will maximize utility, this link between desert and utility is just as frequently absent. Sometimes we deserve things but no one is in a position to provide them. For example, a child who has come down with a painful and fatal disease may deserve to live and to be happy. Yet it may be impossible for anyone to provide these things to the child. Perhaps there is no cure for the disease, and no way to

[21] Duncan-Jones (1952: 137). A few pages later Duncan-Jones adds a sort of emotive element to the analysis, saying that we express repugnance, resentment, moral indignation, etc. in the case in which we say someone deserves punishment. Thus his actual view (or perhaps the view he is attributing to Butler) seems to have been a combination of the consequentialist justification and the appraising attitudes justification.

make the child happy. The same thing might happen in cases of many other sorts: a person might deserve thanks, or expressions of gratitude, or a large cash reward for saving a life; yet it might be impossible to give him any of this, since he died in the effort. A person might deserve punishment for having committed a crime, and yet it might be that since he cannot be caught, no one has the option of giving him that punishment. In all these cases, the act of giving the deserved item to S is not among the alternatives for anyone. Hence giving it to him does not maximize utility for any agent. Nevertheless, the person still deserves that desert.

Sometimes it can be inexpedient to give someone a reward or punishment that he does deserve. The famous boxing match between Jack Johnson and Jim Jeffries provides a good example. Some facts from Wikipedia:

> The fight took place on July 4, 1910 in front of 20,000 people, at a ring built just for the occasion in downtown Reno, Nevada. Jeffries proved unable to impose his will on the younger champion and Johnson dominated the fight. By the 15th round, after Jeffries had been knocked down twice for the first time in his career, Jeffries' corner threw in the towel to end the fight and prevent Jeffries from having a knock out on his record. Johnson later remarked he knew the fight was over in the 4th round when he landed an uppercut and saw the look on Jeffries's face, stating *I knew what that look meant, the old ship was sinking*. The outcome of the fight triggered race riots that evening—the Fourth of July—all across the United States, from Texas and Colorado to New York and Washington, D.C. Johnson's victory over Jeffries had dashed white dreams of finding a "great white hope" to defeat him. Many whites felt humiliated by the defeat of Jeffries.[22]

On this basis we can formulate a counterexample to CD1. Consider the reward of being declared to be heavyweight champion of the world. Johnson deserved this in virtue of his great skill and his defeat of Jeffries. But giving him that reward on that basis had low utility—it caused race riots; people died; racism grew.

In other cases, the failure arises in the opposite way. Suppose a crazed maniac threatens to murder a dozen hostages unless he is given a half-hour of prime time TV to air his grievances. Giving him this airtime might maximize utility for the police chief; it might be the best thing for the chief to do in the circumstances; surely the maniac does not deserve it.

Perhaps a defender of Sidgwick's remark would acknowledge that these examples refute the idea behind CD1, but he might go on to insist that they do not refute the consequentialist thesis that Sidgwick stated in the footnote. It must be admitted that his remarks suggest a slightly different principle:

CD2: The claim that S deserves reward (punishment) for having done A can be justified by pointing out that if it were possible to reward (punish) S for

22 https://en.wikipedia.org/wiki/Jack_Johnson_%28boxer%29.

> having done A, then doing so would have high utility in virtue of inducing others to do (refrain from doing) things relevantly like A.

CD2 differs from CD1 in a couple of respects. In CD2, we specify that what S deserves is reward or punishment; furthermore, we specify that this reward or punishment is intended to be reward or punishment for some particular act, A; furthermore, we specify that the utility arising from punishment or reward must come about because others will be induced to or deterred from performing acts similar to A. Not just any source of utility will count. Finally, we phrase CD2 in such a way that the reward or punishment does not have to be among anyone's alternatives—nor does it have to maximize utility. It need only be such that if it were possible then it would have high utility of the sort specified. This is similar in many ways to what Austin Duncan-Jones said.

CD2 might appear to be an improvement over CD1. However, CD2 is still open to a variety of objections. One serious problem with CD2 is brought out by consideration of the famous telishment case, also known as "The Small Southern Town."[23] The example was presented by Carritt in his *Ethical and Political Thinking*, but gained great notoriety as a result of being quoted at length in Rawls's "Two Concepts of Rules". Here is the passage from Carritt:

> If some kind of very cruel crime becomes common, and none of the criminals can be caught, it might be highly expedient, as an example, to hang an innocent man, if a charge against him could be so framed that he were universally thought guilty; indeed this would only fail to be an ideal instance of utilitarian "punishment" because the victim himself would not have been so likely as a real felon to commit such a crime in the future; in all other respects it would be perfectly deterrent and therefore felicific.

In this example, punishing an innocent person has high utility for precisely the reasons stated—it would have great deterrent effect; but the victim of the punishment does not deserve punishment; after all, he is innocent. This reveals a very deep fact about desert and utility: sometimes it can be expedient to give someone a reward or a punishment that he or she does not deserve.

In the Small Southern Town, the unfortunate victim did not commit any crime. He was innocent. That is the basis for saying that he does not deserve punishment. Yet if enough people believe he was guilty, and are deterred from committing similar acts because of the threat of punishment, there may be great utility in punishing him anyway. This suggests a simple modification of CD2; we can add a clause saying that the person to be punished or rewarded must actually

[23] Rawls (1955: 3–13).

have performed the act for which he is to be deemed to deserve punishment.[24] More exactly:

> CD2+: The claim that S deserves reward (punishment) for having done A can be justified by pointing out (a) that in fact S did do A, and furthermore (b) that if it were possible to reward (punish) S for having done A, then doing so would have high utility in virtue of inducing others to do (refrain from doing) things relevantly like A.

This addition may enable the consequentialist approach to avoid the problem of the Small Southern Town, but the resulting principle is still unacceptable. One problem with CD2+ can be illustrated by a case in which a very popular person has actually done something for which he deserves punishment, but no one believes he is guilty. Imagine that if he were punished for having done the nasty deed, there would be an outpouring of anger from all of the popular person's fans and friends who think he has been framed. If our interest were in producing an outcome with high utility, we would have to refrain from punishing him. But in spite of that, since in fact he did do the nasty deed, he does deserve the punishment.

I think it is especially important to note, finally, that CD2 and CD2+ say nothing about cases of desert not involving reward and punishment. Thus, for example, suppose someone deserves compensation for suffering; an apology for an insult; or a tax refund for having had too much withheld from his paycheck. None of this is reward or punishment, and so the consequentialist principles considered here offer no justification for the desert claims. They are too narrow.

My conclusion is that the consequentialist approach is hopeless. Appeals to the utility of giving someone what he deserves cannot justify a claim to the effect that the possession of a certain feature makes a person deserve a certain sort of treatment. Sometimes deserved treatment is expedient; sometimes it is not. Sometimes undeserved treatment is expedient; sometimes it is not.

2.4.2 Institutional justifications of desert claims

First, some background: an *institution* may be taken to be a system of rules that define positions, moves, penalties, rewards, etc.[25] We might think that we could

[24] In Arneson (2003: 244–5) Richard Arneson discusses a closely related view about moral responsibility. He suggests that Smart was aware of cases in which great utility might be derived from framing an innocent person. He also suggests that one way to avoid this undesirable result would be to add a clause specifying that the person to be held responsible must actually have done the deed for which he is to be held responsible.

[25] I have benefitted from Owen McLeod's "Desert and Institutions," which can be found in Pojman and McLeod (1999: 186–95).

say that an institution exists in a society at a time if a sufficiently large number of members of the society accept the rules in the institution, and intend to be participating in it. But that is vague (how many is a "sufficiently large" number?). In addition it may be false. It could be that a very large number of people accept some set of rules, but the powerful leaders reject them and refuse to set up the institution. Then it does not exist there. And it could be that a majority of citizens reject an institution, but have to face up to the fact that it does exist. An example would be the system of racial segregation that used to exist in the United States—the so-called "Jim Crow" system. It is not easy to say what makes an institution "exist" in a society. I think we have to leave this puzzle to the sociologists.

We may also need to assume that when people set up these institutions, they do so with some intention. They are trying to achieve something; or more likely, they are trying to achieve a whole bunch of different things. Maybe different people have different aims. We can say that the *point* of an institution is the main goal or aim that people have in establishing or maintaining that institution.

A person may be *governed* by some institution even if he does not like it, or does not endorse it. Thus, for example, suppose we have a criminal justice system in a certain society. Suppose some miscreant lives in that society and has violated the laws. He has been charged with some crime. Suppose he is found guilty in a duly established court of law and is sentenced to ten years in prison. He is governed by the rules of the judicial system whether he likes it or not. To be governed by an institution one must live (or perhaps be a visitor) in the society where the institution exists, and one must somehow "fall under" the rules. Those rules must "apply to" the individual. Again, this is a tricky sociological notion, not easily spelled out.

Some philosophers have said things that suggest that it is possible to justify a desert claim by identifying an institution according to which the deserver is entitled to the desert. We can state this idea a bit more clearly:

> AID: The claim that a person, S, deserves something, D, on the basis of the fact that he has a feature, F, can be justified by pointing out that there is some social institution, I; I exists in S's society; S is governed by I; according to the rules of I, those who have F are to receive D; S has F.[26]

This "actual institutional" account of desert is almost universally rejected.[27] There are several independent sources of difficulty. Most of these emerge from

[26] The "A" in "AID" stands for "actual." This version of the thesis claims that desert is determined by the rules of *actual* institutions.

[27] There are a few passages in Rawls's *Theory of Justice* in which he suggests something like this view. See, for example, the passage on p. 103 where he is talking about a just system of cooperation. He imagines that someone has followed the rules and is therefore entitled to some reward. Rawls

its requirement that desert arises always and only when there is an appropriate *actual* social institution. This produces a number of devastating objections. Suppose a thoroughly decent person has suffered a number of horrible misfortunes. He deserves a change of luck; he deserves some good luck for a change. Suppose he lives in a country where there is no social institution that supplies this. If AID were true, we would have no way to justify the claim that he deserves it.

An equally devastating objection arises from the fact that some of the institutions that actually exist are morally indefensible. Let us imagine a thoroughly horrible social institution—slavery. Suppose some unfortunate individual is governed by that institution. Suppose the institution contains rules that say that slaves who are strong and healthy shall be required to work without pay in the cotton fields. Suppose this individual is strong and healthy; then the proposed actual institutional idea about justification says that the claim that he deserves to be forced to work in the fields without pay can be justified by appeal to the fact that there is an actual institution that requires this of him. That is as preposterous as it is offensive.

The general point: we must not lose sight of the fundamental difference between *entitlement* and *desert*. Actual institutionalism seems to confuse these. It seems to say that you deserve something if and only if you are entitled to it by the rules of an actual institution. Since there are bad institutions, and missing institutions, this is clearly a mistake.

We can deal with all of these objections by altering the institutional account of justification. Instead of making desert depend upon the existence of an actual social institution, we can make it depend upon the rules that would be contained in some ideal social institution. The main change is that we no longer require that the social institution be actual. We require instead that it be an ideal institution—an institution that would be in some way desirable. Then we can attempt to justify desert claims by saying that the deservers would be entitled to those deserts by the rules of an ideal social institution.

We can state the thesis this way:

IID: The claim that a person, S, deserves something, G, on the basis of the fact that he has a feature, F, can be justified by pointing out that there is some

says, "But this sense of desert presupposes the existence of the cooperative scheme..." thereby suggesting that there is some sense of "desert" in which it means the same as "entitled [by a just scheme]." I doubt that this was Rawls's considered view. Whether endorsed by Rawls or not, the idea suggested here would induce deep circularity in my project. I intend to explain justice by appeal to the concept of desert; the suggested account of desert would explain desert in part by appeal to justice.

possible social institution, I; I would be ideal for S's society; S would be governed by I; according to the rules of I, those who have F are to receive G; S has F.

Before we can evaluate this proposal, we must have a clearer understanding of what is meant by saying that a possible institution is "ideal" for a society. We might try to define this term by saying that an ideal institution is one that distributes benefits and burdens to people precisely in accord with their deserts. With this account of ideality in place, IID generates quite a few correct results. Unfortunately, it would be inadmissible in the present context. After all, the whole point of this exercise is to find some way to justify desert claims. This account would explain desert by appeal to ideal institutions, and then explain ideal institutions by appeal to desert.

Following the rule utilitarians, we could define ideality in this way: a possible institution is ideal for a society if and only if having it as the society's institutional way of achieving its point would produce more utility than would the having of any alternative institution aimed at achieving the same point. If we proceed in this way, we have an account of justification that seems to incorporate aspects of the utilitarian approach into the institutional approach.

This hybrid approach to justification also fails, as this example shows: Suppose the ideal ice-skating institution would have rules specifying that in order to get the gold medal, you have to perform a seven minute free program; a six minute program of required figures; and that you must wear a regulation team uniform consisting of full length trousers and matching long-sleeved team shirts. But suppose this ideal institution is not in place. In its place is a good, but not ideal actual institution. Suppose Nancy scrupulously follows the rules of the actual institution and puts in a fabulous performance—far better than any of the other competitors. Suppose some of these rules are not the ones in the ideal ice-skating institution. Nancy may deserve the gold medal in fact; but she surely would not be entitled to it under the ideal institution by virtue of her performance here tonight. She did not abide by the rules of the ideal institution; she abided by the rules of the actual institution that does not contain precisely these rules. As a result, IID implies that it is impossible to justify the claim that Nancy deserves the medal.

I am inclined to think that there is no helpful way to justify desert claims by appeal to claims about the entitlements created by institutions, actual or ideal.[28]

[28] Commentators often claim that David Cummiskey defended an institutional justification of desert claims in his "Desert and Institutions," *Analysis* 47, 1 (January 1987), p. 18. It is not clear to me that the attribution is fully supported by the text.

2.4.3 *Appraising attitudes and the justification of desert claims*

Some philosophers have said things that suggest that desert claims can be justified by appeal to facts about "appraising attitudes."[29] In order to understand this idea, we need first to understand what is meant by "appraising attitude."

Miller lists three "positive" appraising attitudes. These are admiration, approval, and gratitude (Pojman and McLeod 1999: 96). Suppose you admire someone; then you must admire him *for something he is or something he did.* Maybe he worked hard; or wrote a good paper; or can run very fast; or is able to play the violin beautifully. Similarly for the other positive appraising attitudes.

There is a corresponding view about "negative" appraising attitudes. Presumably these would be things like disapproval, resentment, contempt, "thinking ill of," condemnation. But they are like the positive ones in this respect: if you disapprove of someone, then you must disapprove of him *for something he is or something he did.* Maybe he plagiarized a paper; maybe he is totally out of shape; maybe he is utterly talentless.

Miller says that the bases of favorable appraising attitudes have to be things that are distinctive of certain individuals. They must be features that are "outstanding or exceptional." Thus, if some feature is uniformly had by everyone, it cannot be a suitable basis for an appraising attitude.[30]

Miller says that if we did not have these attitudes, "we would not and could not use the concept of desert."[31] The words would have no meaning for us. He also says that the range of possible desert bases coincides with the range of bases for appraising attitudes. You cannot deserve something on the basis of your possession of a property, F, unless we could have an appraising attitude toward you on the basis of your possession of F. But what is most important for our present purposes is that, according to Miller, "the existence of these appraising attitudes makes intelligible the connection between a desert judgment and its basis." It may appear, then, that he means to be claiming that something about these appraising attitudes provides the answer to our question about the justification of desert claims.

A bit later in his discussion, Miller states his thesis:

> Desert, then, denotes a relationship between an individual and his conduct, and modes of treatment which are liked or disliked. When we make a judgement of desert we are judging the appropriateness of this particular individual, with his qualities and past

[29] I base what I say here primarily on remarks made by David Miller in Miller (1976). The relevant discussion is reprinted in Pojman and McLeod (1999: 93–100).

[30] Pojman and McLeod (1999: 95).

[31] Pojman and McLeod (1999: 96).

behaviour, receiving a given benefit or harm—an appropriateness which is made intelligible by considering the appraising attitudes that we may take up toward the individual.[32]

This passage suggests that Miller wants to defend a form of "judger relativism" about desert. That is, it suggests that he wants to say that whether a desert judgment is correct depends upon whether the person who makes that judgment personally has the appropriate appraising attitude. But Miller explicitly denies this. "It is not actually necessary for me, the maker of the judgement, to have this attitude of admiration myself."[33] Miller suggests that what is necessary is that "I live in a community in which most people would take up the relevant appraising attitude...."[34]

Let us focus on the case in which what is deserved is a benefit. We can assume that if the theory works adequately in this case, a modest extension will work adequately in the case in which someone deserves a burden. Miller's form of this part of the appraising attitudes view then seems to be something like this:

AAD1: If an evaluator, J, makes the judgment that S deserves some benefit, G, on the basis of S's possession of F then J's judgment is justified if and only if

i. F is a property that S has in virtue of some outstanding or exceptional qualities or past behavior;
ii. Getting G will be a benefit for S;
iii. J lives in a community where the majority have a favorable appraising attitude (admiration, respect, affection) for people in virtue of their having F, and think it appropriate on this basis that these people be given G.

If understood in this way, the proposal seems to me to be clearly wrong. Imagine a thoughtful member—call him "Huck"—of a society in which slavery is very widely accepted. Suppose Huck knows a slave, Jim. Suppose Huck thinks that Jim deserves to be freed from slavery, and suppose he thinks that Jim deserves this simply in virtue of the fact that Jim has not done anything wrong. AAD1 goes dramatically wrong in this case. First of all, Huck's desert claim does not involve a desert base that is "outstanding or exceptional"; quite the contrary, the desert base is something that is common to all who have done nothing wrong. Furthermore, it is not the case that a majority in Huck's community would take up a favorable attitude toward Jim in virtue of his having done nothing wrong—and surely most of them would not think it appropriate for people to be freed from slavery on this basis. Thus, most people along the Mississippi River at that time would reject Huck's appraisal.

32 Pojman and McLeod (1999: 98).
33 Pojman and McLeod (1999: 97).
34 Pojman and McLeod (1999: 98).

It may seem that part of the problem here arises from Miller's appeal to a sort of social relativism. Maybe a better version of the view would simply eliminate the requirement that a majority of compatriots would have the relevant appraising attitude. Furthermore, another part of the problem arises from the requirement that the desert base must be some feature that is "outstanding or exceptional." Perhaps this should be eliminated as well. This would yield a different version of the appraising attitudes view:

AAD2: If an evaluator, J, makes the judgment that S deserves some benefit, G, on the basis of S's possession of F then J's judgment is justified if and only if

i. F is a property (exceptional or not) that S has;
ii. Getting G would be a benefit for S;
iii. J has a favorable appraising attitude (admiration, respect, affection) for people in virtue of their having F, and thinks it would be a good thing that those who have F be given G on the basis of the fact that they have F.

AAD2 may yield more plausible results in the case involving Huck (though this could be debated), but it obviously goes wrong in cases in which an evaluator is mistaken about a desert base. Suppose, for example, that a racist believes that a person of his own race deserves an important benefit simply because of his membership in the preferred race. Suppose he does have admiration for people of that race, and does think that it would be a good thing for people of that race to gain the advantage in question. AAD2 implies that the racist's prejudiced judgment is justified.

A revised version of the idea would not allow justification to turn directly on the possession of the appraising attitude. It would require that the appraising attitude be "correct"—one that the subject deserves. The resulting reformulation might look like this:

AAD3: If an evaluator, J, makes the judgment that S deserves some benefit, G, on the basis of S's possession of F then J's judgment is justified if and only if

i. F is a property (exceptional or not) that S has;
ii. Getting G would be a benefit for S;
iii. It would be appropriate for J to have a favorable appraising attitude (admiration, respect, affection) for people in virtue of their having F, and to think it would be a good thing that those who have F be given G on the basis of the fact that they have F.

One obvious problem with AAD3 is its apparent circularity. When we say (in iii) that it would be "appropriate" for J to have a favorable appraising attitude for people who have F, we seem to mean neither more nor less than that these people deserve to receive this sort of reaction; they deserve to be admired or respected for having F. If this is the case, the alleged justification makes use of the very notion that it is intended to explicate.[35]

But the problems with AAD3 run even deeper than this. Some of us are desertists about justice. We think that there is justice in a community if and only if members are getting what they deserve. My form of desertism is the view that there is political economic distributive justice in a community if members are getting the political economic deserts that they deserve in virtue of their possession of political economic desert bases. Now consider such things as an effective police force; reduced in-state tuition rates; low interest loans for people who live in officially declared disaster areas; functional infrastructure such as highways, water supply systems, postal services, etc. I am inclined to say that people deserve these things, and that there is a higher level of political economic distributive justice in a country if they are made available to members who need them. Let us focus on a simple example: free public education. I think people deserve to have access to schools.

It is hard to think of an appraising attitude that we have (or ought to have) toward people in virtue of which we think they are special and outstanding and meritorious and in virtue of which they deserve public education. Admiration, gratitude, approval, and other such positive appraising attitudes seem out of place in this context. Maybe the desert base is *need*. Maybe it is this: our chances of flourishing as human beings will be much greater if we are educated; none of us is able, entirely on his or her own, to establish an educational system that will provide the education that we need. But if the whole community chips in, we can build schools, hire teachers, buy books and other supplies, and thus have public education. I would say that each of us deserves the opportunity to attend a free public school because we have this sort of need for education. But being needy is not a basis for any suitable appraising attitude.

Miller explicitly rejects need as a desert base, since we neither admire people for being needy, nor hold them in contempt for it. Thus, he thinks that need is not a basis for an appraising attitude. So on his view, it cannot be a desert base.

[35] Owen McLeod made approximately this point in his (1999b: 64).

But in my view, it is a desert base—indeed one of the most important—and so Miller's view must be wrong. In effect, Miller would say:

1. Need is not a basis for an appraising attitude.
2. If need is not a basis for an appraising attitude, then need is not a desert base.
3. Therefore, need is not a desert base.

And I am inclined to accept a different argument:

1. Need is a desert base.
2. If need is a desert base, then some desert bases are not bases for appraising attitudes.
3. Therefore, some desert bases are not bases for appraising attitudes.

I prefer my position since I think a reasonable account of political economic distributive justice would require receipt in accord with features some of which are not bases of appraising attitudes; and so I think that such a theory would require receipt in accord with features that are disallowed as desert bases by Miller's theory. I present and explain a catalogue of these features later in Chapter 4. Several of the features that I list as especially important political economic desert bases would not count as desert bases at all on Miller's view. As I see it, this suggests that Miller has too narrow a conception of desert bases.[36]

2.5 More Concerning the Justification of Desert Claims

I have tried to explain why, in my view, desert claims cannot be justified by appeal to claims about utility, or institutions, or appraising attitudes.[37] As I suggested earlier, I am more inclined to justify desert claims by appeal to claims about requirement. I think that the concept of requirement is somewhat broader and slightly more familiar than the concept of desert. I also think that it is possible to justify the claim that a person, S, deserves some benefit, D, in virtue of having some desert base, DB, by pointing out that the having of DB in general requires

[36] For further helpful discussion of the "appraising attitudes" approach, see McLeod (1995: 74–9). I am especially impressed by his discussion.

[37] Others have attempted to justify desert claims in other ways. In his (1987) *Desert*, George Sher apparently means to claim that in every case in which something is deserved on some basis, there is some fact about some sort of normativity that supports the desert claim. In some cases the relevant sort of normativity is *intrinsic value*. In other cases is it *moral obligation*; and in yet other cases it seems to be something else. I encourage the interested reader to review the details of Sher's pluralistic approach. See also Lamont (1994).

receiving some benefit like D; and the having of DB is a sufficiently intimate fact about S.

At the same time, however, I must acknowledge that the concept of requirement is so closely connected to the concept of desert that this proposed justification amounts almost to a tautology. Some will surely feel that it is no justification at all. Furthermore, given that the concept of requirement is foundational and not open to any deeper grounding, it may seem that the move to requirement yields only a very modest level of increased insight. And thus I am prepared to leave open the possibility that the concept of desert is "semi-autonomous"—it is on approximately the same foundational level as the concept of requirement. Perhaps this will have to suffice.

However, there may be a different way to justify desert claims. Whether this is so or not depends upon what is meant by "justifies." I think there is something that can be said in defense of my approach. It is a variant of the reflective equilibrium approach made famous in the work of Rawls. My use of the method differs in important ways from Rawls's. I discuss this in greater detail in Appendix A "A Note on Method."

3

Four Forms of Desertism

In a remark that I quoted earlier, John Hospers said, "justice is getting what one deserves. What could be simpler?"[1] The suggestion here is that desertism is pretty straightforward. Once you understand the concepts of *desert* and *receipt*, the statement of the theory is obvious: there is perfect distributive justice in a society if and only if in every case in which a member of the society deserves something, he or she receives it. That does seem, prima facie, pretty simple.

However, as so often happens in cases such as this, things are not quite as simple as the remark from Hospers suggests. In fact, there are many different ways in which the desertist conception of justice can be developed. Some of these have been discussed in the literature; others have not yet been noted. In some cases, critics of desertism have interpreted the doctrine in one of these ways, and have apparently assumed that if someone wants to defend desertism, it will have to be desertism of the form that the critic has identified. Their arguments in some cases were relevant only to one form of desertism but were presented as if they would bear on all forms. But there are other options. Some forms of desertism seem to me to be implausible. Others seem to be of limited application. The most interesting form—the form I defend in this book—has not previously been presented or discussed. Let us then consider some forms of desertism, starting with the simplest and most familiar forms.

3.1 Cosmic Desertism about Distributive Justice

Cosmic desertism is the most all-inclusive form of desertism. The idea here is simple:

> CDa: There is perfect distributive justice in a society if and only if every member of that society receives everything that he or she deserves.[2]

[1] Hospers (1961: 433). As I pointed out in the Introduction, Hospers goes on to say that the appearance of simplicity is very misleading.

[2] Miller (1976: 114–15) briefly mentions cosmic desertism. Feinberg uses the term "cosmic justice" but he has a different idea in mind. For him, a cosmic injustice is one that somehow throws

In order to appreciate the implications of this principle, we need to have an account of the things that people deserve. Aristotle suggested that the currencies of justice are "honour or money or the other things that fall to be divided among those who have a share in the constitution."[3] But then we must face the question: what are these "other things that fall to be divided"? A somewhat more extensive list is provided by Feinberg in his "Justice and Personal Desert." Feinberg lists:

1. Awards of prizes;
2. Assignments of grades;
3. Rewards and punishments;
4. Praise, blame, and other informal responses;
5. Reparation, liability and other modes of compensation.

Feinberg goes on to mention another class of possible deserts:

6. Offices and positions of honor.

A large portion of the literature on desert proceeds on the assumption that what we fundamentally deserve is:

7. Economic compensation for work, or rent, or royalties, or anything for which we get paid.

Some who write on justice seem to operate with the assumption that the main thing we deserve is:

8. Welfare, happiness, pleasure, or the opportunity to have a good life.

I would add some further categories:

9. Theological-Moral deserts, including heavenly bliss and infernal suffering.

This category would include whatever things we deserve in the afterlife in virtue of the moral quality of our character and behavior here on earth.

10. Political deserts, including citizenship, the right to vote, freedom of speech, religion, assembly, etc.
11. Etiquettical deserts, including apologies, thank-you notes, invitations, gifts, gold watches, retirement parties, etc.

the cosmos itself "out of kilter." Or, as Feinberg says, it is one "suffered, *inter alia*, by the cosmos itself" Feinberg (1974: 308).

[3] *NE*, bk. 5, ch. 2.

When he presented his list, Feinberg included a disclaimer. He said that he was making "no claim to taxonomic precision or completeness."[4] I am like Feinberg; I also make no such claims.

In any case, when combined with this list of possible deserts, the cosmic desertist principle of distributive justice now has some real content. The principle itself tells us that we have perfect distributive justice in a state when every citizen gets everything he or she deserves. The list then goes on to give us some indication of some of the things we might be thought to deserve. The general principle together with the list of deserts yields a substantive thesis about distributive justice.

3.2 Approximations to Perfect Justice

No group we are likely to encounter here on earth would manifest perfect distributive justice as measured by cosmic desertism. There are sure to be cases in which deserts conflict, so that not everyone can get everything deserved; surely there are shortages of some goods, so that there is not enough to go round. So we need to combine our principle about perfect distributive justice with a comparative principle that tells us when one imperfectly just arrangement is more just than another imperfectly just arrangement. Here is an idea:

CDc: There is greater distributive justice in a group, G1, than there is in another group, G2, if and only if the situation in G1 more closely approximates perfect distributive justice as measured by CDa than does the situation in G2.

But how are we to measure "degrees of approximation"? One immediately attractive idea would make use of the concept of a "receipt/desert ratio." Consider all the basic desert statements[5] concerning things that are deserved by anyone in the group from anyone for any reason at any time. Some portion of those statements will have this feature: the deserver got what he deserved, from the person from whom he deserved it, and at the time when he deserved to get it. When this is the case, the basic desert statement is "requited." Consider, for any time, the ratio of requited basic desert statements to basic desert statements. We

[4] Feinberg (1970: 62).

[5] When I speak here of "basic desert statements" I have in mind simple statements about some person, S, some desert, D, some desert base, DB, some distributor, R, and perhaps some times, t1 and t2, of the form "In virtue of having DB at t1, S deserves D from R at t2." I introduce this simplification mainly just to avoid double-counting of desert facts. Since I do not endorse the idea of measuring approximation by appeal to receipt/desert ratios, I think it is not necessary for me to give a more precise account of the relevant class of statements.

might think that this ratio gives us a way of measuring how closely a distribution approximates perfect justice.

But there is a serious problem with this approach. We can imagine situations in which no one in a group is getting precisely what he deserves from the distributor from whom he deserves it and at the right time, but we can go on to imagine that the level of cosmic justice is nevertheless still very high. To see how this could happen, consider this case: suppose my next door neighbor drove his car across my lawn late last night and put deep ruts into the freshly seeded grass. What I deserve is a prompt, sincere apology from my next door neighbor and an offer to repair the damage he has done to my lawn. But suppose I do not get that. Suppose instead that my neighbor's wife calls—somewhat belatedly—and gives me a somewhat less than fully convincing apology on behalf of her husband. Suppose she offers to give me an amount of money that would be slightly too small to cover the expenses involved in repairing the damage to the lawn. In this case, while I did not get precisely what I deserved, I got instead something fairly close to what I deserved. If lots of people in some country received half-hearted apologies such as these regularly, then the level of cosmic justice would be reduced. It would be lower than it would have been if everyone had gotten precisely the apology he or she deserved—and from the right person, at the right time, and with the right level of sincerity. But it is important to see that the level of distributive justice is not zero. It would be higher than the level of cosmic justice in a country in which some people got precisely what they deserved, but all the rest got nothing. Even though no one in the first country got what precisely what he or she deserved, everyone got something approximating what he or she deserved. This shows that we cannot identify the degree of less than perfect justice in a country as the ratio of perfectly requited desert claims to total desert claims in that country.

There are several different factors that could bear on the question concerning proximity to perfect desert. One of these is *timing*. Justice is most perfectly served if people get what they deserve precisely at the time when they deserve to get it. If they get it before or after that time, then the level of justice in the situation is adversely affected. I assume that in general justice is better served if people receive their deserts at times closer to the time at which they deserve to get them.

Suppose the thing deserved is a measurable item (like money or happiness, for example). Then, other things being equal, it would seem to be more just if the amount of the deserved item that in fact is received were closer to the amount deserved. So if you deserve precisely \$100.00, then it will be more just for you to receive \$99.00 than it would be for you to receive \$50.00. But we have to recognize that this sort of proximity is relevant only in cases in which the deserved item is something that comes in straightforwardly measurable amounts.[6]

In many cases, however, the thing deserved is not so easily measured. In the apology case discussed a few paragraphs back, for example, I deserved a prompt, sincere apology from my neighbor. I got a less prompt and less sincere apology—and I got it from my neighbor's wife instead of from him. It may be difficult to find a clear system of measurement that will allow us to determine how close this apology is to the perfect apology that I actually deserve. But since justice is at least partially served when people get less than perfect apologies, we must assume that it makes sense to speak of the extent to which actual but imperfect receipt approximates receipt of precisely what is deserved.

In other cases, involving other deserved items, other features of the case will combine to determine proximity to perfect justice.[7]

I recognize that what I have said here leaves the concept of approximation somewhat vague. I hope the reader, making use of his or her intuitive grasp of the intended notion, will be able to understand what I mean well enough when I speak of the extent to which an imperfect distribution approximates a perfect one.

We cannot reasonably doubt that there is such a thing as cosmic distributive justice as described by principles CDa and CDc. Indeed, I suspect that some critics of desertism have assumed that desertists had some such thing in mind. But my own view is that this form of desertism is of marginal interest. It seems to me that the concept of cosmic justice blends together too many disparate considerations. In order for there to be perfect cosmic distributive justice in some society, everyone must receive everything he or she deserves. And this would mean that every student would get every grade that he or she deserves, and every athlete would win every competition that he or she deserves to win, and every neighbor would receive every apology and thank-you note that he or she deserves, and everyone would receive the amount of respect, and admiration, and love, and contempt, and good luck that he or she deserves. It would be a veritable wonderland of requited desert in which no one would have any grounds for complaint about being short-changed about anything.

[6] And even when it is a measurable item, many profound problems remain. Among these, for example, is this: suppose you deserve exactly n units of some good. What difference would it make if you got n + 2 units rather than n − 2 units? Does an excess decrease justice just as much as an equal deficiency? Suppose each of several people deserves exactly n units of some good. Suppose there is not enough to go around. Would it be more just to give some exactly what they deserve and others much less? Or would it be more just to give everyone a less-than-deserved share of equal size? Questions such as this are very difficult and deserving of careful attention. The best recent discussion of these issues can be found in Shelly Kagan's *The Geometry of Desert*.

[7] I briefly come back to this problem later in section 9.3.3.

Surely, however, when political philosophers are drawn to the idea that justice is a matter of receipt in accord with desert, they do not have anything quite so fantastic in mind. They do not mean to be endorsing the idea that in a just state, thank-you notes and apologies must be received precisely at the fitting moment. They are not thinking about retirement parties and gold watches. Rather, they must have in mind some restricted class of deserts, and some restricted class of desert bases, and they must be thinking that in a just state, people receive all the deserts in that restricted class, and that they receive them when they have desert bases from that restricted class. They are thinking that the relevant sort of distributive justice requires that these restricted deserts be distributed in accord with these restricted desert bases. They are not thinking of matters of etiquette or other purely personal affairs.

But that leaves us with a question about how the restrictions are to be determined. Precisely what items go into the restricted class of deserts? And what desert bases go into the restricted class of desert bases that is relevant to distributive justice in a state?

3.3 Desertism about Divine Distributive Justice

If we start with a principle of cosmic distributive justice, and then impose certain restrictions on the admissible deserts, desert bases, and distributors, we will arrive at a principle of divine distributive justice. I am thinking of a trio of restrictions that yields a form of desertism that has come in for some discussion in the literature.

i. Instead of considering all possible deserts, we can consider just the ones that fall into two categories: various levels of heavenly bliss; various levels of infernal suffering. If a view like Dante's is correct, then there are very many different levels of heaven and hell; the bliss enjoyed or the suffering endured in these levels is supposed to correspond appropriately to various sorts of virtue and vice that one could manifest in life. But the deserts in question would all fall into these two categories. There are no prizes, trophies, honorific jobs, apologies, cash rewards, extra miles on your credit card, etc. Let us use the term "divine deserts" to indicate this restricted class of deserts.
ii. Instead of considering all possible distributors of deserts, we could focus on one central distributor—God. (Perhaps St. Peter gives him some assistance.) Where divine distributive justice is concerned, bliss and suffering that you get from any other source are not relevant. The only kinds of bliss and suffering that count are bliss and suffering that you get from God.

iii. Instead of considering all possible desert bases, we could focus only on what we may call "moral desert bases." I have in mind here all the traits that can properly be identified as the moral virtues and the moral vices. According to one popular view, these would be things such as lust, gluttony, greed, sloth, wrath, envy, pride, etc. and their "positive" counterparts. For a full accounting, the reader should turn to Dante's *Divine Comedy.*

Now we are in position to state the fundamental principle of the desertist theory of divine distributive justice:

DDa: There is perfect distributive justice in a possible world if and only if in every case in which a resident of that world deserves a divine desert in virtue of having a moral desert base, he or she receives that desert in the afterlife from God.

Associated with DDa would be a comparative principle that says that one possible world has a greater degree of distributive justice than another if and only the quality of the fit between divine deserts and moral desert bases in the first world more closely approximates the perfect quality of fit required by DDa than does the quality of that fit in the second world.

Earlier I cited a passage from Leibniz's "On the Ultimate Origination of Things" in which he seems to endorse a principle about distributive justice that is relevantly like DDa. Leibniz said:

> There couldn't be a better standard in this matter than the *law of justice,* which lays down that everyone is to participate in the perfection of the universe, and to have personal happiness, in proportion to his own virtue and to the extent that his will has contributed to the common good. This vindicates the charity and love of God, which constitutes the entire force and power of the Christian religion, in the judgment of wise theologians.[8]

The whole scheme seems to me to be somewhat far-fetched. I mention it here for a couple of reasons. I want to distinguish between cosmic justice and divine justice. Some writers on these topics seem to use the terminology interchangeably,[9] but if we use the terminology as I suggest, principles of cosmic justice and divine justice would give clearly distinct evaluations. Furthermore, I want to illustrate the technique of restricting deserts, or distributors, or desert bases. I am going to use this same technique in the presentation of a view that I take to be considerably more interesting.

[8] Translation by Jonathan Bennett:.http://www.earlymoderntexts.com/authors/leibniz.

[9] Michael Slote seems to do this in "Desert, Consent, and Justice." Speaking of "our attitudes toward divine or cosmic justice," he remarks that "we feel that if God or the world is just, then people are rewarded according to their merits or worth..." Slote (1973: 337). As I use the terminology, Slote's remark would apply to divine justice, but not to cosmic.

What about the connections between these principles of justice? Is it possible for there to be a situation in which the level of distributive justice as measured by the cosmic principle is very low, but the level of distributive justice as measured by the divine principle is very high? This would happen if people rarely received the things that they deserve here on earth, but if in addition they always received their heavenly rewards from God later on in the afterlife.

It is also possible for there to be a situation in which the level of distributive justice as measured by the cosmic principle is very high, but the level of distributive justice as measured by the divine principle is very low. This would happen if people often received the apologies, thank-you notes, wages, grades, honorific jobs, etc. that they deserve here on earth, but if in addition they never received any heavenly or infernal rewards in an afterlife for the virtue or vice that they manifested while they lived.

If there were *perfect* cosmic distributive justice, then everyone would receive everything he or she deserved; and—assuming that manifestations of virtue and vice make us deserving of rewards from God in the afterlife—it would follow that there would have to be perfect divine distributive justice. The inference in the opposite direction clearly would be mistaken. It seems that God could be doing a perfect job of rewarding us in the afterlife for our virtues and vices, while here on earth we rarely receive the things we deserve. In that case the principle of divine distributive justice would imply that there is perfect distributive justice, but the principle of cosmic distributive justice would imply that there is not anything even close to perfect distributive justice.

While the idea about distributive justice captured by principle DDa might be of interest to some philosophers of religion, I doubt that any social or political philosopher would have any professional interest in it. Social and political philosophers are more interested in *earthly* justice—the kind of justice that obtains in virtue of things that governments do for their citizens here on earth. But a principle of divine justice (such as DDa) focuses exclusively on things that come about as a result of what God does; and benefits or burdens that will be received in the afterlife, rather than here on earth. Virtually any theory of political economic distributive justice could be combined with this view about divine justice. Since I am interested in defending a view about the justice of states here on earth, I shall have nothing further to say about divine distributive justice.

3.4 Desertism about Earthly Moral Justice

A historically important form of desertism emerges if we continue to maintain that the relevant desert bases are all manifestations of moral virtue and vice, but we introduce different restrictions on deserts and distributors. Instead of saying (with Leibniz) that the relevant deserts are levels of happiness and unhappiness that we will experience in heaven or hell, we can say that the relevant deserts are levels of happiness and unhappiness that we experience here on earth, during our lives. Furthermore, instead of saying that the distributor from whom we deserve these rewards is God, we can say that we deserve them from our country. The result is a somewhat more popular form of desertism:

MDa: There is perfect distributive justice in a society if and only if in every case in which a citizen of that society deserves a level of happiness or unhappiness in virtue of having a moral desert base, the government of his or her country ensures that he or she receives that level of happiness or unhappiness.[10]

Associated with MDa there is a principle about imperfect distributive justice. This again would be a matter of approximation.

If there were perfect distributive justice as measured by the cosmic principle, CDa, in a society, then (given one perhaps controversial assumption) there would be perfect distributive justice as measured by the earthly moral principle, MDa, there, too. If people are getting everything they deserve, and they deserve levels of happiness in virtue of their moral excellence (and this last is the controversial assumption mentioned earlier), then they are getting those levels of happiness, too. However, the inference in the other direction obviously fails. We might get all the happiness we deserve while failing to get lots of other things. Perhaps my level of happiness is just right given my level of virtue, but still I have not gotten the income tax refund that I deserve. So perfect earthly moral justice apparently does not entail perfect cosmic justice.

Depending upon some details of interpretation, it may turn out that earthly moral justice entails divine moral justice. Suppose all the governments on earth somehow manage to arrange things so that everyone gets precisely the level of happiness he or she deserves in light of levels of moral virtue. No one goes to his or her grave still deserving more happiness or misery than he or she has already received in life. Then there is perfect earthly moral justice. In this case, it would seem that there is nothing more that God needs to do in order to bring about divine moral justice. Even if there is no god, and no one receives any happiness or misery in the afterlife, there will be no unrequited deserts in that (null) afterlife. So, if we like, we can say that divine moral justice has been done as it were "by

[10] A modest variant of MDa would replace "happiness" with "welfare." I discuss the "happiness" version largely because this is the version that Rawls attacked.

default."[11] On the other hand, as should be obvious, there could be perfect divine justice combined with a painfully low level of earthly moral justice. This would happen if there is a god, and if that god does give us all our heavenly rewards in the afterlife, but our countries never ensure that we have the happiness we deserve here on earth.

Later, in Chapter 7, I will discuss several passages in which John Rawls attacks desertism. I will show that when Rawls attacks desertism, he seems to have something quite like MDa in mind. He mentions what he takes to be the motto of desertism: "justice is happiness according to virtue."[12] Some of his objections to desertism, I will claim, apply to earthly moral desertism as characterized by MDa, though not to the form of desertism that I defend in this book.

The idea that distributive justice should be measured by something like the earthly moral principle, MDa, seems to me to be another non-starter. It does not seem to me that it is the business of governments to try to ensure that happiness is distributed in accord with moral virtue. It may fall to governments to see to the distribution of such things as income tax refunds, tuition remissions for in-state students, and the protection offered by a police force. Admittedly, some of these things may have effects on the level of happiness of some recipients. But it is not the government's business to determine the level of virtue of recipients and then to adjust the distribution of these things so as to ensure that levels of happiness properly correspond to levels of virtue. Consider, for example, income tax refunds. Suppose two citizens are equally morally virtuous. Suppose they file identical income tax returns. Suppose the same amount of money had been withheld from the paychecks of the two citizens. In each case, suppose, the amount withheld was $1000 greater than the citizen's tax liability. Suppose each of them then receives his $1000 tax refund precisely in accord with an entirely fair system of taxation. It seems then that the government has treated them justly. Suppose it then turns out that the receipt of his tax refund makes one citizen very happy, whereas the receipt of his equal-sized tax refund does not make the other citizen happy. Maybe the second citizen is looks at his $1000 check with tears in his eyes, saying "I wish I could have gotten a bigger refund." Surely we would be astonished if the unhappy taxpayer were to insist that he has been treated unjustly—that he is just as virtuous a person as the other taxpayer, but that the IRS has not returned enough to make him as happy as the other taxpayer. Surely the IRS agent would be justified in insisting that his job is merely to see to it that taxpayers receive the refunds that are due to them, not that they

[11] Thanks to Jean-Paul Vessel for helping me to appreciate this point.
[12] Rawls (1971: 310).

are to receive refunds sufficient to make them as happy as they deserve to be. In light of considerations such as these, it seems pretty clear that the concept of distributive justice that is of central interest to social and political philosophers is not properly explicated by a principle like MDa.

Rawls presents a series of objections that might be used to highlight defects in the idea that distributive justice obtains when we have "happiness in accord with virtue." I discuss these objections later in Chapter 7. I claim that Rawls presupposed that desertism must be understood as something like earthly moral desertism. I furthermore claim that some of his objections in fact do reveal something questionable about taking earthly moral desertism as our theory of political economic justice. But, as I show later, those objections have no bearing on the form of desertism that I present and defend in this book.

3.5 Desertism about Political Economic Distributive Justice

We now turn to a different combination of restrictions on deserts, desert bases, and distributors. These restrictions yield a desertist theory of political economic distributive justice. The theory in question is intended to be a competitor to versions of the theories of justice that have been debated in the philosophical literature in recent years. The theories in question are such things as egalitarianism of several forms, as defended by Nielsen (1981a; 1981b) and Ake (1975) among others; sufficientism as defended by Frankfurt (1987) and Crisp (2003), among others; prioritarianism as defended by Parfit (1997) and others; the difference principle as defended by Rawls (1971) and others; libertarianism as defended by Nozick (1974) and others. It is unreasonable to suppose that when the advocates of those theories presented their theories they took themselves to be offering views about what I have identified as cosmic distributive justice, divine distributive justice, or earthly moral distributive justice. When these philosophers spoke of justice, they were thinking of an important evaluative feature of states—a feature that states have in virtue of the way they go about seeing to the distribution of benefits and burdens that it is the business of states to distribute to their citizens.

Theories of justice as presented in this context are presented as views about political and economic matters. Each such theory gives us a proposed way of evaluating states, or institutional frameworks, or communities for the way in which economic items such as money, jobs, taxes, and political items such as political rights and opportunities and obligations are distributed. A theory could purport to give an account of the circumstances under which these things have been distributed justly even though it is silent on the distribution of other very important things such as happiness, or life, or warm loving relationships or apologies. I am confident that none of the abovementioned theories is intended to be a theory about what makes for perfect cosmic justice. Equally, none of those theories is intended to give an account of divine or earthly moral justice. And likewise for the theory I will present.

My aim here is to formulate a theory of distributive justice that is a direct competitor to the theories about political economic distributive justice that I have mentioned.[13] It is intended to offer a system for the evaluation of the distribution of political and economic items in a sufficiently unified political entity such as a country, or a state. When I speak of "unified political entities," I have in mind entities that typically have the power to tax and redistribute wealth; that have the power to require people to do things, and to grant permissions and rights. But the theory I will defend does not make use of the concept of equality, or of a minimum threshold, or of giving priority to worse off citizens. Rather, this theory—as a form of desertism—makes essential use of the concept of desert.

We arrive at my desertist theory of political economic distributive justice by imposing three main restrictions on cosmic distributive justice. The restrictions concern (a) the deserts, (b) the desert bases, and (c) the distributors.

Instead of focusing on all the things that anyone could deserve, I want to focus on what I will be calling "political economic deserts." These include such things as political rights and obligations, other benefits and burdens we get from our countries, security of certain sorts, access to publically owned or regulated infrastructure such as transportation systems, educational systems, judicial systems, communication systems, etc. It excludes things that we may deserve from other sources. We may deserve apologies and thank-you notes from our friends, but they are not political economic deserts. We may deserve good luck in sports or romance, but again, these are not deserts that we deserve from our countries. We may deserve happiness in heaven, but it is not the business of our country to arrange for this and it would be no defect in the level of distributive justice in a country if its citizens rarely received their heavenly rewards from God. Many other deserts fail to be political economic deserts, and hence play no role in my account of distributive justice. Later in Chapter 4 I will give a more detailed list of

[13] I have to acknowledge that it is still possible that the philosophers I mentioned would claim that they were not offering views about what I am calling "political economic distributive justice." Maybe they were thinking of justice broadly conceived. A more careful statement of my thesis might be this: I am proposing a theory that is intended to be a direct competitor to *suitably interpreted* versions of popular theories in the literature.

the things I take to be political economic deserts and I will attempt to justify my claims about which deserts count as political economic deserts.

Instead of focusing on all the desert bases in virtue of which anyone could deserve anything, I want to focus on what I will be calling "political economic desert bases." These will include certain kinds of vulnerability, such as vulnerability to robbers and muggers as well as vulnerability to disease; the need for certain kinds of opportunity, such as the opportunity to be educated and the opportunity to get assistance when starting up a business; the need for defense of certain legitimate rights, such as the right to a fair trial, or to vote. In general, I have in mind desert bases such that it is the business of a government to take note of the fact that its citizens manifest these bases, and it is the business of that government to try to see to it that its citizens receive the things that they deserve on these bases. This category excludes many items that would count as desert bases in other contexts. Thus, for example, suppose a sweet-tempered and sincere fellow has had bad luck in romance. He loved a certain woman, and courted her, and hoped she would agree to marry him. But suppose his efforts failed and he remains single and lonely. In virtue of his sincere and fruitless efforts to find love, he deserves some good luck in romance. But this desert base is not one that his government is called upon to requite. It is not a political economic desert base.[14] Later I will give a more detailed list of the things I take to be political economic desert bases and I will provide a rationale for my claims about what counts as a political economic desert base.

We deserve things from lots of different distributors. Some of us deserve things from our parents, spouses, and children; some of us deserve things from strangers who rudely interact with us in traffic jams; if there is a God, perhaps we deserve something from God. But these distributors are not relevant to political economic distributive justice. I want to focus on what I will call our "political economic distributors." In the typical case, the political economic distributor for a certain person is the government of that person's country, or suitable representatives of that government. Later I will give a more detailed account of the things that I take to be political economic distributors.

However, at this point I just want to state the overall theory that I mean to defend. In later sections I will fill in the details. Here is my view:

PEDa: There is perfect political economic distributive justice in a country if and only if in every case in which a citizen of that country deserves a

[14] I return to this topic in a section on "unfinished business" at the end of the book in section 9.2.1.

> political economic desert in virtue of having a political economic desert base, he or she receives that desert from the appropriate political economic distributor.[15]

PEDa gives necessary and sufficient conditions for there being perfect political economic distributive justice within some group. But no group we are likely to encounter here on earth would be perfectly just in that way. So we need to consider a comparative principle as well:

> PEDc: There is greater political economic distributive justice in a group, G1, than there is in another group, G2, if and only if the situation in G1 more closely approximates perfect political economic distributive justice as measured by PEDa than does the situation in G2.

It should be clear that if there is perfect cosmic distributive justice in some possible world, then there is perfect political economic distributive justice in every country in that world. But the inference in the other direction does not hold. There might be perfect political economic justice in some country even though some citizens fail to get some of the things they deserve. Maybe we are all getting everything we deserve from our country, but some of our neighbors refuse to give us the apologies that we deserve from them. Indeed, there could be perfect political economic distributive justice in every country in some possible world even though many residents of that world fail to receive lots of things that they deserve.

It should also be clear that there is no interesting connection between divine distributive justice and political economic distributive justice. We can easily imagine a situation in which people receive all the political economic deserts that they deserve from their governments, but never receive any of the heavenly rewards they deserve in the afterlife. This would happen most obviously in the case in which earthly governments are well ordered, but there is no god. In such a case, the level of political economic distributive justice would be very high, but the level of divine distributive justice could be very low. The opposite situation is also possible. We might fail to get our political economic deserts here on earth, but it is consistent with this to suppose that we get our just rewards in heaven.

[15] PEDa is stated as a mere biconditional. However, I intend it to be understood as expressing a somewhat stronger connection between perfect justice and receipt in accord with desert. In a fully explicit statement of the view, I would say that receipt in accord with desert is what "makes for" justice; or that when a state is perfectly just, it is so "in virtue of the fact that" citizens receive what they deserve. I have suppressed this extra phrase in the interest of keeping things simple. It is to be understood here and wherever I state a proposed theory of justice.

Suppose the government in some country steadfastly keeps out of the business of tracking the levels of virtue in its citizens. Suppose this government also steadfastly keeps out of the business of worrying about how happy its citizens are.[16] But suppose in addition that the government scrupulously distributes income tax refunds, in-state tuition waivers, voting rights, police protection, and other such things to citizens who deserve to have them. Then the level of distributive justice as measured by the earthly moral principle, MDa, in that country could be very low, but the level of distributive justice as measured by the political economic principle I advocate, PEDa, would be very high. So these are clearly distinct views about what makes for distributive justice.

I am inclined to think that when egalitarians say that justice requires equality of welfare they are advocating a view about distributive justice; their view differs from mine in virtue of the fact that they have a different view about what makes for the relevant sort of distributive justice. They think it requires equality of welfare; I think it requires distribution of political economic deserts in accord with political economic desert bases. If this is the case, then there is a genuine dispute between these egalitarians and me. We are focusing on the same target concept—distributive justice—but we disagree about the distributive fact upon which it depends.

The same would be true of typical sufficientists, prioritarians, believers in the difference principle, libertarians, and Marxists. In each case, if the theorist in question is proposing a view about what makes for distributive justice in a country, then he or she is proposing a view that is a genuine competitor to the view that I am proposing in this book.[17]

In order to fully understand the implications of the proposed theory of distributive justice, we need to have a clearer account of the deserts and desert

[16] Unlike Bhutan, where the government has established a commission to survey and measure the "gross national happiness" of their country. For a brief account of the Bhutanese policies about the measurement of happiness, see the Wikipedia article "Gross National Happiness" at http://en.wikipedia.org/wiki/Gross_national_happiness. So far as I know, the Bhutanese commission does not seek to determine each individual citizen's level of happiness or to take steps to adjust that level so as to make it accord with the citizen's level of virtue.

[17] Later, in various places but mostly in Chapter 5, I will present a series of arguments designed to show that each of these competing theories of justice can be combined with a restrictive view about deserts and desert bases. Thus, for example, consider an egalitarianism of welfare. Suppose we say that the only thing we deserve is to be at the same level of welfare as everyone else. Suppose in addition that we say that the only basis for deserving this is that we are not at the same level of welfare as everyone else. In that case, egalitarianism of welfare would be equivalent to the restricted form of desertism. Thus, I do not mean to say that every competing theory of justice is inconsistent with every form of desertism. Instead, I want to say that *in its typical form*, each competing theory of justice is inconsistent with desertism—except for some sufficiently gerrymandered and restricted "degenerate" forms of desertism.

bases that play an essential role in the formulation of the theory. After all, on this view, it is the receipt of these deserts, on these bases, that makes for distributive justice according to my view. I turn to these questions in Chapter 4.

Before I move on to that, however, I want to summarize the main points I have been making about these four different views about distributive justice:

3.6 Four Forms of Desertism

Here is a little chart that summarizes the main features of the four forms of desertism that I have distinguished in this chapter:

Four Forms of Desertism

	Bases	**Deserts**	**Distributor**	**Discussed by**
Cosmic	All	All	All	?
Divine	Moral virtue and vice	Heavenly bliss; Infernal suffering	God	Leibniz
Earthly Moral	Moral virtue and vice	Earthly happiness and suffering	Governments	Rawls
Political-Economic	PE desert bases	PE deserts	Governments	Feldman

4

Political Economic Deserts and Desert Bases

I want to characterize certain desert bases as the specifically political economic desert bases. I want to characterize certain deserts as the specifically political economic deserts. My desertist theory of distributive justice is that there is perfect political economic distributive justice in a country if and only if the government of that country ensures that its citizens receive the political economic deserts that they deserve to receive in virtue of their possession of the relevant political economic desert bases. My aim in this chapter is first to explain why, in my view, these deserts and bases are the specifically *political economic* deserts and bases. In my effort to explain this, I make use of some ideas I derive from Aristotle. Having done this, I go on to catalog what I take to be the most important of these deserts and desert bases. Later in the chapter I will also mention some things that some of us deserve, but that in my view are not political economic deserts. I begin with Aristotle.

4.1 Aristotle and Community Essential Needs

In a famous passage near the beginning of the *Politics* Aristotle said that we are by nature social animals. Here is the passage, as translated by Benjamin Jowett:

> the individual, when isolated, is not self-sufficing; and therefore he is like a part in relation to the whole. But he who is unable to live in society, or who has no need because he is sufficient for himself, must be either a beast or a god: he is no part of a state. A social instinct is implanted in all men by nature, and yet he who first founded the state was the greatest of benefactors. For man, when perfected, is the best of animals, but, when separated from law and justice, he is the worst of all; since armed injustice is the more dangerous, and he is equipped at birth with arms, meant to be used by intelligence and virtue, which he may use for the worst ends. Wherefore, if he have not virtue, he is the most unholy and the most savage of animals, and the most full of lust and gluttony. But justice is the bond of men in states, for the administration

of justice, which is the determination of what is just, is the principle of order in political society.[1]

Aristotle makes a number of grand and interesting claims in that passage. I mean to focus on one that is most relevant in the present context. That is a claim about ordinary human beings—creatures who, because they are neither gods nor beasts, need to live in communities in order to reach their potential as "the best of animals." I interpret Aristotle's point here to be that we have *community essential needs*—there are certain things that human beings ordinarily need in order to flourish. Among these are certain things that an ordinary person is not able to secure on his or her own. In normal circumstances people will be able to get them only if they live in a civilized community. This fact helps to explain what makes some of our desert bases count as political-economic desert bases. An example may help to make this clearer.

Suppose a hurricane takes a strange path up the Connecticut River valley. Trees and power lines are torn down. Roads are washed out. Suppose a riverside farm suffers enormous damage; the soil in the fields is washed away. In its place there is now a huge pile of rocks and debris. In virtue of having suffered this calamity, the farmers need some assistance. Perhaps they need a low-interest loan that will enable them to afford reconstruction; perhaps they need to have the road to their house repaired or for the banks of the river to be restored; perhaps they need to have a warm, dry place to stay while they work on getting the mud out of their house.

The homeowners in this example have an important desert base—their farm has been devastated by a flood; they are unable to repair the damage on their own. They need to get some help from someone—presumably their community. I think this need generates desert. The homeowners deserve assistance from their community, and they deserve it because they need it. Perhaps others would agree with me about the desert base and the desert in this case, but I want to go a bit further. I want to claim that this is a political economic desert base, and that the help that they deserve is a political economic desert. Thus, the case is relevant to the level of political economic justice in their community. What could justify my claim that having the specified need is a political economic desert base, and that it grounds the specified sorts of support as political economic deserts?

We can move up to a slightly higher level of abstraction. Since many others do not own riverside farms, and have not suffered flood damage, not everyone

[1] Aristotle, *Politics* Book I, Part II. Retrieved from http://classics.mit.edu/Aristotle/politics.1.one.html.

deserves precisely what these farmers deserve (viz., help in the restoration of their farm). But others are like the farmers in this somewhat more abstract respect: since they are vulnerable to natural disasters such as floods, hurricanes, earthquakes, tornadoes, etc. and since they are individually unable to protect themselves against these natural disasters, they deserve to be embedded in a community that will do its best to ensure that help will be provided to members who are adversely affected by such things. The desert base here is *vulnerability to natural disaster*, and the desert is *assurance of assistance guaranteed by the community*. Since the deserved help in this case satisfies these conditions, and would come from the government, it is a political economic desert, and the desert base is a political economic desert base.

One might still wonder what justifies my claim that this more abstract case bears on political economic distributive justice. We can move to a still higher level of abstraction. We can note that these farmers are vulnerable to natural disaster because they are "neither beasts nor gods." They cannot flourish as human beings if they are sheltering in the mud-covered, debris-strewn wreckage of their home. They do not have the power to clear the mud and debris on their own. They need help that they can get only if they live in an organized community that recognizes their community essential needs. As things stand, without such help, they will not be able to flourish as human beings. The government—as representative of the community—is the agency from which they deserve to receive this help. And so the basis on which they deserve this help is a political economic desert base—the fact that the farmers are ordinary human beings with community essential needs. What they deserve from their government—assurance of help in getting back on their feet—is a political economic desert. Hence, if the farmers fail to receive the assurance that they need, the level of political economic distributive justice in their community will be adversely affected.

We do not come to have political economic desert bases *in virtue of the fact that we are citizens of a state*. We can see this if we imagine some farmers living in the state of nature. Suppose there is no government in the region where they live. Suppose they suffer from a natural disaster similar to the one that befell my upriver neighbors. These state-of-nature farmers would be like my Massachusetts neighbors in some important respects. They too would be unable to flourish as human beings without the assurance of help that could come only from some sort of collective action. So they would have a political economic desert base just like the one my neighbors had. In virtue of their need for help in reconstruction, they also deserve to be embedded in a community that can provide assurance to citizens who have been victims of natural disaster. Unfortunately for the state-of-nature farmers, in their case there is no government and no government-like agency that is in position to give them this sort of assurance. So they suffer a political economic injustice, even though there is no state whose level of political economic distributive justice is thereby diminished.[2]

In the more familiar and realistic case, the farmers are citizens of a state. The reader might wonder why the farmers deserve to receive aid *from that state*.[3] Why could not the government officials of that state admit that the farmers deserve some assistance, but at the same time deny that the farmers deserve the assistance *from them*? Why could not those officials insist that it is not the government's problem?

Recall that the farmers have a community essential need—in order to flourish as human beings they need a kind of help that in the normal course of events can come only from some sort of collective effort. They deserve to be embedded in a community where there is some agency that ensures that citizens such as these get the help they need from the group. This is a *de dicto* fact about what the farmers deserve: the farmers deserve to live in a place where there is a government and it assures citizens that they will get the help they need. But in a case where in fact there is a government, then it falls to that government *de re* to ensure that the farmers get the help that they need. The farmers could say: "we deserve to get this help from our government; as things stand, *you* are our government; so we deserve to get this help *from you*."

Later I will describe some other deserts that I will classify as political economic deserts. These will include assurance of assistance that would arise in virtue of other sorts of *vulnerability*. Additionally, I will mention *opportunities* of certain sorts, and *entitlements*. In each case I will maintain that particular low level desert/desert base pairs are instances of slightly more abstract desert/desert base pairs. At the greatest level of abstraction we find the same pair of factors: *being an ordinary human being with community essential needs* as the desert base, and *being embedded in a community that will try to ensure that those needs are met* as the desert. Where the distributor of the desert is the government or some suitable representative, all these desert/desert base pairs are classified as political economic deserts and bases. Accordingly, in my view, the level of political economic distributive justice in a community is determined by the extent to which citizens receive these deserts when they are deserved on these bases.

[2] Thanks to a referee for Oxford University Press for encouraging me to explain my view on this question.

[3] Thanks to Owen McLeod for raising this thorny question and for helping me to see how best to answer it.

Let me make my point in a more general form. Suppose some person, S, deserves to receive something, D; suppose he deserves it because he manifests the desert base, DB. This might be relevant to political economic distributive justice, and it might not. It depends upon whether D is a political economic desert and whether DB is a political economic desert base. I claim that these are matters of political economic concern provided that S has community essential needs, and that S's possession of community essential needs is a desert base that makes S deserve to be embedded in a community that will respond to needs like these—in particular, it makes S deserve to be embedded in a community that will recognize that possession of DB makes S deserve D and will attempt to see to it that S receives D.

Thus, I claim that a certain sort of *need* provides the rationale for counting certain deserts as political economic desert bases. The need in question is *community essential need*. This, as I see it, makes us deserve to be embedded in a community that will recognize and try to requite these needs. Some philosophers have denied that need is ever a desert base. David Miller, for example, claims that in every case in which someone deserves something good, D, in virtue of having a desert base, DB, DB is also the object of a favorable appraising attitude.[4] The person must be worthy of admiration, or respect, or some such "positive" appraising attitude in virtue of having DB. Call that the *appraisal/desert base thesis*. But Miller points out that we do not admire or respect people for being needy. Nor is there any other appraising attitude that is naturally associated with being needy. Hence Miller concludes that need is not a desert base for good treatment. As I said earlier, I disagree with Miller. As I see it, we clearly and often do deserve help, support, sympathy, and other good things in virtue of need; and since this would be impossible if the appraisal/desert base thesis were true, I conclude that the thesis is false.[5]

Many other philosophers would present a different argument for the conclusion that (at least in many typical cases) need is not a basis upon which we could deserve something. Instead of appealing to some alleged fact about appraising attitudes, these philosophers appeal to an alleged fact about *responsibility*. These philosophers (as I mentioned earlier[6]) claim that no one ever deserves anything in virtue of the possession of some feature unless the person is responsible for

[4] See Miller (1976: 85–7). Miller says, "What disqualifies needs from being taken as grounds for desert is [among other things] that no one wishes to have them, or admires others for having them" (86). Geoffrey Cupit accepts a similar claim about desert bases: "what does not affect the status of the deserver—what does not make the deserver more or less worthy of respect, admiration, and so on—cannot function as a basis of desert" Cupit (1996b: 38). My reaction to Cupit's claim is relevantly like my reaction to Miller's.

[5] For a good discussion of this point, see McLeod (2008).

[6] Chapter 2, Section 2.3.

having that feature. Thus, in any case in which a person bears no responsibility for having a certain need, he or she cannot deserve anything in virtue of having that need.

But the Responsibility Condition seems to me to be false. Cases involving etiquettical deserts form an obvious class of counterexamples. Suppose we are at a dinner party; suppose I suddenly and uncontrollably start to cough; suppose my coughing disrupts the party for a moment before I am able to leave the table. Surely I owe an apology to my fellow diners. They deserve this from me simply as a matter of courtesy. But in any ordinary case they would bear no responsibility for the fact that I coughed.

Suppose a malnourished and sickly infant is found abandoned in a basket on the steps of Town Hall. As I see it, an infant like this would deserve some food, a clean diaper, a warm, dry place to sleep, and perhaps medical attention. The desert base in this case would be overwhelming need; if the infant does not receive these things, she will suffer and die. Surely no thoughtful person would respond to this case by saying that since the infant is not responsible for being in this sorry state, she deserves nothing from the community.

The general point should be clear: I claim that our most fundamental political economic desert base is a special kind of *need*. I characterized this as community essential need. I mentioned (and soon will discuss) some specific forms of this need: the need for security; the need for opportunity; the need for certain political rights. Some philosophers would claim that since we are not responsible for having our community essential needs, we cannot deserve anything in virtue of having these needs. I grant that we are not responsible for having our community essential needs. We are not gods. We are mere human beings who have these needs more or less "by nature." But I see no connection between that fact and the claim that we cannot deserve anything in virtue of having those needs. That claim seems to me to be obviously false.

4.2 What We Deserve From Our Countries

I turn now to descriptions of what I take to be the main groups of political economic deserts and their bases.

4.2.1 Security

In his legendary description of the horrors of the state of nature, Hobbes mentions a series of disasters that we would suffer if we were to live without an organized government. He concludes his account by telling us about the horror that he takes to be "worst of all," and that is "continuall feare, and danger of violent death." And he concludes by saying that in the state of nature "the life of man [would be] solitary, poore, nasty, brutish, and short."[7]

I think that reflection on this passage—especially the remarks about "continuall feare and danger of violent death"—naturally suggests a collection of some of the most important political deserts. These are deserts that fall under the general category of *security*. As I see it, we deserve security of several different sorts. We deserve security against foreign invaders who might come into our country and attack us. We also deserve security against thugs who already live in our neighborhood. We also deserve security against natural disasters such as hurricanes, floods, earthquakes, and tornadoes. Finally, we deserve security against the disasters associated with illness and injury. Let us consider these in turn.

Each of us, operating solely on his or her own, would be unable to mount a successful defense against foreign marauders. If enemies from outside our country were to invade, and if at the time of the invasion each of us were left to improvise his or her own defense, we would quickly find ourselves captured, or injured, or perhaps dead. Our property might be taken from us. We might be sold into slavery. As a fundamental matter of political justice, we deserve to have some measure of defense against such attacks; and in order to be effective, this defense would most likely have to be organized by our community. This may come in the form of a police force, or an army, or a government that somehow sees to it that we are not attacked, that our property is not stolen, and that we are not killed or dragged off into slavery.

We might at first assume that we deserve to have the services of a police force to provide security against neighborhood thugs. But maybe you do not want a fully armed SWAT team parked in the street in front of your house every night. Maybe there is no immediate reason for them to be there in any case. Maybe you are very rich and you prefer to be protected by your own squad of private security guards. I am not claiming that what you deserve is that security actually be provided by the government. As I see it, what you deserve is something a bit more abstract. It is rather that you deserve to have fairly ready access to some sort of police-like protection if you need it. It must be the case that if you find yourself needing and wanting that sort of protection, you can sound some sort of alarm and it will—fairly promptly—be provided.

Suppose the top brass at the Police Department are trying to figure out how to deploy their forces. Suppose they reflect on your neighborhood and they see that there have been no burglaries over there in several years. Suppose they know that you have a neighborhood watch team in place, that some of your neighbors are

[7] Hobbes, *Leviathan*, pp. 57–8 in Bennett version.

very keen on making sure that no troublemakers start hanging out in your neighborhood. Suppose they also know that burglar alarms have been installed in most homes in your neighborhood. The Chief might then conclude that your need for police protection has been met. There is no need for the Department to do any more for you. It is consistent with this to suppose that the Chief steadfastly maintains a policy according to which if trouble arises in your neighborhood or if citizens there should call in asking for assistance, then the Department will promptly dispatch a car to check it out. In this case, the government has ensured that you will get police-like security if you need it or ask for it. Although the government has not given you any actual officers in your driveway, it has seen to it that you have gotten what you deserve by way of this sort of security.

I mention all of this to illustrate a general point about deserts. It might be natural to think that what you deserve by way of security would be the actual presence of a police officer in your driveway. But I think this misconstrues the item that you deserve. What you actually deserve, as I see it, is to live in a place where the government sees to it that you have suitable *access* to some sort of police-like security—that such security should be *readily available* to you.

We can see the significance of this distinction if we reflect on the implications for justice. Suppose a wealthy citizen chooses to hire his own security guards. He prefers to have no police officers hanging around his property. Suppose he explains this to the Chief and, accordingly, the Chief does not deploy any police officers to the wealthy citizen's property. Now we can see how the distinction makes a difference. If we were to say that the wealthy citizen deserves actual police protection, then we would be forced to conclude that he has not gotten what he deserved. There are no cruisers parked in his driveway. A desertist like me would then have to say (implausibly) that this situation detracts from the level of justice in the community. On the other hand, if we say that what the wealthy citizen deserves is instead that *the government sees to it that police-like protection is readily available to him* or that *he lives in a community where the government sees to it that citizens have access to police-like security*, then we can conclude that the wealthy citizen has received precisely what he deserves from his community. Appropriate representatives of the community have ensured that the wealthy citizen already has, or promptly could get, the sort of security he might need. In that case, we would not have any reason to say that the level of political economic distributive justice in the community has been adversely affected.

The political economic desert base in this case is something like this: merely being an ordinary human being who, if left entirely on his own, would not be able to defend himself against threats to his personal safety or his possessions. We can call this "vulnerability to attack."

Our vulnerability makes us deserve another closely related item. This is, roughly speaking, that we live in a place where the government takes sufficiently aggressive and well-publicized steps to deter would-be attackers from attacking in the first place. When there is a well-organized police force, and their capacity to capture and see to the prosecution of burglars and other miscreants is well publicized, those who otherwise might be inclined to engage in theft or mayhem will have reason to reconsider. This helps to provide security for us by deterring criminal activity by which we would be harmed.

Closely associated with this is another and profoundly important desert: *we deserve to have a reasonable system of laws against such invasions in place and enforced.* If the laws are established in a reasonable way, and penalties for their violation are not too wildly incommensurate with the harm that would be done by violations, then we deserve for it to be the case that those who violate the laws are required to suffer the penalties. Each of us deserves to live in a community in which there are laws, and penalties for the violation thereof, that are likely to deter potential malefactors from taking advantage of our individual weakness. We deserve all this from our countries because we are vulnerable, and having this apparatus in place helps to protect us (or at least to give us some hope of rectification in case the deterrence fails). The need in this case is another community essential need. Hence it is a political economic desert base, and the deserved security is a political economic desert. Whether we get it affects the level of political economic distributive justice in our community.

If left to our own defenses, we would be vulnerable to predations from enemies foreign and domestic. I claim that this provides the basis on which we deserve to live in a place where the government ensures that we have access to the sorts of security that we need. We are similarly vulnerable to threats to our health. None of us is individually capable of diagnosing and treating every illness that might strike. Some, of course, are experts at medical diagnosis. Such experts might be able to figure out what diseases they have. But even the best informed doctor may not personally own a big medical center with all the requisite equipment and personnel that would be needed to treat him if he were to fall ill. Surely, it would be a rare surgeon who would be capable of performing open heart surgery on herself, and an equally rare dentist who could drill out his own infected root canal.

In light of these facts, I maintain that each of us deserves to live in a place where the community sees to it that members have ready access to medical assistance. In the already-discussed case involving help from the police, I distinguished between the claim (which I reject) that everyone deserves to have a police officer on guard at her house, and the more plausible claim (which I accept) that everyone deserves to live in a community that ensures that citizens have ready access to police-like security if they need it. Similarly in the present case I distinguish between the claim (which I reject) that everyone deserves actually to receive medical care for every disease or injury he or she might suffer, and the more plausible claim that everyone deserves to live in a community that sees to it that citizens have ready access to such medical care if they need it. If such medical care is readily available, but a person chooses to forego it, there is no injustice. If what she deserved was *to live in a community that ensures ready access to medical care if needed* then such a person has received what she deserves even in the case in which she chooses not to make use of that access.[8]

The desert base in this case is again a sort of *vulnerability*. In the example involving the police force, the vulnerability specifically involved predations from human attackers. In this present case, the vulnerability involves medical harms arising from infection, injury, and other related medical problems. Again, this need is a community essential need. The desert base arising from it is a political economic desert base, and the benefits needed are political economic deserts.

We have other vulnerabilities. We are all vulnerable to calamities such as would be brought about by natural disasters such as hurricanes, earthquakes, tornadoes, floods, forest fires, etc. If we had to defend against such things on our own, any of them could drive us into poverty or death. This gives rise to another category of political economic deserts. As I see it, each of us *deserves to live in a community that has ensured that there is some sort of safety net that will provide assistance to citizens who are adversely affected by natural disasters*. This may come in the form of a governmental agency such as FEMA, or it might come in the form of a well-regulated system of flood insurance. It might also involve such things as a fire department or an emergency relief program. Again, I am not claiming that the government must provide these services itself. If government officials determine that non-governmental organizations are in place and are ready to provide relief to those who need it, then the government has done its job. It has ensured that citizens live in a place where such relief is available to those who need it.

In all these cases involving security, the political economic desert base is some sort of *vulnerability* and the political economic desert is the corresponding sort of *access to security*. The distributor is our community or suitable representatives. The level of distributive justice in a community is directly affected by the extent to which citizens receive these political economic deserts.

[8] I give more detail about my view concerning the amount of medical care that we deserve below in section 4.3.

4.2.2 *Opportunity*

At a campaign event in Roanoke, Virginia on July 13, 2012, United States President Barack Obama made some remarks about the role of government in providing components of the built infrastructure such as roads and bridges and the internet. Speaking of successful business people, the President said:

> If you were successful, somebody along the line gave you some help . . . Somebody helped to create this unbelievable American system that we have that allowed you to thrive. Somebody invested in roads and bridges. If you've got a business—you didn't build that. Somebody else made that happen. The Internet didn't get invented on its own. Government research created the Internet so that all the companies could make money off the Internet. The point is, is that when we succeed, we succeed because of our individual initiative, but also because we do things together.[9]

I think the President's remarks highlight a very important collection of political economic deserts. Although we might reasonably disagree about the precise extent of these deserts, their general character is fairly clear. In order for us to flourish as human beings, we may need to make use of various items that can be roughly characterized as "community owned or regulated infrastructure." The President mentioned roads, bridges, and the internet. It is easy to think of other items that fall into the same category: the electric grid, the water supply system, the system for getting rid of sewage. Of course plenty of people manage to eke out a living without these things, and in former times even rich and comfortable people managed to make do. But in light of the fact that these things are in place in other countries, it would be much harder to be successful in business nowadays if you lived in a country where these things were not available.

No one, working solely on his or her own, would be able to build the roads and bridges and other such components of the infrastructure. It requires the efforts of a community to build such things. Without these things we would lose the opportunity to open a business (as the President emphasized), or to gain satisfying employment, or even to travel, learn, and thrive. No one is able to construct such things on his or her own. Rich and energetic as he is, even Mitt Romney could not have built the interstate highway system with his own hands. It requires the cooperative effort of a community to construct such things. In light of these facts, I maintain that each of us deserves, as a matter of political economic justice, to live in a country where the government ensures that access to such things is made available.

[9] Retrieved on November 4, 2013 from: https://www.whitehouse.gov/the-press-office/2012/07/13/remarks-president-campaign-event-roanoke-virginia.

There are other items that satisfy a similar set of conditions. Consider, for example, an educational system. This might consist of a mixture of public and private schools, colleges, and universities. The system as a whole would be complex and far-reaching. It might involve teachers, administrators, school psychologists, nurses, librarians, school buildings, and all the support staff needed to keep the buildings comfortable and safe. Without some such educational system, many people would be unable to learn the things they need to understand in order to improve themselves economically. Perhaps more importantly, without an educational system, our intellectual lives would be much poorer. Thus, if we are to have the opportunity to develop in these ways, we need to live in a country in which the government ensures that we have access to an educational system. Lack of such access, or barriers to access, would detract from the level of political economic distributive justice in a country.

Similar things can be said about a financial system. We need banks and a reliable form of money.

In virtue of the fact that we are members of our communities, we deserve the opportunity to take advantage of these items of public infrastructure. Thus, we deserve a chance to attend public schools, to travel on public roads, to get water and electricity and internet connections, and otherwise to make use of facilities that are owned or regulated collectively by our communities. I will refer to these deserts collectively as matters of *opportunity*. When they are in place and functioning smoothly, we have the opportunity to travel, to turn on the lights, to get a drink of water, to flush the toilet, to learn how to read and write, to get a loan, etc. In my view, every one of these things is a political economic desert, and in each case the distributor is our government or a suitable representative.

4.2.3 Legitimate entitlement

There is a lively debate about whether the mere fact that you are legally entitled to something makes you deserve to get it. Some emphasize the fact that when you are legally entitled to something, someone or some institution has in effect promised it to you. Then, following the notion (mentioned by Chisholm earlier) that promise making requires promise keeping, and noting that desert is a form of requirement, we may conclude that if you are legally entitled to something, then in effect someone has promised it to you, and since promising engenders desert, you deserve to get it. Others, claiming perhaps that all desert bases must also be bases for appraising attitudes, insist that legal entitlement cannot engender desert. After all, we do not admire a person for being legally entitled to a refund on his income tax, or to be eligible as a resident for reduced tuition at his state's university. So we need to understand when (if at all) legitimate entitlement gives rise to desert; and, assuming that such desert arises in some cases, we furthermore need to understand when the desert is *political economic desert.* On the view I mean to defend here, it is only such desert that bears on the level of political economic distributive justice in a country.

I want to begin by describing three cases. My aim here is to drive home the puzzling feature of legitimate entitlement as a desert base. I do this by describing three cases that may seem to suggest different views about the connection between entitlement and justice. Subsequently, I will present my view and try to explain how a single view can account for the intuitions that arise in these three cases.

Case One: The Refunds. Suppose you filed your income tax forms honestly and on time. Suppose that in virtue of a variety of facts about your income, the amount of money that was withheld from your paycheck, the number of dependents you are claiming, etc., it turns out that you are legally entitled to a tax refund of $1000. This would be a relatively straightforward matter of tax law and the facts about your income, the size of your family, the amount withheld, and other factors spelled out in the tax code. Let us assume that there is no deeper legal question about your case; any competent tax accountant could quickly determine that you are entitled to this refund. It is not a hard question.

Suppose your identical twin brother had exactly the same amount of income, had the same amount withheld, and was for similar reasons due an exactly equivalent $1000 refund. Suppose strangely enough that an agent from the IRS writes back to you, saying that even though you are legally entitled to the $1000, they have decided to give you a refund of only $500. The agent admits that in other cases they generally try their best to give the refunds to which taxpayers are entitled, but in your case they have decided to give just half. Your brother tells you that he has just received his full refund of $1000.

This treatment by the IRS would probably appear to you to be an outrage. It is not just that the IRS arbitrarily decided to give you less than the amount to which you are legally entitled; it goes beyond that. There is an injustice here. It is not fair. It seems to me that this injustice constitutes a black mark against the country—your desert of the refund was a political economic desert; the refusal of the IRS to give you the refund detracts from the level of political economic justice in your country. If they did it frequently, an impartial observer would likely say that a certain kind of political injustice seems to be rampant in your country.

Case Two: The Inheritance. Suppose you have always been a respectful grandchild to your crotchety old grandfather. Suppose that after he became somewhat disabled, you often agreed to drive him to his medical appointments and sometimes stayed with him when he was ill. Suppose you did this all cheerfully and mostly out of grandfilial respect. After all, he was your grandfather. Your brother, on the other hand, never treated your grandfather with respect. He never drove him anywhere and never stayed with him when he was ill. Instead, he often ridiculed the old man behind his back and sometimes even insulted him to his face. Suppose then that when your grandfather dies, you discover that he has cut you out of his will entirely. You are to get nothing, while your brother is to inherit the entire estate. Your grandfather gave no explanation.

It seems to me that in this case many would want to say that you deserved at least half of the estate, if not quite a bit more. Something seems to have gone wrong; there has been an injustice here. Although your brother is legally entitled to his inheritance, we may feel that he does not deserve to get quite so much. And though you are not legally entitled to anything, we may feel that you deserve some of it.

However, it does not seem to me that this injustice would adversely affect the level of political economic distributive justice in your country. Imagine a group of External Justice Auditors. Suppose they have come to your country to give it a rating for political economic distributive justice. Suppose they learn about this will. I am inclined to think that while they would recognize the unfairness of your grandfather's arbitrary decision, it would not be reasonable for them to take it into account when determining the ranking of your country for political economic distributive justice. They might conclude that if the will was written and filed in accord with all the existing (and, let us suppose, fundamentally reasonable) legal requirements, then political economic distributive justice was done when your brother got the whole estate.

So in this case your brother is legally entitled to the inheritance; nevertheless, it may seem that he does not deserve it. His receipt of the money decreases the level of some kind of justice in your country, but it does not decrease the level of political economic justice. In Case One, the situation seems different. In that case you are entitled to a $1000 refund from the IRS, and their failure to provide it seems to constitute a violation of political economic distributive justice. Thus, the two examples seem to illustrate different ways in which legal entitlement, desert, and political economic distributive justice can be connected.

Case Three: Suppose two young assistant professors of philosophy are hired by a private college. Suppose the professors are equally qualified for their jobs. Suppose they worked equally hard in graduate school and have compiled equally impressive resumes. Suppose they are fairly well matched when it comes to teaching success, conference participation, and ability to engage in a successful interview. But suppose the college decides to offer one new assistant professor a larger salary simply because he is male, while the other professor is female. The dean explains that the college has had a long tradition of giving men larger starting salaries than they give women, and they see no reason to depart from tradition in the current case.

It seems to me that even though the male professor is legally entitled to his larger salary, he may not deserve to be getting more than his new colleague. It also seems to me that the disparity in wages in this case indicates that there is a political economic injustice somewhere in the vicinity. Even though the professors are not working for the government, the fact that they are being treated in this discriminatory way somehow detracts from the level of political economic distributive justice in their country.

These examples are intended to highlight some questions about the connection between legitimate entitlement, desert, political economic desert, and justice. I think we would like to see a general theory that sorts these cases out in a reasonable way. We want to know whether the mere fact of legal entitlement generates desert; we want to know if failure to receive legally entitled deserts automatically affects the level of justice in a country; and, assuming that it does affect the level of justice in a country, we want to know if failure to receive legally entitled deserts affects the level of political economic distributive justice in a country.

My answers to these questions make use of some assumptions and some technical terminology. I start with:

1. Entitlement Generating Institutions (EGIs). Entitlement is essentially institutional.[10] When we say that a person is entitled to some benefit, we imply that the person has some feature, F; that there is some institution in effect in his society; that that institution has some rules; that those rules apply to people who have F and say that those who have F shall be entitled to receive the benefit in question. Thus, as I use the terminology, claims about entitlement always allude to *institutions*. When the rules of an institution specify conditions under which someone will be entitled to something, then the institution is *entitlement generating*.

Some institutions are highly articulated systems of rules designed to determine in a relatively precise way who is entitled to what. The legal code of a country might be such an institution. It specifies, for example, the conditions under which a person is entitled to vote, or to get access to elementary school education, or to get a refund on his income taxes. Other institutions are less formalized and may be open to a variety of interpretations. The rules of etiquette in effect in some

[10] Some connections between desert and entitlement were discussed earlier in section 2.2.

society may loosely suggest that those who give wedding gifts of a certain value are to receive hand-written thank-you notes within a certain period of time after the wedding. If you satisfy those conditions, you are entitled by the etiquettical institution to get the thank-you note.

2. The point of an EGI. In some cases, when establishing an EGI, a legislature may start by holding hearings on some problem. Analyses of the problem may be suggested. Suggestions for dealing with the problem may be offered. In each case, if the suggestions involve the establishment of various possible EGIs, then those EGIs would have the same point, or aim. There is a certain recognized problem, such that each of the EGIs was taken to provide a possible way of dealing with that problem. In virtue of the fact that they all have the same point, the various EGIs are alternatives.

In other cases the identification of the point of an institution can be more difficult. There may be a variety of different answers to the question "why do we have this institution?" In some cases it may not be easy to determine which answer is correct. Perhaps the institution has several different overlapping purposes. Perhaps some of these are more important than others. This would be a matter to be sorted out by thoughtful sociologists.

3. There are many ways in which EGIs can be evaluated. Once we know the point of an EGI, we may try to figure out how effective it would be in helping to achieve its goal. Also, we might want to know the costs that would be associated with the establishment and maintenance of the EGI in the society. We also might want to know if the establishment of an EGI would raise conflicts with other well-established and already successful EGIs.

4. For a variety of reasons that I have described elsewhere, I think it would be a mistake to evaluate EGIs simply in terms of utility.[11] The danger is that a utility maximizing EGI might turn out to impose very unfair burdens on some participants. We must keep in mind that our aim here is to explain how entitlement generates desert, and how desert affects justice. Thus, it would be a mistake to evaluate EGIs in the present case simply on the basis of their utilities. The utility maximizing EGI might impose seriously unjust burdens on some participants.

We might be tempted to evaluate EGIs by appeal to the concept of desert. We might focus on the entitlements that a possible EGI would generate. We might say that a really good EGI would generate entitlements in such a way that those who become entitled to things according to the rules in the EGI always deserve them.

[11] I allude here to section 2.4.1.

I think this claim about good EGIs is near enough true, but I think it would be a mistake to appeal to it as we try to characterize the good EGIs. That is because I am going to claim that facts about the entitlements generated by good EGIs can be used to explain why, in some cases, we deserve the things to which we are entitled. The proposed evaluation of EGIs would make my explanation circular.

Furthermore, since we want to use some fact about the EGIs to explain the justice of the entitlements they generate, it would also be a mistake to evaluate EGIs simply by appeal to the extent that the distributions permitted by the EGI would be just. It also would make the present project circular.

I propose to make use of the concept of desert in a different way in the attempt to evaluate EGIs. I will say that a "deserved EGI" for a country is one such that citizens of that country deserve to have that EGI in effect there. Suppose there are several possible alternative EGIs for some country. Since they are alternatives, there is some point, such that each of them would constitute a way of achieving that point. Among these EGIs there might be several that share this feature: the citizens of the country deserve (to some reasonably high positive extent) to have that EGI be in effect in their country. I will say that all of these EGIs fall into the "deserved range."

5. Suppose in fact one of the EGIs from the deserved range is in effect in your country, and furthermore suppose that it applies to you in your present situation, and furthermore that in accord with the rules of that EGI you are entitled to a certain benefit (for example, a $1000 refund on your income tax). Then in my view, not only are you entitled by that EGI to have that refund, you also deserve it; and in addition, since the distributor is your government (and your desert base and the desert are political economic desert and base) it follows that your receipt of this benefit affects not only the level of justice in your country, but the level of specifically *political economic distributive justice.*

Hence, if you do not get the money that is owed to you, that will detract from the level of political economic distributive justice of your country; if you do get the money, that will enhance the level of political economic distributive justice. In general terms: if the government of a country has seen to it that an EGI from the deserved range is actually in effect in that country, and if under the terms of that EGI a citizen is entitled to some benefit, then (a) the citizen is *entitled* to the benefit because he satisfies the conditions laid out in some actual EGI; but also (b) the citizen *deserves* that benefit, because he is entitled to it by a deserved EGI. Furthermore, (c) the citizen deserves to have that EGI in effect in his society, and his desert of this EGI counts as *political economic desert.* Finally, (d) if the distributor of the benefit is the government, then his desert of the benefit to which he is entitled according to the rules of the EGI also counts as *political economic desert*. As a result of all this, if the citizen fails to get the benefit to which he is entitled, the level of political economic justice in his society will be adversely affected.

6. Suppose in fact some other EGI is in effect in your country, and suppose this actual EGI is one that does not fall into a range such that people in your country deserve to have in effect some EGI from that range. Suppose the rules of the actual, non-deserved EGI say that you are to have possession of a certain slave. Then you are entitled to the ownership of that slave according to the actual EGI, but since people do not deserve to live in a country with that EGI, entitlements generated by that EGI give rise to only a minuscule amount of desert. Thus, unless you deserve to own the slave for some other reason, you probably do not deserve on balance to own him at all in spite of your legal entitlement.

7. One thing to note: everyone deserves to live in a country in which an EGI from a certain range is in effect, and we are imagining a case in which no such EGI is in effect. If the government failed to establish a suitable EGI, then there is a decrease in political economic distributive justice. Citizens of the country deserved a political economic desert from their government, and the government did not produce.

8. If you anyway go ahead and own the slave, then the level of political economic distributive justice in your country will go *down* even more, since the government will in effect be preventing the slave from receiving several political economic deserts such as freedom, education, security, etc. The government will be doing this by allowing the actual undeserved EGI to remain in effect.

With all of this as background,[12] let us now reconsider the three examples that I introduced earlier. My aim is to explain how my proposed account of the connections between legal entitlement, desert, and political economic desert justifies our (or maybe just *my*) intuitions about the ways in which the described distributions affect the level of political economic distributive justice in the country.

Case One involved some income tax refunds. You and your brother were legally entitled to refunds of $1000; however, the IRS arbitrarily decided to give you only $500. The principles I have proposed give what seems to me to be a correct account of the situation. In virtue of the fact that you are legally entitled to

[12] In a fuller exposition of my view, I would acknowledge that even within the deserved range, some EGIs would be *more deserved* than others. Accordingly, the level of political economic distributive justice in some country would be *even greater* if citizens were to receive the deserts to which they would be entitled by the more highly deserved EGI. I suppress discussion of this point in the text. I trust that the interested reader can readily imagine how the view could be developed.

$1000 by the actual EGI in your country, you deserve to some small extent to get it. But if we assume in addition that the actual EGI in your country (roughly speaking, the one involving all the regulations governing income tax withholding and refunds) is in the deserved range, then your entitlement is based on a deserved, actual EGI. In that case, your desert of the refund is far more substantial.

Furthermore, given these assumptions, we can conclude that the desert in this case is political economic desert: your desert base is legitimate entitlement as specified by a deserved EGI and hence is political economic desert; the distributor is the government of your country. Thus, not only do you deserve the refund, your desert of it counts as political economic desert. Your failure to receive the refund thus detracts from the level of political economic distributive justice in your country. These implications coincide with my intuitions about the case. If outside justice auditors were evaluating your country for political economic distributive justice, they would have to take this episode as a serious injustice. It is a black mark against your country; your outrage would be entirely justified.

In Case Two, a grandfather gave his whole estate to his nasty grandson rather than to his decent grandson. The EGI in this case is constituted by the legal structure concerning inheritance. That would involve a lot of laws and regulations, as well as less formal policies concerning standard procedures. It was stipulated that the will was drawn up entirely in accord with the rules governing such things in the EGI. As a result, the nasty grandson is legally entitled to the whole estate. His legal entitlement generates a certain amount of desert; but his nasty behavior might counteract that desert. Maybe on balance he has only very slight desert of the money. Maybe on balance the decent grandson has greater all-things-considered desert. So it may turn out that from the perspective of cosmic justice, something has gone wrong. The less deserving grandson got the money. Let us assume that the actual EGI is one from the deserved range. Thus, insofar as the establishment of a deserved EGI is concerned, there seems to be no violation of political economic distributive justice.

Note in this case that the government is not the distributor of the inheritance. The role of the government was to establish an EGI from the deserved range, and to ensure that citizens making use of that EGI receive the benefits and burdens to which they are legally entitled by its rules. We assume in this case that the government did its duty. But it is essential in this case to note that the distributor of the estate was not the government. No government official decided that the nasty grandson was to receive the money. The grandfather was responsible for that. So, while there was a violation of cosmic justice (the wrong grandson got the money) there was no violation of political economic distributive justice. If the decent grandson has a complaint, it should not be a complaint about anything the government did; it should be a complaint about something his grandfather did.

Case Three involved two young assistant professors. I stipulated that the professors are equally qualified for their jobs. The college that hired them, appealing to its long-standing traditional policy, agreed to a contract that would give the male applicant a higher salary than his female colleague. The assistant professors were then legally entitled to their salaries.

In virtue of the fact that each professor was legally entitled to his or her salary, each had at least some desert of that salary. However, the EGI under which they received their salaries (the rules of the long-standing hiring policy of their college) was not in the deserved range. People do not deserve to be governed by hiring policies that discriminate in this way on the basis of a factor (in this case, gender) that does not bear on their qualifications or ability to perform the job. As a result, there are several injustices here. First, the female applicant did not have the opportunity to be governed in this case by an EGI from the deserved range. She deserved that opportunity, and so the failure to receive it detracts from the level of cosmic justice in her country.

Furthermore, there is a political economic injustice here as well. Although the female applicant was not paid by the government, the government still played an important role in this injustice. The applicant deserved to live in a country where the government would ensure that job applicants would be offered salaries according to the rules of deserved EGIs. The government fell down on the job. It allowed an undeserved EGI to remain in place. Hence, the discriminatory wage received by the female assistant professor was (a) precisely the wage to which she was legally entitled, but (b) probably lower than the wage that she deserved all things considered, and (c) lower than the wage to which she would have been entitled by an EGI from the deserved range. Furthermore, since the applicant deserved to live in a country where the government ensured that wages would be determined by deserved EGIs, and the government did not fulfil this obligation, the level of political economic distributive justice in her country was adversely affected by this episode. Again, I think these results are acceptable.

4.2.4 Political rights

The level of political economic distributive justice in a country is profoundly affected by facts about the way in which political rights are distributed there. If citizens are denied their rights, justice takes a beating. If the state fails to recognize certain important rights, justice again takes a beating. In an ideally just state—one that has a very high level of political economic distributive justice—institutions will be in place that properly allocate political rights to citizens. Thus, my account of the things we deserve from our countries must include *political rights*.

We have two importantly different ways of talking about political rights. In some cases, when we say that someone has a right to some benefit, we presuppose that there is some right-protecting institution in place and that that institution contains provisions that imply that no one is to interfere with his receipt of the specified benefit. For example, consider the familiar claim that someone who has been arrested has the right to remain silent. In such a case, we expect to hear someone say "read him his rights." If a police officer attempts to force the person to give incriminating evidence against himself, his rights will have been violated. Talk of rights, when in this pattern, is talk of a sociological, political, empirical fact. Whether you have a certain right is not a normative question; it is a factual question (perhaps requiring a trip to court in order to be determined in hard cases). Let us say that when we talk in this way about rights, we are speaking *factually* about rights.

In other cases, when we say that someone has a right to some benefit, our remark is not entirely factual; it has a normative component. Thus, for example, if we deplore the fact that girls in some countries are not permitted to attend public schools, we may say the laws must be changed, because after all those girls have a right to an education. Our remark cannot be understood in the factual way. Careful scrutiny of the relevant laws in their country might reveal that our statement is simply false—false, that is, if taken as a claim to the effect that there is an institution in place in their country that guarantees them this benefit. Scrutiny of those laws might reveal that they explicitly deny them the right to an education. So our remark has some sort of normative force. We are not saying that the laws in fact guarantee this right; we are saying that it would somehow be a "good thing" if the laws were changed so as to guarantee them the right. Let us say that when we talk in this way about rights, we are speaking *normatively* about rights.

Several different accounts have been offered of the normative force of such talk about rights. Some are based on consequentialist intuitions. They maintain (roughly) that people have a right to a certain benefit if and only if utility would be maximized by the establishment of an institution that would ensure that people would receive that benefit. Other accounts make use of Kantian intuitions about the nature of persons. Such accounts focus on some alleged feature of persons—their dignity, or autonomy, or rationality, for example—and go on to claim that in virtue of having this feature, people deserve to have a certain benefit. People have a right to a benefit if and only if they deserve to receive that benefit in virtue of their dignity, or autonomy, or whatever.

I have already explained my misgivings about the consequentialist approach in closely related contexts. We can easily imagine a possible institution (such as the Rawlsian "Telishment") that would maximize utility but that would also impose grotesquely unjust burdens on some citizens. I am also doubtful about the Kantian approach. I think that even those who lack dignity, autonomy, and rationality may have political rights. Consider the case of a very sick old person who is suffering from profound senile dementia. He is no longer rational; his autonomy (however this is to be defined) is seriously compromised; I am not sure if he has retained his dignity; yet he still has some important political rights. Among these, perhaps, the right to be allowed to die in accord with his previously expressed wishes. A similar situation might arise in the case of the abandoned infant discovered on the front steps of Town Hall. She is too young to have much autonomy and rationality. Again I am not so sure of her dignity. Yet I am inclined to think that she might have a right to be cared for by the community at least until she is old enough to care for herself.

I propose instead to make use of the concept of *desert* in my account of normative talk about rights. The view I mean to defend is just a modest extension of things I have already said about legitimate entitlement.

First I need to introduce the concept of a Legal Entitlement Granting Institution (or "LEGI"). Such an institution may be said to exist in a country if a suitable set of laws or regulations are in place in that country; these laws establish a complex of positions and procedures and (perhaps) penalties; and they stipulate that citizens who satisfy certain stated conditions shall be entitled to certain benefits. Thus, for example, there is in fact a set of regulations in place here in Massachusetts that creates and regulates the Department of Children and Families.[13] Those rules include rules about how the Commissioner is to be chosen as well as rules governing the circumstances under which a child will come under the protection of the Department. Most importantly, they specify the conditions that a child must satisfy in order to be entitled to certain benefits such as foster care.

Similar state agencies exist in other states. They differ from the Massachusetts Department in various ways but are generally intended to achieve the same point: the protection of the interests of children against abuse and neglect. It is reasonable to assume that there are many different ways—some slightly better, some slightly worse—in which such an agency could be set up. I assume that some of these possible agencies would be able to achieve this goal reasonably well. Many of these LEGIs satisfy this condition: innocent children who could be vulnerable

[13] Information about the Massachusetts DCF can be found here: http://www.mass.gov/eohhs/gov/departments/dcf/about-the-department-of-children-and-families.html.

to abuse or neglect deserve to live in a community in which something like that LEGI is in place. Any possible LEGI that satisfies this condition is in the "deserved range."

Suppose a person lives in a country in which some LEGI is in place. Suppose that that LEGI contains rules that imply that people with feature F are entitled to be treated in some way, W. Suppose the person in fact has feature F. Then the person is legally entitled to be treated in way W. He has a factual right to be treated in way W. In itself this fact would have no bearing on political economic distributive justice.

If the actual LEGI is not in the deserved range, then there is an injustice. Similarly if there is no LEGI in place. The citizens deserved to live in a community in which there is a LEGI from the deserved range in place; the government did not set up such a LEGI. So in either case there is an unrequited political economic desert base and, as a result, the level of political economic distributive justice is decreased. If abused children fail to receive the benefits they would have received if a LEGI from the deserved range had been in place, then there is a further violation of rights and a further political economic injustice

On the other hand, suppose that the actual LEGI is in the deserved range. Good. Then since the government has established a LEGI from the deserved range, citizens are getting something they deserve from their government (viz., the existence of the deserved LEGI). Political economic distributive justice is enhanced. If a citizen is entitled under that LEGI to some benefit, then he deserves to get it, and his desert is political economic desert. In this case, we can say that he has a normative right to the specified treatment. If he gets the benefit to which he is entitled, then the level of political economic distributive justice in the country is increased.[14] If he fails to get it, there is a political

[14] In his article "Desert" in the *Stanford Encyclopedia of Philosophy*, Owen McLeod points out a difficulty that would arise if we were to say that whenever a person is entitled to some benefit by an actual LEGI, he fully deserves to get it. McLeod also discusses this difficulty in section VI of his "Desert and Institutions," which appears on pp. 193–4 in *What Do We Deserve?* McLeod points out that if this view were true, "evil or morally repugnant rules [would be] capable of generating desert. Suppose, for example, that Nazi laws entitled officers of the SS to property confiscated from Jews. Even so, it hardly seems correct to say that, in virtue of this, the Nazi officers came to deserve (even prima facie) the stolen property." The objection highlights a serious difficulty with some possible views about entitlement and desert, but it does not bear on the view I am defending here. On my view, though the Nazi law might make the officers legally entitled to the stolen property, those laws were not part of a deserved LEGI. No one deserves to live in a country that has "evil or morally repugnant" laws such as those. As a result, entitlements under those laws do not generate political economic desert. Indeed, in my view, people deserve to live in countries with LEGIs that prohibit such repugnant theft, and as a result the mere existence of the Nazi laws was an affront to political economic distributive justice. The acts performed under those laws were still further violations of political economic deserts.

economic injustice and the overall level of political economic distributive justice in the country goes down accordingly.

One might wonder about other rights that would enhance the level of justice in a country. Abstractly, we can say that citizens have a normative political right to do something if they deserve to live in a country in which the government has established an institutional setting that ensures that citizens will have the opportunity to do that thing. Citizens deserve in the relevant way to live in such a country if normal people need to be able to do that thing in order to flourish as human beings, and individuals acting on their own do not have the power to guarantee it for themselves. This abstract part of the answer is relatively easily explained. It is much harder to defend a detailed list cataloging precisely which things are in this way our political rights.

Amendment One of the Bill of Rights may be a good place to start. I think it would be reasonable to agree that we deserve to live in a country that guarantees some version of the right to participate (or not) in religious activities; the right to speak your mind; the right to a free press; the right to assemble together with like-minded others. Each of these rights is open to a variety of interpretations, restrictions, and provisos. Thus, for example, while we may agree that we all deserve a right to freedom of speech, we may not agree on the details. Do we deserve to have a right to use racial slurs? Do we deserve to have a right to advocate the overthrow of the government or to express our support for violent terrorist gangs?

Perhaps it will suffice here to say that there are many different institutional frameworks that would ensure some form of the right of freedom of speech. Each of these is deserved to some degree; presumably some of them fall into the deserved range. We deserve to live in a place where one or another of these is in place. Precisely which one? That is a matter of debate. Since my central aim here is to describe the broad outlines of a desertist theory of justice, it does not seem to me that it is incumbent on me to advocate for a specific, detailed version of the rules concerning precisely which forms of speech will be permitted in a just state. Similarly for the other freedoms.[15]

[15] Amendment Two specifies that citizens of the United States have a right to bear arms. I find it difficult to see precisely why we would need to possess high-power assault weapons in order to flourish as human beings. If in fact we do not have that as a community essential need, then we do not deserve to live in a country that ensures us the right to own such weapons. Justice would not be adversely affected if there were restrictions of the possession of such weapons by ordinary citizens. I think it may be sufficient here to say that my theory of political economic distributive justice, on its own, does not incorporate any definitive position on this thorny question.

An especially interesting question concerns the citizen's right to vote or otherwise participate in the affairs of government.[16] In one form, the question is this: does political economic justice require that citizens have significant input into the decisions made by their government? Or does justice merely require that those decisions be made in such a way that the welfare of the citizens remains high?

It may appear that the view I am advocating implies that it is not essential for citizens to vote, or to serve in any sort of legislative body. It may appear that my view implies that there could be perfect political economic distributive justice even in a country in which the citizens play no role in governmental affairs. Surely we can imagine a very benevolent dictator who sees to it that his subjects have the benefits that they need in order to be happy. This would suggest that the citizens do not have a community essential need to participate in the affairs of government; and in turn that would suggest that they suffer no political economic injustice if they are forced to live in a place where they lack the power to participate meaningfully in their government. Yet many would surely feel that such citizens, merely in virtue of the fact that they are barred from any role in decision-making, are suffering an injustice.

By way of reply, I must first point out that the question—as I have formulated it here—seems to be based on a misunderstanding of my view. I do not maintain that justice requires that people receive the benefits they need in order to be *happy*. I maintain instead that justice requires that people receive certain of the benefits they need in order to *flourish as human beings*. So the relevant question here must be the slightly different question: could there be a benevolent dictator who sees to it that his subjects flourish as human beings even though they are not permitted to play any meaningful role in the decisions of their government? Their happiness or unhappiness is perhaps only indirectly relevant to the question.

I think it is reasonable to maintain that human flourishing involves, among other things, having the opportunity to participate in the decisions of one's government. This may take many different forms. In my case, it involves the right to attend and vote in annual town meetings. It also involves having an opportunity to serve as a public official.[17] In another case, it might involve having the right to vote for representatives who will then debate and vote in a parliament or house of representatives or senate.

Given this view about human flourishing, it would follow that people in general deserve to be embedded in countries where citizens have the right to

[16] The question was raised by a reader for Oxford University Press. I thank Owen McLeod for extensive helpful further discussion.

[17] Which I do. I am one of three Pound Keepers in the Town of Leyden, Massachusetts.

participate in governmental decisions.[18] The precise form of their participation could vary from case to case, but it would presumably be determined by the details of the rules contained in some Entitlement Granting Institution from the deserved range in their country. Where no such institution is in place, or where the institution in place does not come from the deserved range, there is injustice. And this injustice would persist even if a benevolent dictator consistently made decisions that managed to make the citizens happy.

This may be a good point to say something about our desert of compensation, and how failures of compensation affect justice. Governments often engage in activities that are harmful to some citizens. For example, there are cases in which a government determines that it is important to build a new highway in a place where people are currently living. Houses must be taken; homeowners will be evicted. In the ideal case, it is all for the public good, but at the same time it might impose significant harm on certain citizens.

If left entirely to their own devices, citizens would have a hard time forcing the government to compensate them for their losses in such cases. Accordingly, they deserve to have access to some sort of legal process that will help them to make their claims. Again, there are many different ways in which this sort of protection could be provided. Let us say that any institutional arrangement that would perform this function is a "Legal Compensation Granting Institution" or LCGI. Some LCGIs would perform this function well, and others would do it poorly. An LCGI is in the deserved range if and only if it is one such that people deserve to live in a country in which such an institution is in place.

If a citizen is entitled, under the provisions of an existing LCGI from the deserved range, to compensation for some harm inflicted upon him by the government, then he deserves this compensation. His desert of the compensation is political economic desert and the distributor of the benefit should be the government. Hence, if the deserving citizen fails to get the deserved benefit from the government, he has suffered a political economic injustice. If the government has neglected to establish an LCGI from the deserved range, then there is a different sort of injustice—citizens deserved to live in a place where the government has established such an institution, and the government has not done its job. Again, political economic distributive justice is adversely affected.

[18] I recognize that I have not formulated a detailed account of human flourishing. I return to this topic in section 9.2.1 "Flourishing as a human being."

4.2.5 Burdens we deserve to bear

According to one familiar form of desertism there is perfect justice in a country if benefits and burdens are distributed to citizens according to their virtues and vices.[19] On views of this sort, the possession of moral virtues makes a person deserve benefits from the state; the possession of moral vices makes a person deserve burdens from the state. So long as we do not reflect too deeply on the "vice/burden" side of the ledger, this may seem to have at least some plausibility. But when we do look at the "vice/burden" side, we quickly see that views of this sort are deeply problematic.

Among the burdens that a state may impose on its citizens are such things as taxes, obligations for military or community service, and obligations for jury duty. Some high-school students would probably insist that the obligation to attend school should be counted as a burden imposed upon citizens by the state. It should immediately strike the reader that there is a problem here. It makes no sense to suppose that citizens deserve to suffer these burdens because they have been bad. Surely, it is preposterous to say that the burden of income taxes falls harder on those who have been morally worse! Moral vice does not make us deserve to be required to pay taxes. At once this indicates that the familiar form of desertism will have a hard time explaining why morally upright citizens deserve the burdens of taxation, military or other public service, and other such things that are justly imposed on citizens. The attempt to explain desert of political burdens by appeal to vice simply cannot succeed.

According to the view I am defending in this book, moral virtue and vice are not political economic desert bases. Thus, I would not attempt to explain why we deserve to pay income taxes by appeal to facts about our moral failings. Such considerations play no role in my theory. Nevertheless, I recognize that in a perfectly just state, citizens will be required to bear certain burdens. So a question remains: if citizens do not deserve burdens because they have been bad, then what does make them deserve these burdens? What is the political economic desert base in virtue of which citizens in a just state deserve these political economic "deserts"?

My answer here follows the pattern that was discussed in connection with legitimate entitlements and deserved compensation. In those cases I started with the idea that there are many different institutional arrangements that could be put in place in order to deal with a recognized community need. Thus, for example, since experience teaches us that some parents will fail to provide proper

[19] This view is a minor variant of a view that I earlier dubbed "earthly moral desertism." It seems be relevantly similar to the form of desertism that Rawls attacked in *A Theory of Justice*.

nurturance to their children, we need a way to distribute child protective services. There are many different ways in which it can be done. Some of these are better than others. Really good institutional arrangements fall into the deserved range—people deserve to live in a country in which one of these arrangements is in place. Suppose some such arrangement is in place, and suppose it contains a rule that says that abused or neglected children are entitled to foster care or other services. Then abused or neglected children deserve, as a matter of political economic justice, to get the specified services. If the community does not establish an institutional arrangement from the deserved range, there is a failure of political economic distributive justice. If such an arrangement is in place, and some child is entitled to its services but does not receive those services, then there is a different sort of failure of political economic distributive justice. The child deserved something from his community and did not receive it. For justice to reign, there must be a decent institutional arrangement, and citizens who are entitled to services according to its rules must be receiving them.

A similar rationale explains why we deserve to pay taxes. First, the community recognizes that it confronts a fiscal problem: there are many services that citizens deserve from the community—an army, a law-enforcement system, a judicial system, an educational system, an interstate highway system, water supply and treatment systems, medical care for the elderly and needy, etc. Each of these things will cost a lot of money. Some system for gathering the funds must be established. Clearly, there are a lot of different ways in which this can be done. Property taxes, sales taxes, usage fees, income taxes, taxes on savings, etc. Each of these can be arranged in any of indefinitely many different ways. There are lots of different ways in which these fiscal systems can be evaluated.

We could evaluate each such arrangement on purely utilitarian grounds. If we choose to proceed in this way, we would declare the utility-maximizing arrangement to be ideal. This idea is open to familiar objections. Maybe the arrangement that would maximize utility would do this by imposing grotesque injustices on some citizens. (Think of "fiscal telishment.") On the other hand, we could evaluate the arrangements by appeal to the extent to which they would distribute tax burdens to those who deserve those burdens. But this would not answer our question, since we are trying to figure out what makes a person deserve to pay taxes.

I prefer to evaluate each fiscal institution by the extent to which people deserve to live in a country in which it is in place. In other words, thinking of some possible system of taxation, we ask "do people deserve to live in a place where *this* is the way in which the government collects taxes?" Some fiscal institutions would fail this test in virtue of the fact that they would not generate enough revenue. Others would fail because they would ruin the economy. Yet others would fail if they would provoke citizens into thoughts of leaving the country. But a wide variety of fiscal institutions might pass this test. Of each of these, we could plausibly claim that people deserve to some significant extent to live in a country in which this is the system by which the government is funded. Let us say that any such system of taxation is in the "deserved range."

Now we can see one way in which this bears on political economic distributive justice. Everyone deserves to live in a country in which the system of taxation is from the deserved range. If some country has so far neglected to set up a system of taxation, or has set up a system not in the deserved range, then the level of political economic distributive justice in that country is adversely affected. Citizens deserved something from their government; they did not get it.

But suppose that the fiscal institution in place in some country is from the deserved range. Then the government has given its citizens something that they deserve, and to that extent there is political economic distributive justice. Going further, we note that the rules of that system will imply, together with facts about income, number of dependents, or other such relevant factors, how much each citizen owes in taxes. We can then say (using the terminology in a somewhat awkward way) that each citizen is legally entitled to pay a certain amount in taxes. Perhaps more naturally we can say that the government is legally entitled to receive that much money from the citizen. Since the fiscal institution is itself from the deserved range, the legal entitlements it generates support political economic desert. We can then say that each citizen deserves to pay the taxes to which he or she is legally entitled, and the government deserves to receive them. If citizens pay those taxes, then the level of political economic distributive justice is again enhanced.

I think that each citizen has a further political economic desert that bears crucially on this case. Suppose we live in a country in which the fiscal system is from the deserved range; then each of us deserves for it to be the case that the rules of the system are enforced. Most importantly, this implies that each of us deserves assurance that our fellow citizens will be required to pay their taxes.

One of the interesting implications of this approach emerges from the possibility that the citizens of one country are legally required to pay their taxes in accord with one set of regulations while the citizens of another country are required to pay quite different taxes in accord with a significantly different set of regulations. What may be surprising here is that this could happen even though neither group of citizens is suffering any political economic injustice. This would happen if the fiscal system from the first country is from the deserved range and the different fiscal system for the second country is also from the deserved range. The citizens of each country could then deserve—perhaps even to a very high extent—to have in place the system that in fact is in place in their country. In that case, though their tax bills would be quite different, every one of these citizens fully deserves to confront the tax bill that he or she confronts, and political economic justice will be done if the different sets of regulations are efficiently enforced in their respective countries.

This introduces an important sort of relativism into the discussion of taxation. Suppose the tax code of some country is highly progressive, so that people with big incomes pay at a much higher rate than people with smaller incomes. But suppose that tax code is included in an overall system of taxation that is from the deserved range. Suppose the tax code of another country is far less progressive. People with big incomes pay at nearly the same rate as people with small incomes. Yet the second country's overall system of taxation is also from the deserved range. Now consider a comparison of a high-income resident of the first country with an equally high-income resident of the second country. The resident of the first country is paying far more in income taxes than is the equally wealthy resident of the second country. The resident of the first country might wonder how both countries could enjoy equally high levels of political economic distributive justice while he is required to pay so much more in taxes than an equally wealthy citizen of the other country. But the answer is simple: each system of taxation is from the deserved range; hence, the citizens deserve to pay the taxes that have been levied on them by their respective governments. In each case, it is a matter of political economic distributive justice.

4.3 Justice, Healthcare, and a Clarification of My Aims

Earlier, near the end of section 4.2.1, I said that in my view justice requires that citizens have access to healthcare. The reader might want greater detail. More precisely, the reader might want to know the extent of the healthcare benefits that citizens deserve from their countries. Since—in my view—what they deserve depends upon what they need in a certain way, the reader might also want a more extensive account of the relevant sort of need. Clearly, the general principles that apply in the case involving healthcare will also apply in other cases involving other alleged deserts. The example involving healthcare is intended to be illustrative.

The view defended in this book does not imply that whenever someone needs something, political economic justice requires that he be given it. According to my view, political economic justice comes into play only in cases of "community essential need." A person has this sort of need for something only if (a) the item in question is something that people need to have in order to flourish as human beings, and (b) people are not able to secure this thing on their own; they typically need to band together into communities in order to secure this thing. I have characterized these needs as "community essential needs."

As I see it, we have this sort of need for access to healthcare. That explains why it is a matter bearing on political economic distributive justice. But readers might want further information. They might raise the question: precisely how much healthcare do we deserve in this way? My answer is in a way simple: we deserve the amount that people need in order to flourish as human beings and cannot get on their own.

But this requires the answer to a further and much more difficult question: "precisely how much healthcare do people need in this distinctive way?" But this further question lies beyond what I want to say about the nature of political economic distributive justice. I have presented an account of what I take to be the nature of this sort of justice. Advocates of different views about healthcare can agree about this conception of justice while disagreeing about the precise amount of healthcare we deserve. They will do this if they disagree about what it takes to flourish as a human being or if they disagree about whether individuals are able on their own to secure the things that they need in order to flourish or if they disagree about whether we really need to be embedded in a civilized community in order to get these needed things.

Suppose someone thinks that people are seriously incapable of dealing with their health problems on their own. Suppose this person thinks that individuals have very little control over their weight or their smoking or drinking habits. Suppose this person also thinks that you cannot flourish as a human being if you have diabetes or heart trouble or liver disease brought about by overeating or smoking or drinking. Suppose he thinks that in all such cases individuals have community essential needs for healthcare arising from illnesses brought about by their own poor behavior—which, in this person's view, the individuals had no power to control. Then this person, accepting my theory of political economic distributive justice, will claim that justice requires that this person should get access to healthcare to help him out with these medical problems.

Suppose another person thinks that people are able to control their own eating, drinking, and smoking habits. Suppose he thinks, for example, that you do not need to be embedded in a helpful community in order to quit smoking or to moderate your alcohol intake. Then this person will think that health problems arising from irresponsible behavior are not matters of community essential needs. And so, even if this second person also accepts my theory of political economic distributive justice, he will not agree that justice requires the same high level of access to healthcare in these cases.

I take this to be one of the good features of my view: people often disagree about what justice requires. In some cases they seem to end up shouting at each other; they seem to be arguing from mere "intuitions." But if they were all to accept my theory of political economic distributive justice, they would agree on what must be the case in order for this sort of justice to obtain. Instead of merely confronting each other with bare intuitions, they could focus on the underlying factors that (given my view) would determine whether the disputed item satisfies the conditions. I acknowledge of course that disputants might still dispute. I am not claiming that acceptance of my theory would eliminate differences of opinion about justice. I am making a different claim: I claim that my theory offers a systematic structure within which debates about justice can take place. It invites disputants to look at deeper underlying factors that affect justice. Of course, they may disagree about these things as well. But they can disagree about these deeper things while agreeing about the nature of justice.[20,21]

What I say here about desert of healthcare carries over, with fairly obvious changes in detail, to desert of other kinds of benefit. In every case, one's view about the precise amount of the benefit deserved will depend upon one's view about what is required for human flourishing and one's view about the extent to which individuals are capable of securing these things on their own.

4.4 Some Things that are Not Political Economic Deserts and Bases

My list of political economy deserts and desert bases *excludes* a lot of things that probably are deserts and desert bases that would be taken into account by a theory of cosmic distributive justice. I have in mind such things as these:

Moral virtue and vice as desert bases; heaven or hell as deserts. If there is a God, and if He cares about such things, maybe He will see to it that the virtuous are rewarded and the vicious penalized. In that case, divine justice will reign. I have my doubts. But I am confident that this is not a matter over which the government (or the community) has much responsibility. It is not the case that we have these deserts or desert bases in virtue of the fact that we are social

[20] We should not overlook the fact that there are plenty of non-justice related reasons for a government to provide access to healthcare to its citizens. Some of these are matters of sheer benevolence. Others are matters of utility. Others might be matters of fidelity (maybe someone promised the citizens that they would get health insurance).

[21] My thanks to Jean-Paul Vessel, Mark Walker, and Danny Scoccia for raising the questions about healthcare that I discuss in this section.

animals, or the fact that we have community essential needs. They are not political economic deserts and desert bases.[22]

Here is a brief (and undoubtedly incomplete) list of further desert bases and deserts that are *not* political economy desert bases and deserts:

> Being a nice guy—having friends
> Having had quite a lot of bad luck—some good luck
> Having neglected to study hard in school—a second chance
> Being smart and creative—getting your paper published in a good journal; getting your screenplay turned into a real movie
> Having been insulted—getting an apology
> Being a very fast runner—winning a medal or trophy
> Working diligently in business—having financial success
> Being the better candidate—winning the election.

Some philosophers seem to think that there is political economic distributive justice in a community only if *welfare* or *happiness* is distributed appropriately. Thus, for example, Crisp (2003), Parfit (1997), and Arneson (2000) at one time or another explicitly formulated their views about justice by speaking of the distribution of welfare. I disagree. Although I can appreciate the idea that people deserve to be at least minimally happy, I do not think that the level of political economic distributive justice in a community depends upon the extent to which welfare or happiness is allocated to the deserving. I do not think that *being a human being* or *being a citizen* is a political economic desert base on the basis of which citizens deserve to have governments that distribute happiness to them. My view on this is straightforward: having higher welfare would be nice, but it is not something that we need in order to flourish as human beings. We can easily imagine an individual who grows and thrives and makes great achievements, but

[22] Rawls presented several arguments against desertism in *A Theory of Justice* (1971: 100–8, 310–15). Several of those arguments turn essentially on the presupposition that desertism incorporates the view that moral virtue is the main desert base and happiness is the main desert. Rawls indicates that this is how he understands desertism when he remarks that, on this view, "justice is happiness according to virtue" (1971: 310). He gives a series of objections. One of these objections turns on the notion that since it is so hard to determine who is virtuous, it would be hard for the state to ensure that justice is done. Rawls also points out that this conception of justice would not be chosen in the original position. He also claims that we are not responsible for our levels of moral virtue and vice and so we can't deserve anything on this basis. I think the Rawlsian arguments have no relevance to my form of desertism about political economic justice. As I see it, moral virtue and vice are not political economic desert bases, and happiness is not a political economic desert. As a result, insofar as justice is concerned, there is no need for the state to try to measure these things, and the level of political economic justice is not affected by them. As I see it, the Rawlsian objections might be relevant to a theory of justice that claims that justice obtains when citizens receive political economic deserts from their governments in virtue of their possession of moral virtue and vice. The objections are not relevant to PEDa. The Rawlsian arguments are discussed in much greater detail in Chapter 7.

who nevertheless is not very happy. Such an individual could flourish as human being while not being very happy.[23] We can imagine individuals who are alike with respect to levels of happiness but unlike with respect to levels of flourishing. So our need for happiness (assuming that we have such a need) is not a community essential need. Hence, these are not political economic deserts and desert bases, and the level of political economic distributive justice in our community is not directly affected by the extent to which these desert claims are requited.

I think it is possible for there to be a country in which there is a very high level of political economic distributive justice even though the citizens are not as happy as they deserve to be. I think it is possible for there to be two countries exactly alike with respect to political economic distributive justice even though the citizens of one country are happier than the citizens of the other country. So I add to the list of excluded deserts and desert bases:

Being a human being—being happy.

This concludes my discussion of political economic desert bases and deserts.[24] By presenting this catalogue in conjunction with my fundamental principle

[23] I return to this point later in section 9.2.1 "Flourishing as a human being."

[24] A reader for Oxford University Press suggested that it would be helpful to say a few words about the relations between my concept of political economic deserts and the Rawlsian concept of primary social goods. I define political economic deserts by appeal to two considerations: (a) these are things that normal people need in order to flourish as human beings; and (b) they are also things that in the normal course of events individuals cannot secure on their own—they need to be embedded in a suitable community in order to get them. In the first (1971) edition of *A Theory of Justice* Rawls defined primary social goods as "things that every rational man is presumed to want. These goods normally have a use whatever a person's rational plan of life" (62). Elsewhere Rawls seemed to be thinking of this same view when he said that primary goods are things that rational persons want whatever else they want. As Rawls himself later acknowledged in the revised (1999) edition of the book, this definition of primary goods is unacceptable. It makes what counts as a primary good depend too much on contingent facts about human psychology. Perhaps Rawls was troubled by cases like this: suppose a rational person decides to join an ascetic monastic order; suppose that when he joins, he sincerely renounces all worldly goods. As a result, he no longer wants money, or a job, or the right to vote. As a result, it appears that many of the things that Rawls wants to count as primary goods do not satisfy the definition: they are not things that any rational person would want no matter what else he wants. A more extreme case can be imagined: suppose a rational person has a painful and incurable disease; suppose things have reached the point where all he wants is a quick and painless death. This unfortunate person no longer wants money, or a job, or the right to vote. Shall we conclude, then, that these items are not primary goods?

In his "Social Unity and Primary Goods," which appears in Sen and Williams (1982: 159–85), as well as in the revised (1999) edition of *A Theory of Justice* Rawls proposed a different account of primary goods. There he said that primary goods are "what persons need in their status as free and equal citizens, and as normal and fully cooperating members of society over a complete life" (xiii). In Rawls (2001: 58–9), he went on to list some of the items he then took to be primary social goods. These include:

PEDa, I hope to have given a clearer picture of what it would be like for there to be perfect political economic distributive justice in some community. Roughly, it would be like this: in each case in which a person had a political economic desert base for some political economic desert, his political economic distributor would ensure that it is provided in a timely way.

Appendix: Digression: Desert of Wages

Some philosophers write as if they think that the question about political economic distributive justice is largely a question about the distribution of wealth. Accordingly, they seem to think that the question about just compensation for work is at the core of the debate about justice. Recall the Marxist slogan "From each according to his ability, to each according to his need."[25] It certainly

The basic rights and liberties;
Freedom of movement; freedom in choice of a job;
The powers of offices and positions of responsibility;
Income and wealth;
The social bases of self-respect: the recognition by social institutions that gives citizens a sense of self-worth and the confidence to carry out their plans.

I think it is interesting that Rawls defines primary goods by appeal to the concept of *need*. My definition of political economic deserts also makes use of the concept of need, though in a slightly different way. I also think it is interesting that Rawls specifically mentions things that people need "as citizens." This also makes the broad outlines of the revised Rawlsian concept of primary goods similar to my concept of political economic deserts. Perhaps even more relevant is the fact that several of the items that Rawls counted as primary social goods (for example, basic rights; freedom; [access to] income and wealth) also appear on my list of political economic deserts. My list includes some things that Rawls did not mention in this context. Specifically, the security that comes from having a competent police force in the neighborhood; the security that comes from having a social safety net; access to healthcare; access to publically owned or regulated infrastructure that makes education, growth, health, etc., possible.

The reader for Oxford University Press suggested that I might be embarrassed if the things I count as political economic deserts should turn out to be the same as the things that Rawls counted as primary social goods. The reader recognized that my view could still count as a form of desertism even if it claimed that justice is enhanced when primary social goods are distributed in accord with desert; but he went on to say that I would want my theory to be "more thorough-going desertist"; that I would prefer a theory according to which what gets distributed is "deserts" rather than primary social goods. But I see no reason for embarrassment. Suppose my list of political economic deserts turned out to be exactly the same as Rawls's list of primary social goods. That would not make my view any less a thorough-going form of desertism. The theory would still say that we have perfect political economic distributive justice when political economic deserts are distributed in accord with political economic desert bases. The fact (if it were a fact) that the political economic deserts are all and only things that Rawls called "primary social goods" would not detract from the theory's status as a pure form of desertism . After all, it would still say that what makes for justice is that deserved things are distributed in accord with desert.

25 Karl Marx, "Critique of the Gotha Program," 1875.

seems natural to interpret this as a claim about political economic distributive justice, and it seems just as natural to understand it to be claiming (or at least suggesting) that in a just regime workers would be paid wages commensurate with their needs. If one needs more than another, the one is to receive a greater wage than the other. Recall the contrary claim as made by the sufficientist: "what is important is that everyone should have a sufficiently large amount of money." Again, (assuming that the sufficientist means to be talking about political economic distributive justice) the idea seems to be that there is justice in a country if wages and other economic matters are organized in such a way that every citizen has at least a sufficiently large amount of money. An egalitarian of wealth would presumably maintain that political economic justice requires that wages be structured so as to yield outcomes in which each citizen has the same amount of money as each other.

For present purposes this question about desert of wages is important, since I have claimed that justice is a matter of receipt in accord with desert. If people are getting wages either greater than, or less than, what they deserve, this could adversely affect the level of justice in their country. Thus, it would be good to have a general account of our desert of wages. Then, provided that this desert is *political economic desert*, we could see how it fits into my general account of political economic distributive justice. So we need to consider what explains a person's desert of some wage.

Many different explanations have been given for our desert of wages. Perhaps it will be convenient to divide these into three main categories—the Unitarian, the Pluralist, and the Universalist. Let us consider them in turn.

A Unitarian maintains that there is some single desert base that explains desert of wages in all cases. Unitarians disagree about what this desert base is. Among the most popular candidates are effort, contribution, difficulty of the job, and amount of training required. Each of these ideas has its difficulties.

a. Effort. Some jobs are easy to do. Someone who has such a job would not work up a sweat doing the job; nor would he have to scrunch up his forehead thinking really hard trying to figure out how to proceed. Virtually anyone could do the job. A good example of an easy job might be the job of a person who is required from time to time to watch TV to see what shows are on his favorite channel. Another person might have a much harder job. For example, consider the difficulties confronted by a professional boxer who is required to step into the ring to do battle with powerful and punishing opponents. The boxer also has to train diligently for many hours. It requires great dedication and sacrifice. Even a purely intellectual job might require a lot of effort. For example, consider writing this book. I am finding it very difficult. Although I do not often work up a sweat, I do find that I often have to scrunch up my forehead. If effort were the sole basis for the desert of wages, we could endorse a general principle: those who do harder jobs deserve higher wages.

b. Contribution. Those who perform certain jobs make great economic contributions to their employers. Thus, an insightful (and perhaps lucky) portfolio manager might succeed in choosing investments that pay off for her company. Imagine that the stocks and bonds that she selects always gain in value. Another portfolio manager might choose investments that regularly decline in value. In such a case, we could say that the former manager makes a greater economic contribution to her company. Although in some cases it would not be quite so easy to determine the monetary value of an employee's work, it is at least reasonable to suppose that workers generally make some such contribution. If economic contribution were the sole basis for desert of wages, then we could endorse a different general principle: those who make greater economic contributions to their employers deserve higher wages.

c. Onerousness of job. Some jobs are definitely *onerous*. They involve doing things that are distasteful or disgusting. For example, there are jobs in slaughterhouses that any sensitive person would find very unpleasant. Consider, for another example, the job of a medical examiner who has to probe into the rotting remains of accident victims. Other jobs are enjoyable and pleasant. Imagine a person whose job involves constructing beautiful flower arrangements. She might love her job and find it so much fun that she would do it even if there were no pay. If onerousness were the sole criterion for the desert of wages, we could say that those who have more onerous jobs deserve higher wages.

d. Lengthy training. Medical doctors in the United States make relatively large salaries. Some claim that these high salaries are deserved because the doctors had to go through college and then medical school; then had to serve as tired, overworked, and underpaid interns or residents before they could finally start to earn some money (most of which would at first go toward paying back the loans that financed the long education). Other jobs require only the briefest of training. An eager young person who wants a job in the medical profession but who has no time for medical school might be able to get a job as an orderly. The job involves making beds and clearing up soiled bedpans. It is dirty, smelly, and often boring work, but it does not require any advanced degrees. If length of training were the sole criterion for the desert of wages, we could endorse this: those who take jobs that require longer periods of training deserve higher wages.

Although some philosophers have expressed support for one or another of these criteria for desert of wages, none of them is plausible. That is, none of them is plausible *if taken as the sole criterion by which desert of wages is to be determined.* Each of these criteria has this feature: it is easy to think of cases in which the criterion implies that Worker A deserves a greater wage than Worker B, but as we reflect on the cases, we find the implication wholly implausible.[26]

Thus, for example, if a clumsy and muddleheaded worker finds a certain job to be very difficult—he sweats hard from 9am until 5pm—and an efficient and skilled worker finds the same job to be smooth sailing, then the difficulty criterion implies that the sweaty worker deserves a higher wage than the skilled worker. If they are equally productive and have agreed to the same pay scale, it seems hard to justify the notion that one deserves more than the other. Or suppose that it takes longer to get a PhD in Comparative Literature than it does to get an MD and do an internship. The "lengthy training" criterion implies that someone who has completed the especially tedious training in Comparative Literature deserves more pay than someone who has completed the slightly less tedious training in medicine; yet many would find this implausible. If the PhD in Comparative Literature goes on to a job teaching in a college, he may deserve nothing more than the modest salary befitting an assistant professor. If the MD is doing a decent job as a pediatric neuro-oncologist, she deserves every penny of her huge salary.

Universalism. Whereas the Unitarian selects exactly one desert base, and claims that all desert of wages is to be explained by appeal to it, the Universalist takes the opposite tack. He claims that the wage that a worker deserves depends on the complex interaction of an indeterminately large number of bases. On this view, every one of the above-mentioned desert bases may bear on a person's desert of wages. But in addition, there are such factors as "the wage to which one is entitled by contract or custom, the fact that one is a person, certain needs one may have, one's moral worth, one's past receipt of goods and evils, and perhaps others."[27] Although McLeod (who maintains a view like this) does not explicitly commit himself to a full-fledged form of Universalism, his remarks suggest it. On such a view, there is no limit to the number of desert bases in virtue of which someone might deserve a certain wage. In each case, every one of these desert bases makes its contribution to the worker's overall desert.

[26] See Owen McLeod's paper "Desert and Wages" (reprinted in *What Do We Deserve?* ed. McLeod and Pojman, 1999, pp. 271–82) for a multitude of persuasive examples.

[27] McLeod "Desert and Wages," 277.

While I believe that Universalism points us toward an important insight about a certain form of justice, I think it does not figure in the best account of political economic distributive justice. I will attempt to explain this by appeal to an example. Imagine a comparison of two brand-new assistant professors getting their first jobs. Let them be virtually indiscernible with respect to the commonly cited job related desert bases—how hard they have to work on the job, how onerous their jobs are, the magnitude of the contributions they make to their respective colleges, and the length of time it took them to earn their PhDs. But suppose Professor A had some fairly serious health problems in his youth whereas Professor B never confronted such problems; suppose Professor A is universally recognized as a very nice guy with a sweet temperament, whereas Professor B is somewhat aloof and sometimes makes biting remarks; suppose Professor A's family is considerably less wealthy than Professor B's. Given natural assumptions about desert bases, Universalism implies in this case that Professor A deserves to have a higher wage than Professor B. I acknowledge that there is some merit to this idea. If we learn that Professors A and B are getting the same wage, we might feel that that is somehow unfortunate. It might have been fairer, all things considered, if some way could have been found to give Professor A a bit more.

But on the other hand, if an international body were trying to rank countries for their level of political economic justice, they very well might see nothing worrisome about the way Professors A and B have been treated. Even if they felt that it would be nice if Professor A could be given some sort of encouragement, I doubt that they would think that it falls to the nation as a whole to see to it that cases such as this not be permitted. All this suggests that while there might be a cosmic injustice here, there is no specifically political economic injustice. So, when we take a broad view of the situation, we may feel that there is something to be said in favor of giving Professor A a higher wage; but on the other hand, when we consider the question from the perspective of political economic distributive justice, we may conclude that the nation as a whole has not failed in allowing Professor A simply to get the wage specified in his seemingly fair contract.

Since I am interested in political economic distributive justice, and Universalism seems more naturally associated with what I have dubbed cosmic distributive justice, I prefer to find some different account of desert of wages—or perhaps more accurately—a better account of *political economic desert of wages.*

Pluralism. An intermediate position might seem attractive here. One popular reaction to cases like the ones I have discussed involves admitting that none of the Unitarian principles provides a satisfactory account of our desert of wages *on its own*. Instead, each of them identifies a factor that helps to determine the appropriate wage. If we add "other things being equal" to each of the principles, and combine the amended principles, then we can say that the resulting complex principle is a plausible account of desert of wages. The result is a form of Pluralism about the desert of wages. According to views of this sort, there are several different factors, each of which bears on desert of wages; taken jointly, they provide a multi-factorial criterion of desert.

One form of Pluralism would say that the operative factors are just the four I mentioned earlier: difficulty of the job, onerousness of the work, economic contribution, and length of training. It seems to me, however, that there is reason to doubt that this form of pluralism gives us the needed insight into the desert of wages that bears on political economic distributive justice. Suppose again that there are two philosophy professors. Suppose they are indiscernible with respect to all of the cited factors. They work equally hard; they make equivalent contributions to the bottom lines at their private colleges; they do similar work, so that the work of one is just as onerous as the work of the other; each of them took exactly seven years to complete the PhD. If the cited form of Pluralism were true, the professors would deserve equal pay.

However, we can go on to imagine that each of the professors negotiated independently with his or her own college administration. Suppose that one negotiated a contract for \$100,000 per year and the other negotiated a contract for \$105,000 per year. Each of the professors is happy with his or her deal. In this case, other things are equal, yet they have different wages. I cannot see why anyone would think that there is any political economic injustice in this case. The professors are satisfied; the colleges are satisfied. This shows that even if you add "ceteris paribus" to each of the principles and then combine them, there is something wrong with the multi-factorial principle.

But the example brings out an ever deeper problem with this form of Pluralism. In my example, I stipulated that the professors were working for private colleges. Neither was a government employee. Thus, even if there is something unfair about the wages of the professors, this unfairness does not indicate that the *government* or *the society as a whole* has somehow fallen down on the job of ensuring political economic distributive justice. How could it be a black mark against a country if similarly qualified citizens freely enter into reasonable contracts that happen to give them different wages? It seems to me to be no fault of the government. The professor who is earning the lower wage cannot claim that he is being treated unjustly *by the government* or *by the society*. If he is being treated unjustly, it is by his employer. So this leaves us with our question unanswered: what are a worker's political economic desert bases? And what does a worker politically economically deserve, by way of wages, from his government as distributor, on the basis of his or her political economic desert bases?

It is not the business of a government to pay the wages of private sector workers. The philosophy professors in my most recent example receive their pay from their respective private colleges, not from the government. Furthermore, in the typical case, it is not the business of the government to dictate what the wages will be. No government agency oversees and regulates the payscales for the professors at private colleges. As a result, in all these cases, the wages themselves are not *political economic deserts*. Thus we have not yet identified anything that private sector workers deserve *from their government*, or from their society as a whole. Accordingly, if these wages are somehow unfair, that unfairness does not directly affect the level of political economic distributive justice in the country.

So what is the government's business with respect to private sector wages? What do workers deserve from their governments when it comes to paychecks? As I see it, the government's job in this area is to establish an institutional setting within which employers and employees will be able to reach reasonable contractual agreements about wages, benefits, and working conditions. In connection with this, it is the business of government to ensure that certain labor abuses are not tolerated in these contracts. Additionally, the government must ensure that if employers and employees enter into reasonable contracts, those contracts will be honored. If the government succeeds in seeing to it that labor contracts pass some minimum standards, and if the government also provides ready access to a judicial system that provides a forum for the resolution of disputes about allegedly abusive contracts, then the government has seen to its business. When this is the case, citizens have received the political economic deserts that they deserve from their governments. To that extent, there is political economic distributive justice even if people who are indiscernible with respect to the traditional wage-determining factors are getting different wages.

I have made use of a variety of normative expressions in my sketch of the institutional setting that bears on desert of wages. Thus, for example, I spoke of "reasonable contracts," and "minimum standards," and "abuses." I think that different institutional settings could spell these things out in different ways. Quite a few different ones could provide for these things in ways that are acceptable—that is, in ways that are consistent with distributive justice. I want to appeal (as I did in my discussion of legal rights) to the idea of there being a *deserved range* of institutional settings with respect to wages. This is the range of settings such that workers deserve to live in a country where the government sees to it that some institutional setting from that range is in place.

This desert of an institutional setting is a matter of political economic justice. So here we have the first thing that a worker deserves as a matter of political economic justice: *that the institutional setting with respect to wages that is in place in his or her country is one from the deserved range*. Workers deserve this desert because they have a kind of *vulnerability*—they are *vulnerable to exploitation by employers*. No one, working entirely on his own, would be able to protect himself against possible exploitation. It takes a collective entity such as the Labor Relations Board to mount a successful defense.[28] And so, if some country fails to establish such an institutional setting, it has failed to provide something to its citizens that they deserve. Political economic distributive justice is adversely affected.

This view about desert of wages makes use of the idea of a minimally reasonable contract between employer and employee. Such a contract would have to be consistent with child labor laws, workplace safety laws, minimum wage laws, anti-discrimination laws, and other such safeguards. But so long as it does not violate any of these fairly modest limitations, there is considerable freedom for employer and employee to negotiate and agree on wages, hours, benefits, working conditions, etc. In my view, institutional settings from the deserved range could spell these things out in different ways. But, so long as an institutional setting is in the deserved range, its way of spelling out such things is acceptable. So when I say that an employment contract is "reasonable," I mean that it is one that is spelled out in an institutional setting from the deserved range; and similarly when I say that contracts must meet at least "minimum standards," I mean to be indicating the standards of an institutional setting from the deserved range.

Now suppose the government has fulfilled its duty with respect to the provision of a system for the enforcement of reasonable labor contracts. Suppose further that a worker has contracted with an employer to work for a certain wage, the contract itself was reasonable, and the person has done the job according to the contract. In this case, the worker is legitimately entitled to the agreed wage. If an employee is legitimately entitled to a certain wage under some reasonable contract, and he has fulfilled his side of the bargain, then he deserves to get the agreed wage. He deserves the wage in part because it was promised to him on condition that he perform certain work, and he has performed as agreed. Promises in general engender desert. Furthermore, in the present case, in virtue of the fact that the government oversees and regulates important features of the contract, and the contract itself is reasonable, the worker deserves to have the government ensure that the employer will pay the agreed wage if the worker performs the agreed work. Indirectly, then, desert of the wage almost becomes a political economic desert. It is not that the worker deserves the paycheck from the

[28] This indicates that I could have discussed desert of wages in the section in which I was describing political economic deserts in the general category of *security*.

government. He deserves something slightly different. He deserves that the government see to it that his employer pays him the amount specified in their reasonable labor contract. So now we can say that when it comes to wages, the worker politically economically deserves a couple of things from the government. One is that there be regulations governing what shall count as an acceptable labor contract. Another is that when employer and employee have entered into a reasonable contract, and the employee has done the specified work, the employer shall pay the agreed wage. If the government sees to these things, it has done its role with respect to the desert of wages.

Earlier I described a situation in which there were two philosophy professors. I stipulated that they did work that required the same effort and that made the same economic contribution to their respective private colleges. I stipulated that the jobs were equally onerous and required the same long, drawn-out, underpaid training. I claimed that even if one professor earned quite a bit more than the other, this fact might not detract from the level of political economic distributive justice in their country. Now we can see why this is the case. Each professor deserved to live in a country in which a system was in place that ensured that reasonable labor contracts would be enforced; and each professor in fact does live in such a place. Each professor deserved this because without it he or she would be economically vulnerable. Since this is one of the central political economic deserts and one of the central political economic desert bases, and the country distributed that desert to the professors on that base, it follows that insofar as desert of wages is concerned, the level of political economic distributive justice is looking good—even if the two professors agreed to contracts that specify different wages.

Furthermore, since the professors were entitled to these different wages by reasonable contracts, they deserved their agreed wages. In each case, when the professor receives that wage, we have yet a bit more distributive justice. I am not claiming that each professor has political economic desert of precisely the wage he or she receives. That is a private matter between the professors and their respective colleges. The additional political economic distributive justice arises as a result of the fact that the government stands ready to ensure that the terms of reasonable labor contracts will be enforced. Again, it is consistent with all this that the professors receive significantly different wages. After all, they are entitled to different wages by their respective reasonable contracts.

5

Desertism and Some Competitors

In this chapter I sketch some forms of egalitarianism, luck egalitarianism, sufficientism, the difference principle, and libertarianism. For each of these theories of justice, I mention some objections. I explain why these objections do not reveal any difficulties for my desertist theory of political economic distributive justice.

Versions of the views I discuss in this chapter have been defended in print. In some cases a distinguished philosopher is well known as one of the main advocates of the view. However, in many cases, it is not clear that the version of the view that was defended in print by the well-known advocate is a direct competitor to the desertist theory that I want to defend. In some extreme cases, it was not clear that the philosopher in question was actually talking about *justice*. For example, a form of sufficientism was defended by Frankfurt in an important paper (1997). But Frankfurt did not say that he was presenting a theory of distributive justice; he did not mention justice in that paper. Instead, he indicated that he was presenting a view about what would be "important from the point of view of morality" (1997: 21). For another example, a form of egalitarianism was defended by Nielsen. But he did not say that he was presenting a theory about distributive justice. Instead, he talked about "what we seek" (1981: 261).

I want to explain why the desertist theory that I prefer is superior to these competing theories. In order to have meaningful comparisons, I have to develop new versions of the well-known theories that we can find in the literature. I state my versions of these theories as theories explicitly about what makes for perfect political economic distributive justice in a society (rather than as theories about intrinsic value, or moral obligation, or "importance from the point of view of morality," or "what we seek"). Thus, the theories to be discussed here are in my preferred style, rather than in the styles in which they appeared in the literature. In my reformulations, the theories are explicitly about *political economic distributive justice.* I have recast the theories in this way so as to make it clear that, as I understand them, they are intended to be competing theories about the same subject matter as the theory I advocate. As a result, it remains possible that the original versions of the theories were not intended to be theories about the subject that I take to be of central importance to social and political philosophy. I acknowledge that my objections may have no application to the versions of these theories that were originally presented by their advocates.

5.1 Egalitarianism

The basic idea behind the most fundamentally *egalitarian* forms of egalitarianism is that justice obtains when the currency of justice is distributed equally.[1] Different choices concerning the currency of justice yield different forms of egalitarianism.

Some have suggested that we can take the currency of justice to be *wealth* or *money*.[2] If we base our formulation of egalitarianism on that assumption, we get:

> Em: There is perfect political economic distributive justice in a society if and only if every member of the society has the same amount of wealth as every other member.

Em has implications concerning justice that are dramatically different from the implications of my proposed desertist theory. A single extreme example should make this obvious if it is not obvious already. Imagine a strange country in which the government monitors each citizen's bank account, investments, and other holdings on a regular basis. Suppose the IRS in this country imposes taxes on everyone who has above-average wealth, and on a monthly basis redistributes the revenue to those who have below-average wealth. As a result, the government manages to see to it that wealth is equally distributed among the citizens. Em declares that there is perfect distributive justice in this country (at least during the first few minutes following each month's redistribution).

Suppose, in addition, that the government meddles in other matters. Suppose that according to strictly enforced laws in this country, women are not permitted

[1] Some forms of egalitarianism are apparently not theories of distributive justice at all. So, for example, someone might claim that all people are equally worthy of moral consideration. Mill states "Bentham's Dictum" in this way: "Everybody to count for one, nobody for more than one" (*Utilitarianism* Chapter 5). Views such as these might be categorized as forms of egalitarianism, but they have no immediate implications for the justice or otherwise of possible distributions of the currency of justice. I focus exclusively on forms of egalitarianism that are intended to be theories of distributive justice.

[2] As, for example, Frankfurt seems to do, though not in connection with egalitarianism.

to engage in any sort of interesting employment. They are required to stay at home at first being dutiful daughters to their fathers, and then being obedient wives to their husbands. Furthermore, suppose that women are not permitted to drive cars. If they need to go to the mall, they must get a male relative to drive them there, and then to monitor their behavior as they shop. In addition, women are not permitted to attend schools. As a result, most women are illiterate. Suppose finally that women are not permitted to vote. Men in this country, on the other hand, enjoy all these rights that are denied to women. Men can travel, go to school, hold down interesting jobs, and vote.

My theory of distributive justice, PED, implies that there is a very low level of political economic distributive justice in this country. Half the population is being denied many of the political benefits that they deserve to have. The government itself is preventing the women from receiving these benefits. In itself, this would be sufficient to drive the level of justice down very significantly. Furthermore, in virtue of the aggressive policy of redistribution of wealth, those who deserve to have very little money will have just as much money as those who deserve to have a lot. Thus, for example, consider an unproductive, lazy, corrupt wastrel who squanders every penny of his government stipend on drugs and gambling. He is guaranteed the same level of wealth as a hard-working, productive, altruistic person who devotes his life to caring for sick children. Each month the wastrel will receive a check sufficient to get him up to the equalized standard for the country. This, as I see it, would drive the level of justice in this strange country even further downward.

I find the implications of Em so counterintuitive that I am inclined to think that no one could have proposed it as a theory of *justice*. Perhaps it would be proposed as a theory about some other virtue of states. I have no idea what that virtue would be, and I shall have nothing further to say about Em here. A different form of egalitarianism would assume a different currency of justice. That would be *welfare* instead of *wealth*. The resulting theory would be:

> Ew: There is perfect political economic distributive justice in a society if and only if every member of the society has the same level of welfare as every other member.

Ew is incomplete as it stands. It does not say what makes the situation in one imperfect society more just than the situation in another imperfect society. It would be natural to assume that associated with Ew is a principle about comparative degrees of distributive justice that provides the explanation. I will assume that it says that the level of distributive justice in one society, S1, is greater than the level in another society, S2, if the distribution of welfare in S1 more closely approximates an equal distribution than does the distribution of welfare in S2.[3]

The concept of welfare is a matter of dispute. Eudaimonists about welfare would say that a person's level of welfare is equal to his level of happiness. Preferentists about welfare would say instead that a person's level of welfare is equal to the net extent to which her preferences are satisfied (perhaps weighted for strength of preferences; perhaps focusing on ideal preferences instead of actual ones). Hedonists about welfare would say that a person's level of welfare is entirely determined by the amounts of pleasure and pain that the person experiences. Pluralists about welfare might say that welfare is a complex matter involving health, wealth, loving personal relationships, job satisfaction, and perhaps other items. Perfectionists about welfare might say that a person's level of welfare is somehow a matter of the extent to which the person approaches the ideal of human perfection.

The fact that the concept of welfare is so controversial makes it difficult to compare Ew—when taken in this abstract form—with PED. However, it may be interesting to consider some differences that would emerge if we understand welfare as happiness. Perhaps the implications of this case would carry over to other interpretations of Ew.

Imagine a country in which political economic deserts are distributed as far as possible in accord with political economic desert bases. Those who deserve security and opportunity of various sorts receive it; those who are legally entitled to benefits in accord with deserved entitlement generating institutions receive those benefits. PED implies that there is a very high level of political economic distributive justice in the country. But suppose in addition that quite a few of the citizens of this country are naturally inclined to be somewhat glum.[4] They have no complaints about the benefits they receive from their country, but on the other hand the receipt of these benefits does not make them especially happy. When they reflect on the fact that they have health insurance, free public education, and the right to vote, these citizens are emotionally unmoved. Additionally, suppose that another portion of the population is naturally inclined to be cheerful. They delight in the things that leave their fellow citizens cold.[5]

[3] For an insightful explanation of the difficulties that emerge when we try to give a precise account of approximations to equality, see Temkin (1993).

[4] I am not imagining that these citizens are suffering from clinical depression. They are not miserable, or suicidal. They simply have a natural tendency to be somewhat glum.

[5] I am not imagining that these citizens are suffering from mania. Again, it is just a matter of being outliers on the "normal" spectrum.

If a person's welfare level is determined by his or her level of happiness, then we must conclude that welfare is unequally distributed in this country.[6] Because they are less happy, the unhappy citizens have lower levels of welfare than the happy citizens. Ew then implies that the level of distributive justice is low. PED, on the other hand, reaches the opposite conclusion. Since the citizens are getting the political economic deserts that they deserve, and they are getting them from their country, PED implies that the level of distributive justice is quite high. Since I think that considerations of justice do not require governments to monitor and adjust levels of happiness—certainly not to try to make these levels *equal*—I do not see any political economic injustice in this imagined country. I think the implications of PED are closer to the truth.

For present purposes, it might make more sense to compare my form of desertism to a different form of egalitarianism. That is because my form of desertism presupposes that the currency of justice is *political economic deserts.* We get a kind of "apples and oranges" lack of parallel if we compare my form of desertism with a form of egalitarianism that presupposes a different currency of justice. Some of the differences between the theories arise because of this difference about currency, rather than simply because of the difference between a theory based on equality and a theory based on receipt in accord with desert.

A different form of egalitarianism makes for a more revealing comparison. That would be:

> Eped: There is perfect political economic distributive justice in a society if and only if every member of the society has the same collection of political economic benefits and burdens as every other member.

Associated with Eped is the expected comparative principle about approximations to perfect justice.

Here is something that I find interesting: suppose you start with my desertist theory of distributive justice. Suppose you say (contrary to what I have said) that there is really only one political economic desert—and that is *having the same collection of political economic benefits and burdens as everyone else in your community;* suppose you say (also contrary to what I have said) that there is really only one political economic desert base—and that is the property of *having a collection of political economic benefits and burdens that is different from that had by others in your community.* In effect then you are saying that in any case in

[6] My argument here depends upon the assumption that cheerful people are happier than glum ones. In *What is This Thing Called Happiness?* I explain and defend a theory of happiness that is intended to support these intuitions.

which political economic benefits and burdens are distributed unequally, everyone deserves for it to be the case that the distribution of these things is adjusted so as to make each person's share equal to that of each other person in the community. Let us use the expression "PED + 1" to refer to the combination of PED and the assumptions (a) that there is only one desert base and that is inequality of political economic benefits and burdens and (b) there is only one desert and that is equality of political economic benefits and burdens.

It would be presumptuous of me to speculate about the thought processes that led any particular philosopher to believe in egalitarianism. But there is no harm in imagining something that could possibly have happened in some possible case. A philosopher might start out thinking that justice is a matter of receipt in accord with desert. This could seem almost analytic. But then she could come to think also that there is only one thing that people deserve, and that is being at the same level of receipt as their fellow citizens. She could then recognize that, given her beliefs, she is committed to the view that justice obtains when there is equality of receipt. She could then take herself to be an egalitarian, but in fact she would at heart be a desertist who has combined her desertism with an implausible view about desert bases. Did any actual philosophy wander down this particular garden path? I have no idea.[7] I mention this in part because I find it interesting to consider the idea that we are all desertists at heart; we differ about justice largely because we have different views about what people deserve. Given a sufficiently extreme view about what we deserve, a desertist could end up looking quite like an egalitarian.

I have assumed that there are very many distinct political economic desert bases. In normal cases, each person will have quite a few of them, and in any reasonably large society, different people will have different collections of them. As a result, in most normal situations Eped and PED yield different judgments about justice. But we can at least imagine that there might be a situation in which all the members of some society have exactly the same collection of political economic desert bases. In such an admittedly unlikely situation, Eped and PED would yield the same implications about distributive justice. Suppose there is a country in which citizens are exactly alike with respect to all political economic desert bases. They all equally deserve the right to vote, in-state tuition refunds, government sponsored healthcare, and assistance with respect to free legal counsel, etc. In that case, PED implies that there will be perfect distributive

[7] Ingmar Persson and Thomas Christiano seem to argue in something like this way for egalitarianism in their essays *Egalitarianism: New Essays on the Nature and Value of Equality*, ed. Nils Holtug and Kasper Lippert-Rasmussen, 2007.

justice in their country only if all citizens receive the same collection of political economic deserts. Eped has the same implication. However, the two theories explain the justice of this equality of distribution in different ways. Eped explains it by saying that justice requires that everyone receive the same collection of political economic deserts in this case because justice requires that everyone receive the same collection of political economic deserts *in every case*. My theory, on the other hand, explains it by saying that justice requires that everyone in this example receive the same collection of political economic deserts because in this extraordinary case the citizens are alike with respect to all political economic desert bases. If one citizen deserves in-state tuition refunds because he is going to State U., then every other citizen deserves the same refund because every other citizen is going to State U. as well.

I think it is interesting to note in this example that there is only one distribution of political economic deserts that would be declared perfectly just by PED, but there are indefinitely many such distributions that would be declared perfectly just by Eped. PED calls for the unique distribution in which each citizen gets what he or she deserves—and in this case it would be an equal distribution. Eped, on the other hand, would declare *any* equal distribution, whether in accord with desert or not, to be perfectly just.

As I see it, in the vast majority of real-life cases, citizens of a country are not equally deserving of political economic deserts. In virtue of special needs that they may have, or legitimate entitlements they have earned, some may deserve special benefits. In virtue of their failure to need certain benefits, or having done something that diminishes or eliminates desert of some benefit, others may deserve smaller collections of benefits. In any such case, as I see it, Eped yields the wrong results about justice, whereas PED yields the right results.

Eped is open to a version of the leveling down objection.[8] If Eped were true, then it would not matter (as far as distributive justice is concerned) whether people's political economic receipt levels were equalized at a high level, or at a low level, or at a negative level. So long as everyone ends up with *the same* level of political economic deserts, this theory implies that we have perfect distributive justice. Some critics may think they can see that egalitarianism goes wrong because it says that there is perfect political economic distributive justice when everyone ends up equalized at a low level of the currency of justice. It is not clear to me that that is precisely the problem. For as I see it, if everyone deserved to be at a low level, then it would be just for them to be at it.

[8] The leveling down objection originates in Parfit (1997).

A better version of the objection works more like this: imagine a community in which some are at high levels of receipt of political economic deserts and others are at low levels. Then imagine two possible transitions: we could transition up so that everyone would be equalized at the higher level of receipt; or we could transition down so that everyone would be equalized at the lower level. Assume that aside from the changes in levels of receipt of political economic deserts, nothing else (as far as possible) is changed. Eped implies that it makes no difference whether we transition upward or downward; either transition yields perfect distributive justice. But, as I see it, so long as we keep the levels that people deserve constant, it cannot be the case that transitioning down would be as just as transitioning up. We cannot have perfect distributive justice both at the higher level and at the lower level. In at least one case, people will not be getting what they deserve.

My desertist theory does not have any difficulty with these considerations. My theory does not imply that there is anything distinctive about equality from the point of view of justice. (Of course, in the extraordinary case in which people are alike with respect to all the political economic desert bases, my theory implies that justice would require that they be alike with respect to receipt of political economic deserts.) As I see it, the transition upward might be a move toward greater political economic distributive justice. This would be the case if the members of the community uniformly deserved to be at the higher level. On the other hand, the transition downward might be a move toward greater distributive justice. If the members of the community uniformly deserved to be at the lower level, then this would be the case. But in real-life cases it would be more likely that distributive justice would call for an unequal distribution of political economic deserts; that is because in real-life cases people are all over the map with respect to their possession of political economic desert bases.

I turn at this point to a certain form of argument that is now familiar in the literature on distributive justice. Roughly, the arguments go like this: we start with some situation that all parties are prepared to accept as being perfectly just. Then we imagine certain innocent changes occurring in the situation. The changes appear to be "justice neutral"—they seem to have no effect on the level of justice in the situation, but the theory under consideration implies that these changes would decrease the level of justice. This shows that the theory is mistaken. Rawls presented some arguments in this form in *A Theory of Justice*.[9] Subsequently, Nozick made use of the same argument pattern in his "Wilt

[9] The example in section 48 of the singer whose talents decline could be used for this purpose.

Chamberlain" argument.[10] I think an interesting argument in the same style against egalitarianism can be developed.

Suppose there is a country in which political economic deserts are distributed equally and in accord with the extent to which citizens deserve to have them. No one has any grounds for complaint about injustice. It seems like a perfectly just situation. Then suppose that one citizen commits some crime, is properly convicted, and as a result loses his freedom and his right to vote. Since the convict has lost some of his political economic deserts while all his fellow citizens retained theirs, these deserts are no longer distributed equally. Egalitarianism of political economic deserts (if understood as Eped) has to say that the level of distributive justice in the society has decreased, but an impartial observer would naturally say that the move toward a less equal distribution of political economic deserts does not detract from the level of justice in this country. Indeed, some would say that considerations of justice *require* that there be an unequal distribution of political economic deserts in this case. This reveals a problem for egalitarianism if understood as Eped.

PED, on the other hand, has no difficulty with this case. When the criminal commits his crime, he starts deserving some penalty, and he stops deserving to be treated as a law-abiding citizen. Since he now has a different collection of desert bases, it is to be expected that justice requires that he have a different collection of deserts. My sense of the situation is thus clear: after this individual commits his crime, it is no longer the case that all citizens in this country are equally deserving of political economic deserts. PED correctly implies that justice requires that citizens receive different collections of these deserts, while Eped incorrectly implies that justice requires that they continue to receive the same collection of deserts.

5.2 Luck Egalitarianism

In recent years a substantial amount of attention has been directed toward a collection of modified forms of egalitarianism. According to these views, not all inequalities detract from the level of distributive justice in a country; only certain ones matter. The ones that matter are inequalities due to the operation of bad luck.[11] If some are worse off through no fault of their own, but simply as a

[10] Nozick (1974: 161–4).

[11] Commentators often cite two papers by Ronald Dworkin as early statements of luck egalitarianism. These are "What Is Equality? Part 1: Equality of Welfare," *Philosophy and Public Affairs* 10 (1981), 185–246; and "What is Equality? Part 2: Equality of Resources," *Philosophy and Public Affairs* 10 (1981), 283–345. These papers were later reprinted in Dworkin's *Sovereign Virtue: The*

result of bad luck, then it falls to the government to compensate them. This would happen, for example, in a case in which one person is worse off than others entirely because he was born with a handicap that makes it harder for him to earn a living, or because—quite out of the blue—she came down with an unpredictable disease.

Carl Knight gives a relatively clear statement of the leading idea behind one form of luck egalitarianism in this passage:

> Variations in the levels of advantage held by different persons (i.e., inequalities) are permitted by justice if and only if those persons are *responsible* for those (or equivalent) variations. On this principle, disadvantages that arise from congenital disability, poor native endowment of talent, and birth into unfavorable social or economic circumstance are typically said to give rise to entitlements for compensation, for they derive from inequalities of opportunity, whereas those that arise from choices to make more or less effort, or to pursue some goals rather than others, do not, for they reflect different uses of opportunity.[12]

Arneson provides a much briefer "summary formulation" of the view in this passage:

> Distributive justice according to the luck egalitarian requires that unchosen or uncourted inequalities be undone and that chosen or courted [in]equalities should be let alone.[13]

One of the attractions of this sort of view is that it provides a more satisfactory evaluation of cases like the one involving the criminal who lost some of his advantages as a result of having been found guilty of a crime. The luck egalitarian can say that while equality of advantage would otherwise be required by justice, when a person is responsible for getting himself in a situation of disadvantage, justice no longer requires that he be brought back into equality with his law-abiding fellow citizens. Justice allows inequalities such as these to stand.

Like any egalitarian, the luck egalitarian thinks that justice requires that inequalities be eliminated. But in virtue of the way luck egalitarianism is typically formulated, it evades the leveling down objection. As standardly formulated, luck egalitarianism specifies that when an inequality is to be rectified, it

Theory and Practice of Equality, Cambridge: Harvard University Press, 2000. Also often cited is G. A. Cohen's "On the Currency of Egalitarian Justice," *Ethics* 99 (1989), 906–44 and Richard Arneson's "Equality and Equal Opportunity for Welfare," *Philosophical Studies* 56 (1989) 77–93. For a comprehensive recent bibliography, see Kasper Lippert-Rasmussen,"Justice and Bad Luck," *The Stanford Encyclopedia of Philosophy* (Summer 2014 Edition), Edward N. Zalta (ed.): http://plato.stanford.edu/archives/sum2014/entries/justice-bad-luck.

[12] Knight (2006: 173). [13] Arneson (2011: 34).

is to be rectified by improving the situation of the worse-off citizen, rather than by worsening the situation of the better off.

The theory has been formulated in many different ways, but these various formulations are variations on a common theme. For justice to obtain, the state must rectify inequalities—except in the case of inequalities for which the worse-off citizen bears the responsibility for being worse off. In such cases, the worse-off citizen can be left where he or she is without any injustice. In virtue of its focus on inequalities for which the worse-off citizen is responsible, the view is sometimes called "responsibility sensitive egalitarianism."

Luck egalitarianism thus seems to combine two attractive ideas. On the one hand, there is an assumption that, as a default position, justice requires an equal distribution of the preferred currency of justice. Taken alone, this might suggest that in order to maintain distributive justice, the state must compensate everyone who falls below the uniform standard. But associated with this is a second leading idea, and this concerns responsibility. If a person falls below the uniform standard simply as a matter of bad luck, then he is due compensation. He bears no responsibility for his poor standing. But if a person "courted inequality" and made a foolish choice that landed him below the uniform standard, then he is responsible for his poor standing. The state is not required to compensate him. He may remain relatively badly off without thereby lowering the level of distributive justice in the community.

Here is an example intended to illustrate the difference between cases in which someone is worse off through some fault of his own and cases in which someone is worse off as a result of bad luck. Suppose Timm and Tomm are identical twins. Suppose they start off with equal $1000 bundles of money, but Timm voluntarily squanders most of his money on tacky knick-knacks that turn out to have no market value. No one forces Timm to waste his money in this way; he is not suffering from any mental disorder. His shopping decisions are voluntary and foolish. Additionally, let us suppose, Timm refuses to work and so has no income and no savings. Tomm, on the other hand, has been far more cautious with his money. He has hidden his original stash under the mattress. He goes to work regularly and uses his salary to pay for daily expenses. At the end of a year, we find that Timm is broke but Tomm has more than a thousand dollars. A straightforward egalitarianism of wealth would say that this inequality constitutes an injustice; steps must be taken to restore the former equality—perhaps the government could impose a tax on Tomm and then redistribute the money to Timm so that they will again have equal amounts of wealth. The demand for compensation in a case such as this will strike many as being unreasonable. Why should the frugal Tomm be required to subsidize the thoughtless shopping decisions of his irresponsible brother? The implausibility of simple egalitarianism is even more apparent if we imagine that after receiving his compensation, Timm immediately goes out and purchases another batch of worthless trinkets, thus again making him worse off than Tomm. Is the government required again to compensate Timm? And how many times must the government step in to compensate Timm for his irresponsible behavior?

A simple form of luck egalitarianism of wealth would say in this case (which we may call "Case 1") that since Timm is worse off entirely as a result of his own foolish spendthrift ways and not just because of bad luck, there is no injustice and there is no need to compensate him.

On the other hand, imagine a different situation (Case 2) involving Timm and Tomm. Suppose again that the twins start off with equal bundles of money, but that Timm is hit by a freak bolt of lightning while walking to his car in the supermarket parking lot. Suppose that there had been no warning. Timm had no reason to anticipate lightning. However, as a result of his injuries, Timm has extra expenses and is unable to go to work. Nothing happens to Tomm. At the end of a year, as in Case 1, Timm is broke but Tomm still has plenty of money.

The imagined form of luck egalitarianism would say that since Timm is worse off in Case 2 entirely as a matter of bad luck, there is an injustice, and there is a need for him to be compensated. It is not at all his fault that he is in a relatively worse condition. The luck egalitarian has the intuition that it is unjust for some people to be worse off through no fault of their own but simply as a result of bad luck, and so it seems to him that it is unjust for Timm to be so much worse off than his brother in this case.[14]

So far I have been imagining a form of luck egalitarianism that incorporates the idea that the currency of justice is wealth. The theory might look like this:

> LE$1: There is perfect political economic distributive justice in a country, S, if and only if every citizen of S has the same amount of wealth as every other citizen of S, except in cases in which some have less than others and their having less is not a matter of bad luck but is their own fault.

Associated with LE$1 would be some principle concerning relative degrees of imperfect distributive justice. Presumably the principle would say that one country, S1, is more just than another country, S2, if and only if the situation

[14] Parfit may have been hinting at this view when he spoke of "the Principle of Equality," which, according to him, "claims that it is bad if, through no fault of theirs, some people are worse off than others" Parfit (1984: 26). As I am understanding it, luck egalitarianism is not a view about what is bad but rather a view about what is unjust.

in S1 more closely approximates the perfect justice described in LE$1. Approximation in this case would be a complex matter somehow involving a couple of factors: the number of individuals who have less wealth as a result of bad luck; the size of the discrepancies between what these individuals actually have and the amount that would come to them if justice were done in their case.

As I pointed out earlier, there are many options concerning the currency of justice. Other forms of luck egalitarianism would differ from LE$1 simply in virtue of making different assumptions about this currency. Some forms of luck egalitarianism would take the currency of justice to be "resources," where this can be understood narrowly to include money and holdings;[15] or it can be understood more broadly to include intangible resources such as valuable family relationships, talents, health, etc. Other forms of luck egalitarianism take welfare or the opportunity to gain welfare to be the item whose distribution matters for justice.[16] For each view about what makes for welfare (for example, happiness, pleasure, desire satisfaction, etc.) we have a different form of luck egalitarianism. And still other forms would focus not on the amount of welfare that each citizen actually has, but on the amount of welfare to which the citizen has access.[17] The variations all follow the structural pattern of LE$1; my critical comments apply equally to all forms; thus I think it is not necessary to burden the patient reader with a review of all these options.[18]

Some luck egalitarians are troubled by cases in which citizens are worse off as a result of bad luck in chancy gambles. In cases of this sort, the worse-off citizen is worse off as a result of bad luck, but he seems responsible for having put himself in a position where his status would likely be adversely affected by bad luck. It is not clear that this sort of misfortune calls for compensation. Consider yet a third case involving Timm and Tomm. Suppose each twin starts out with a bundle of $1000. Suppose each goes to the convenience store and spends all of his money on lottery tickets. Suppose that at the end of the day Timm has lost all his money and is broke, while Tomm comes out even and still has $1000. Though there is an inequality of wealth in this case, and it seems to have come about as a result of

[15] A view along these lines is often said to have its roots in the Rawlsian idea that the currency of justice is "primary social goods." It is also said to be found in Ronald Dworkin's papers "What Is Equality? Part 1" and "What is Equality? Part 2."

[16] For a defense of the idea that welfare should be the currency of justice according to a form of luck egalitarianism, see "Welfare Should Be the Currency of Justice" Arneson (2000: 497–524).

[17] In his "Equality and Equal Opportunity for Welfare," Arneson presents arguments against the resourcist view and the straightforward welfarist view. Instead, he defends the idea that it is the opportunity for welfare that should be equalized. See Arneson (1989: 497–524).

[18] A thorough-going review of the options can be found in Carl Knight's *Luck Egalitarianism: Equality, Responsibility, and Justice*, Edinburgh: Edinburgh University Press, 2009.

Timm's bad luck, the case seems different in an important way from the case in which Timm is hit by a freak bolt of lightning. Many luck egalitarians would want to say, in Case 3 (the lottery case), that Timm bears an important responsibility for his poor financial situation. After all, he chose to risk all of his money on lottery tickets. He knew (or should have known) that there was a good chance that he would lose it all. Many share the intuition that the government has no obligation to compensate worse-off citizens who are worse off (as Timm is) as a result of having lost out on foolish gambles.

In order to deal appropriately with cases like this, some luck egalitarians want to distinguish between "brute bad luck" (as in the case of the lightning bolt) and "option bad luck" (as in the lottery case).[19] They want to formulate the theory in such a way that justice does not require the government to compensate people like Timm in Case 3 for their losses due to option bad luck, but it does require the government to compensate people for their losses due to brute bad luck (like Timm in Case 2). The variant form of luck egalitarianism may be formulated in this way:

> LE$2: There is perfect distributive justice in a country, S, if and only if every citizen of S has the same amount of money as every other citizen of S, except in cases in which some have less than others and their having less is not a matter of brute bad luck but is their own fault or due to option bad luck.

The distinction between brute bad luck (which is compensable) and option bad luck (which is not compensable) is a very tricky business. The rough idea may seem clear enough: in the lottery case, Timm voluntarily chose to put his money at risk. He chose to purchase the lottery tickets, knowing that there was a good chance that he would lose his money. His loss was due to bad luck, but it was his own fault that he took the chance. Justice does not require that he be compensated. But in the lightning case, Timm was just walking back to his car in the parking lot. He was not gambling. His loss was due to brute bad luck. Justice requires compensation in this case.

Or so it may seem at first glance. However, since there is always some slight chance that lightning will strike if you walk across a parking lot, we may say that even in the lightning case, Timm was taking a (very slight) gamble. He was risking his safety on the near certainty that he would not be hit by lightning. In the example, he lost that gamble. This shows that we cannot distinguish between brute bad luck and option bad luck by saying that option bad luck is bad luck that involves taking a risk, while brute bad luck is bad luck that does not involve

[19] See Vallentyne (2002) for references to advocates and near-advocates.

taking any risk.[20] To draw the distinction in this way would put too many cases into the non-compensable option luck category.

In order to have a form of luck egalitarianism that we can profitably discuss, let us make two assumptions. First, let us assume in spite of the difficulties just mentioned, that we understand the intended distinction between brute bad luck and option bad luck well enough. Second, let us assume that in any case in which someone suffers a loss as a result of bad luck, some component of the bad luck is brute bad luck and some component of the bad luck is option bad luck. Obviously, it would be unrealistic to assume that we could in practice actually determine the relative weights of these two components. The idea here is just that some portion of a person's bad luck is compensable and some portion is not. Thus, in the lottery example, we can say that Timm's losses were almost entirely due to option bad luck—he chose to buy the tickets knowing full well that he was running a big risk. On the other hand, in the lightning example, Timm's losses were almost entirely due to brute bad luck—he had no reason to expect that he would be hit by lightning; the chance of being hit was (on the evidence available to him as he headed out toward the parking lot) vanishingly small.

Now we can say that the idea behind a more nuanced form of luck egalitarianism is that when a person is worse off than others, and he is worse off in part because of brute bad luck, then justice requires that he be compensated for the share of his deficit that is due to brute bad luck. But if some component of his deficit is due to his own perhaps foolish decision to take a risk, then that component may be attributed to option bad luck. Justice allows that portion of the deficit to stand. In other words:

> LE$3: There is perfect political economic distributive justice in a country, S, if and only if every citizen of S has the same amount of money as every other citizen of S, except in cases in which some have less than others and the component of the amount by which they have less is not due to brute bad luck but is their own fault or due to option bad luck.

Recall Case 2 in which Timm's deficit arose because of his injuries in the lightning strike. The total deficit (as compared to Tomm) was $1000. We cannot say that the entire loss was due to brute bad luck, since Timm was taking a gamble by choosing to walk across the parking lot. Let us say that 1 percent of the loss was Timm's own fault, due to his taking of a risk. So 1 percent of his loss counts as option bad luck. In this case, LE$3 implies that justice would be done if Timm

[20] For an outstandingly clear and enlightening discussion of the difficulties we confront when trying to distinguish brute bad luck and option bad luck, see Peter Vallentyne (2002: 529–57).

were to receive $990 in compensation. Suppose this happens, and Timm ends up with $10 less than Tomm. Then we can say that the $10 differential does not detract from the justice of the situation, since that component of Timm's deficit was his own fault, and attributable to option bad luck. It reflects the chance he was taking when he risked walking across the parking lot.

In Case 3—the lottery case—Timm's deficit arose because he foolishly squandered his money on lottery tickets. Although his total deficit is still $1000, virtually all of it is his own fault, due to taking a foolish risk. It counts as option bad luck and justice does not require that it be compensated. If we imagine that Timm has some hard-to-control emotional problems that make it difficult for him to resist the temptation to gamble, we may say that to the extent that his losses were due to these problems for which he bears no responsibility, justice requires that he be compensated. In one case, we can imagine, justice might require that Timm receive $100.00 to compensate for his brute bad luck in being afflicted with some emotional problems that make it harder for him to resist gambling. But LE$3 would say, in this case, that if he receives the $100.00, then justice has been done. There is equality of wealth except for the $900.00 deficit that Timm is suffering—but that component is due to Timm's foolish decision to gamble, and that gets categorized as option bad luck.

Here is something I find interesting. There are striking affinities between luck egalitarianism and desertism. One interesting connection emerges if we make a strong assumption about desert. Specifically, we may assume that everyone deserves to have an amount of wealth equal to everyone else's, except for cases in which some have less due to their own voluntary choice. In those cases, the worse-off person deserves to be worse off. It is his own fault. Additionally, we may assume that if a person has a less-than-equal share of wealth, and some component of his deficit is due entirely to bad luck, then he deserves compensation for the component for which he bears no responsibility—the brute luck component. But no one deserves compensation for the part of the deficit for which he is responsible. A desertism of wealth, when combined with these assumptions about what we deserve, would yield results equivalent to those yielded by LE$3. This suggests, but of course does not entail, that defenders of luck egalitarianism might be desertists at heart, but have been moved to defend luck egalitarianism as a result of holding a very narrow and restrictive view about what people deserve.[21]

[21] In fact, at least one defender of luck egalitarianism has drawn attention to the idea that luck egalitarianism is intended to match benefits to desert. In his "Luck Egalitarianism: A Primer," Richard Arneson says: "I have described the luck egalitarian position as though it consisted of some

But there are important differences between LE$3 and the form of desertism that I have been defending in this book. My form of desertism assumes that there are many different *political economic* deserts—roughly deserts such that it is the business of our government to see to it that we receive them. My form of desertism also assumes that there are many different *political economic* desert bases. There are many desert bases such that it is the business of government to see to that they are taken into account when distributing the relevant deserts. Furthermore, my form of desertism assumes that the deserts that matter for justice are deserts that we deserve to get *from our government*. This last difference points up what seems to me to be another problem with luck egalitarianism.

We can easily imagine a case in which someone innocently suffers a deficit, but the deficit arises "privately"—in a way such that it is not the business of government to interfere. With such a case before us, we will see one interesting way in which my theory differs from luck egalitarianism.

Consider yet another case (Case 4) involving Timm and Tomm. Suppose again that Timm and Tomm are identical twins; each has $1000. Although the twins are not aware of him, they have a long-lost rich uncle. When the uncle makes out his will, he flips a coin to decide whether to give $1000 to Timm or to give it to Tomm. The coin comes up heads and the will specifies that Tomm is to receive the whole $1000. Then, when the uncle dies, Tomm is notified of his inheritance. Timm ends up having $1000 less than Tomm. Although the concept of luck is tricky, it would be reasonable to maintain that the deficit in Case 4 is entirely due to brute bad luck. Timm did not even walk across a parking lot. As a result, LE$3 implies that there is an injustice here, and that Timm's deficit is entirely compensable. Not one cent of it is due to his own foolish gambling.

I certainly appreciate the intuition that Timm has suffered an injustice here. It seems unfair that the uncle would choose to give $1000 to Tomm, and nothing to Timm. Given natural and plausible assumptions about the twins, we could conclude that it would have been more fair to give each of them $500. However, it does not seem to me that this is an injustice that calls for governmental intervention. Note that the government did not distribute the inheritance. It was the uncle's money, not the government's. The government's role here is different. It might want to ensure—in the courts if necessary—that all relevant procedures associated with inheritance have been followed. Did the uncle file the will properly? Was he of sound mind when he drew up the will? Did he actually have the money in the first place? Were all appropriate taxes paid in a timely

form of egalitarianism modified by responsiveness to desert. Justice should favor the deserving. This is not how the doctrine is standardly portrayed" Arneson (2011: 142).

manner? If the government stands ready to make sure that there were no irregularities, and the regulations governing inheritances are within the deserved range, then it seems to me that the government has done its job. There is no need for the government to do more. Thus, as I see it, Timm's unfortunate deficit does not adversely affect the level of political economic justice in their country.

My proposed theory of political economic distributive justice has implications in Case 4 that seem to me to be more attractive than those of LE$3. We may agree that Timm deserves $500 in this case, but since he does not deserve it *from the government* or *from the community as a whole* it does not count as a political economic desert. He deserved to get that money from his long-lost rich uncle. I stipulated that Timm did get from the government the procedural safeguards that he deserved to get from the government. So on my theory while there is an injustice, it is not a political economic injustice. It is not a "black mark" against the government. That result seems to me to be correct.

I want next to consider an example that illustrates a different aspect of the problem just discussed. This example bears on a form of luck egalitarianism that takes welfare to be the currency of justice. The theory can be stated in this way:

> LEw: There is perfect political economic distributive justice in a country, S, if and only if every citizen of S has the same level of welfare as every other citizen of S, except in cases in which some have less than others and the component of the amount by which they have less is not due to brute bad luck but is their own fault or due to option bad luck.

For purposes of this discussion, I will assume that a person's welfare is determined by his level of happiness; the happier you are, the higher your welfare. Other views about what makes for welfare have similar implications; nothing turns on my choice of happiness.

Suppose Timm and Tomm are shopping in the supermarket. Timm finds himself in line just ahead of Ginny, a young lady whom he has never previously met. Tomm also finds himself in line just ahead of a young lady he had never previously met, Jenny. Since the lines are moving very slowly, Timm engages in conversation with Ginny and Tomm engages in conversation with Jenny. Suppose each of the brothers falls in love at first sight with the woman he meets in the supermarket. But suppose the similarity ends here. Tomm is lucky in love; Jenny returns his love, they get married, and live happily ever after. On the other hand Timm is unlucky in love. Though he falls in love with Ginny, she does not fall in love with him. After she pays for her groceries she goes on her way, never to meet Timm again. They do not get married. Timm is disappointed about this unfortunate turn of events. Although Timm is sad, his sadness does not rise to the level of clinical depression. In a case such as this it should be clear that Timm's happiness deficit is entirely a matter of brute bad luck. He did not choose to fall in love with Ginny; he did enter into any gambling; it is just his bad luck that things did not work out for him. Similarly for Tomm. He did not choose to fall in love with Jenny; he did not enter into any gambling. It was just his good luck that things did work out well for him.

In this case LEw implies that there is an injustice in Timm and Tomm's country. One citizen is happier than another, and the difference is not at all the fault of the less happy citizen. Surely we cannot blame Timm for falling in love; surely no thoughtful person would say that he is responsible for his own unhappiness. It was just tough luck that he fell in love at first sight with a person who did not love him in return. This explains why, according to LEw, Timm's happiness deficit is compensable. If LEw were true, some agency of the government (perhaps the "Department of Romantic Affairs") would be required to step in and bring Timm's happiness level up to Tomm's. That seems to me to place an absurdly great burden on the government. Surely, if there were an external justice review board, it would not fault the government for failing to do its duty as a matter of justice to ensure that its citizens are all equally happy in their love lives.[22]

As I see it, if Timm and Tomm really are identical twins, and in virtue of being equally nice people are equally deserving of happiness, then it is unfair for Timm to be so much less happy than Tomm. I can imagine a form of desertism that would count this disparity in welfare as unjust. But neither the desert base nor desert bears on political economic distributive justice according to PED. We may assume that Timm and Tomm are indiscernible with respect to political economic desert bases (they are equally vulnerable to attack and natural disaster; they are equally in need of access to roads and bridges; they are equally entitled to tax refunds, etc.). In this case, PED implies that they are equally deserving of political economic deserts, and they deserve to live in a community in which the government ensures that citizens receive these deserts in accord with their

[22] Elizabeth Anderson makes a closely related point in Anderson (1999: 287–337) on p. 305 when, in a passage in which she presents several insightful criticisms of luck egalitarianism, she says: "Even if everyone thought that A was so ugly or socially unappealing that they preferred socially attractive B's personal qualities, it is none of the state's business to attach an official stamp of recognition on such private judgments." Anderson goes on to emphasize the humiliation that would be involved in receiving compensation for such features. Thus, her objection seems to focus at least in part on an aspect of the case that I have not discussed. My point concerns the question whether a state that allowed such differential levels of happiness would thereby deserve to be rated lower on a scale of political economic distributive justice. I claim that it would not. Kok-Chor Tan replied to Anderson in Tan (2008: 665–90). See especially pp. 679–83. The form of luck egalitarianism that Tan defends incorporates a variety of further complexities that make it seem somewhat far removed from familiar forms of the view.

political economic desert bases. In spite of their different levels of happiness, we may assume that they have gotten precisely the political economic deserts that they deserve from their government. In that case, PED implies that while there might be some sort of injustice in this case, it would not be political economic injustice, and that seems right to me.

Before moving on, I would like to discuss an admittedly far-fetched example. I discuss this example in order to bring out a feature of luck egalitarianism that (so far as I know) is not discussed in the critical literature. In my view, this feature deserves attention.

Imagine a country deeply in the grip of some sort of religious fanaticism. Imagine that the government strictly sees to it that no one has access to schools of any sort, and no one gets any sort of health insurance, and no one has access to a banking system or a judicial system. Imagine that the citizens are all mired in ignorance, illness, and poverty. Imagine that the citizens have low welfare and low opportunity for welfare. Suppose the fanatics who run this country are so committed to their religious ideal that they have set things up so that they themselves will also be deprived of all these benefits. And imagine as well that the country is sufficiently well stocked with natural resources so that, with some concerted effort, everyone could be made to be much better off.

The essential feature of my example is that the institutions of this country are set up in such a way that there is complete equality of welfare, resources, opportunity for welfare, and political economic deserts—all of these things are distributed in such a way that everyone gets a supply that is precisely as pathetically small as everyone else's. As a result, there are no inequalities of welfare, resources, opportunity or anything else that might be thought to be the currency of justice.

Now recall what luck egalitarianism says:

> variations in the levels of advantage held by different persons (i.e., inequalities) are permitted by justice if and only if those persons are *responsible* for those (or equivalent) variations.[23]

I take this to suggest that there would be perfect distributive justice in a country if and only if in every case in which someone was worse off than others, he or she would be compensated to an extent equal to the component of his or her deficit due to bad brute luck. The point of my example, as should be obvious, is to raise a question about what happens when all the variations in the levels of advantage have been rectified—when, as a result of this rectification, there are no remaining

[23] Knight (2009: 1).

inequalities due to brute bad luck or anything else. In my example there are no variations in the levels of advantage. Everyone is equally badly off.

My impression is that the luck egalitarian will have to say, in such a case, that the imagined state is enjoying perfect distributive justice even though everyone is mired in unnecessary ignorance, illness, and poverty. The luck egalitarian will have to say this because he or she is, after all, an *egalitarian*. The view seems to focus on what justice requires when there are inequalities; in that case, it may require that some of them be eliminated. But if all of these inequalities have been eliminated, then the view seems to imply that all the demands of justice have been met—we have perfect justice. This seems to me to be very implausible.

My own view has dramatically different implications for this sort of case. As I see it, if everyone is getting less than he or she deserves, then justice requires that everyone get a boost. The fact that everyone is equally shortchanged makes no difference as far as justice is concerned. Since everyone is getting less than he or she deserves, everyone would be justified in complaining about the injustice. The luck egalitarian, on the other hand, seems to be stuck. He uses equality as his benchmark. His theory requires redistributions, compensation, adjustment, only when there is inequality. On my view, on the other hand, redistributions may be required in any case in which some are getting less than they deserve. Such redistributions may be required even if *all* are uniformly getting less than they deserve. Recall the anecdote about Vince Lombardi: "He treated us all the same; like dogs."[24]

5.3 Sufficientism

Frankfurt (1987) formulated his sufficientist doctrine by appeal to the idea of a sufficient amount of *wealth*, and Crisp (2003) formulated another version by appeal to the idea of a sufficient amount of *welfare*. These formulations differ from PED in two ways. First, each of them presupposes a view about the currency of justice that is different from the view built into PED. Second, they advocate a different view about what makes for justice. They say it is a matter of ensuring that everyone has "enough" of the currency of justice.[25] PED says it is a matter of getting political economic deserts received to be in accord with political economic deserts deserved. These extra differences about currency make for

[24] Attributed to Henry Jordan. See the *New York Times* Op-Classic by Jerry Kramer "Winning Wasn't Everything" republished February 5, 2011. Available at: http://www.nytimes.com/ref/opinion/06opclassic.html?_r=0.

[25] For more on how a sufficientist might understand "enough," see Frankfurt (1987: 37–41).

another "apples and oranges" comparison. Suppose we reinterpret sufficientism to be a theory about political economic distributive justice; suppose we assume that it takes the currency of justice to be political economic deserts, just as we do in PED. So understood, the theory implies that if everyone has a sufficient amount of political economic deserts, we have perfect political economic distributive justice.

Now consider this form of sufficientism:

> Sped: There is perfect political economic distributive justice in a society if and only if every member of the society has at least a sufficient amount of political economic deserts.[26]

I introduce Sped here primarily because it will make a more appropriate competitor for PED—these theories agree about the currency of justice. They disagree about how that currency is to be distributed. According to Sped, justice requires that political economic deserts be distributed in such a way that everyone has at least a sufficiently large amount; according to PED, justice requires that these deserts be distributed in such a way that everyone has the deserts that he or she deserves.

Associated with Sped is a doctrine concerning situations in which there is less than perfect distributive justice in a country. The doctrine says that one society is more just than another if the situation in one more closely approximates perfect distributive justice than does the situation in the other. The concept of *approximation* again is left somewhat vague.[27]

[26] Again, I have to apologize about the use of the term "deserts" in the formulation of Sped. I mean to be talking about the political economic benefits, burdens, and neutrals that it falls to a government to distribute to its citizens. Furthermore, in this context we must assume that talk of political economic "deserts" is to be understood as referring to the net amount of such benefits—that is, the amount of such benefits *minus the amount of political economic burdens*.

[27] Reflection on some examples should make it clear that some simple accounts of approximation will not work. We do not want to say that degrees of justice depend upon the absolute number of individuals at or above the threshold; this approach would yield absurd relative evaluations in cases in which we are comparing societies of different sizes. Nor do we want to say that it depends upon the proportion of individuals above the threshold. Suppose exactly half the citizens in Society S1 are above the threshold; suppose exactly half in S2 are above the threshold, but suppose that everyone below the threshold in S1 is *very close* to the threshold, whereas everyone below the threshold in S2 is *very far* below. We want to say that the situation in S1 is more just than the situation in S2, but the proportion above the threshold is the same in the two cases. So approximation must be a more complicated measure involving other matters, such as possibly the distance below the threshold at which some individuals are suffering. I leave it to the sufficientists to work out the details. For an insightful critical survey of some proposed ways of evaluating less than perfectly just distributions, see Casal (2007). See especially pp. 298–9.

Here is something that I find interesting: if you start with a robust form of political economic desertism, but then you say that there is really only one political economic desert base, and that is *having an insufficient amount of political economic deserts*; and if you go on to say that having this desert base makes people who have it deserve a boost in political economic deserts sufficient to get them up to the threshold, then you will have a severely restricted form of desertism. That restricted form of desertism would yield the same judgments about perfect distributive justice as Sped. Thus, someone could take himself to be a sufficientist when in reality he is a desertist who has combined his commitment to desertism with a very narrow view about what we deserve.

Again, it would be presumptuous of me to claim that any actual philosopher came to believe in sufficientism in this way. My claim is merely that sufficientism may be seen as the combination of an abstract form of desertism (which I take to be true) with the view that the only thing we deserve is to have a sufficient amount of political economic deserts (which I take to be false).

Sufficientism seems to me to be open to a variety of serious objections. Some of these concern the theory's implications concerning redistributions involving people who are above the threshold for their society. Imagine a society in which everyone deserves +100 units of political economic deserts. Suppose in addition that +25 units of political economic deserts would be minimally sufficient for each of these citizens. Suppose there are three ethnic groups in the society—the Blues, the Greens, and the Reds. Now imagine that we start with a situation like this:

	Deserve	Receive
Blue	+100	+100
Green	+100	+100
Red	+100	+24

The "Before" Situation

Note that in this case the Reds are slightly below the threshold and the Blues and Greens are equally far above. Suppose the government steps in and redistributes political economic deserts so that we end up with a situation like this:

	Deserve	Receive
Blue	+100	+150
Green	+100	+25
Red	+100	+25

The "After" Situation

In this scenario, we might imagine that the government has taxed the Greens by some large amount so that they lose 75 units of political economic deserts—all units that they deserve to have. The government then turns around and gives 50 of these deserts to the Blues. As a result, the Blues end up having 150 units—much more than the 100 they deserve. With a few remaining units, the government manages to get the Reds up to their level of sufficiency. Note that everyone is above their threshold in the After situation. If Sped were true, this transition would therefore be a move from an unjust state to a perfectly just state. And that seems to me to be a very unpalatable result.

PED has different implications for this case. The Before situation is declared to be less than perfectly distributively just, since the Reds have quite a bit less than they deserve (in fact, 76 units less). But the After situation is declared to be even more unjust, since now the Blues have more than they deserve (also a departure from perfect justice from the perspective of a desertist theory of distributive justice) and now both the Greens and the Reds are getting much less than they deserve. So the implications of my theory are just the reverse of the implications of sufficientism. My theory implies that the transition from Before to After is a move in the wrong direction as far as political economic distributive justice is concerned. I trust that the reader's intuitions will coincide with mine here, and not with those of the imagined sufficientist.

There are other cases that seem to be problematic for sufficientism. Some of these involve citizens who fall below the level of sufficiency. Imagine, to begin with, a society in which everyone has a sufficient amount of political economic deserts. Suppose that no one has any complaints about injustice and the situation seems fair. But then suppose that some citizens decide that they want to join together to form a violent, drug-dealing motorcycle gang. Suppose they do this and for a while make a lot of money and injure a lot of innocent bystanders. At last they are captured by the police, prosecuted for their crimes, found guilty in a duly authorized court of law, and sentenced to suitably long prison terms. They then lose the right to vote, and the right to move around freely, and the right to associate with their former colleagues. As a result of legal expenses and fines, they also lose all of their ill-gotten wealth.

We may assume that the incarceration of the members of the motorcycle gang leads to a situation in which those gang members have fallen below their thresholds for political economic deserts. Whereas political economic deserts were formerly distributed in such a way as to give everyone a sufficiently large net amount, now they are distributed differently. Now some have less than enough. Sped is then forced to say that there is an injustice here. This seems to me to be unwarranted, and I hope the reader will share my intuition. I will not appeal to

PED to support my view here; to do so would be to beg the question against Sped and in favor of PED. So instead of arguing from PED for my view, I will simply say this: it seems to me that if the gang members committed the crimes, and were found guilty in legitimate courts of law, and were given penalties that are fitting in light of their crimes, then they have not suffered any injustice. I think PED has considerable intuitive appeal in this case.[28]

As I see it, Sped focuses exclusively on one factor: whether some members of a community have less than a sufficient amount of the political economic items that governments are called upon to distribute to their citizens. I recognize that in many cases justice does call for an adjustment when someone has less than enough; but it seems obvious that justice sometimes makes demands of other sorts. Sped, because of its exclusive focus on those below the threshold, ignores what happens to those above the threshold. Thus, Sped would have no basis for condemning any redistribution of political economic deserts if that redistribution affected only those who were above the threshold at the outset and remained there afterward. Thus, taxing the moderately rich so as to provide benefits for the super-rich would be declared to have no bearing on justice.[29] On the other hand, Sped's exclusive focus on those under the threshold and its insistence that all such citizens be brought up to the threshold seems to ignore the possibility that some who are below the threshold belong there. In some cases, as I have tried to show, justice does not require us to provide extra benefits to individuals whose below-threshold standing is entirely deserved. In all these cases, PED provides far more intuitive assessments.

5.4 The Difference Principle

In one place in *A Theory of Justice* Rawls states the difference principle in this way:

> The higher expectations of those better situated are just if and only if they work as part of a scheme which improves the expectations of the least advantaged members of society. The intuitive idea is that the social order is not to establish and secure the more attractive prospects of those better off unless doing so is to the advantage of those less fortunate.[30]

[28] Another sort of case makes trouble for sufficientism. These are cases that involve voluntary relinquishment of political economic deserts. This could happen, for example, when a bunch of citizens decide to join a religious order that requires them to swear vows of poverty and silence. Once they join, they have smaller collections of political economic deserts, and yet this sort of transition does not seem to engender any injustice.

[29] Roger Crisp discusses arguments relevantly like this in his (2003: 745–63).

[30] Rawls (1971: 75).

There are many factors that explain why it would be difficult to make a head-to-head comparison of the actual Rawlsian difference principle with my desertist theory of political economic distributive justice. First of all, note that in this formulation, the difference principle does not say anything about the level of justice in a society. It merely states alleged necessary and sufficient conditions for the justice of "the higher expectations of those better situated." Could there be a society in which the expectations of the better situated are just, but the society considered as a whole is unjust?

Second, as here stated, the difference principle is a complex and elusive doctrine. It makes use of the concepts of *expectations*, and *better situations* and *least advantaged* and *prospects*. It assumes that in every society there is some class that is properly identified as the "least advantaged" and some other class that includes the "better situated." How are these classes to be identified? How is "advantage" to be measured? What is the relation between this "advantage" and whatever accounts for the ranking of the "better situated"? Are the "least advantaged" the lowest ten percent on this scale of advantage, or the lowest one percent, or some other group? Is Rawls serious about "expectations" and "prospects"? Does he mean to be referring to a measure of value weighted for likelihood on someone's evidence? And if so, *whose* evidence are we talking about?[31]

A simplified version of the principle would have to clarify and (I would hope) streamline these ideas.

Third, another serious problem in the present context is that the difference principle is embedded in a complex combination of other principles (for example, the liberty principle). The level of justice in a society is presumably determined in some way by the combined operation of this whole set of principles. The difference principle is just part of the story.

In order to have a suitable comparison, I will formulate a theory that departs fairly significantly from what Rawls actually said. Any criticism I then present

[31] I think it is interesting to note, mostly as a historical sidelight, that Rawls seems to have softened his commitment to the difference principle in later writings. Thus, for example, in his "Some Reasons for the Maximin Criterion" (1987) he mentions some practical considerations that might favor the difference principle over Average Utilitarianism. For example, it is easier for ordinary citizens to gather the information they would need in order to figure out what is required by the difference principle; it would be easier for them to understand the idea behind the difference principle; it would be easier for them to stick to their commitment to the difference principle when, later on, they discover its implications for their own welfare. But at the end of the paper, Rawls seems to indicate that he is not fully committed to it: "But I do not wish to overemphasize this criterion: a deeper investigation covering more pair-wise comparisons [with other possible conceptions of justice] may show that some other conception of justice is more reasonable" (145). For further discussion of Rawls's softening with respect to the difference principle, see section 4 of Fried (2014: 430–49).

must be understood to be criticism of the view I state; not the view that Rawls actually stated. I leave it to the interested reader to determine the extent to which these comments apply to the actual Rawlsian view.[32]

I am going to formulate a version of the difference principle that is based on the idea that the currency of justice is political economic deserts. My version of the principle will also assume that within each society there is some set of citizens that is properly characterized as the "worst-off" class. The members of that class are worst off with respect to desirable political economic deserts. So these people will presumably be the poorest and least powerful members of the society.

There is of course a difficulty in determining where to draw the line delimiting the worst-off class. In any modestly large real-life society, the members will be spread out at thousands of different levels of political economic deserts. If we say that the worst-off class contains the lowest ten percent of the population, then the worst-off class will be much larger (and much better off on average) than it would be if we said that the worst-off class contains just the lowest one percent of the population. I will assume that there is a way to draw this line.[33]

As I pointed out, in his statement, Rawls seems to think that the difference principle is intended to assess the justice of "the expectations of the better situated." I will discuss a version of the principle that assesses something different; it will provide necessary and sufficient conditions for there being perfect political economic distributive justice in a society. I do this in part because I want to have a version of the difference principle that is a direct competitor with PED. I also do it in part because I am not sufficiently clear about the item evaluated by the Rawlsian version of the principle.[34]

As I reinterpret it, the difference principle does not straightforwardly evaluate societies for levels of political economic distributive justice. Instead, in the first instance it evaluates *transitions*. It operates in cases in which we have a "before" situation, or "starting point." Suppose we have a society; suppose political economic goods are already distributed among the members, so that there is already a lowest class as determined by the members' modest receipt of political economic goods; suppose there are a couple of different ways in which political

[32] One of Rawls's most extended discussions of the difference principle appears in (1971, ch. 2).

[33] Rawls briefly discusses this problem in section 16 "Relevant Social Positions." He concludes his discussion by acknowledging that it is a problem and making the (optimistic) assumption that people in the original position would find some way to deal with it. In "Luck Egalitarianism: A Primer," Arneson says that Rawls later suggested that the lowest class should be identified as those whose incomes are less than one half of the median (p. 142). See also Van Parijs (2003: 200–40).

[34] The official position, as explained in *A Theory of Justice*, section 15 "Primary Social Goods as the Basis of Expectations," is that the currency of justice is "primary social goods."

economic goods could be redistributed; then we can appeal to the difference principle for a judgment. It will tell us which of the possible redistributions has the greatest level of political economic distributive justice.

This gives us an indirect way of evaluating societies for something like perfect political economic distributive justice. Suppose we have a starting point—a situation in which political economic goods are already distributed to the members of a society. If there is no feasible[35] way to redistribute political economic goods that would improve the condition of the worst-off class in that society, then the "before" distribution is about as just as it can be. In sufficiently serious conditions of scarcity, even the most just available redistribution may fall far short of anything that we would naturally describe as "perfect distributive justice."

The principle can be formulated in this way:

DPped: There is maximal political economic distributive justice in a society if and only if there is no feasible way to redistribute political economic goods that would improve the condition of the members of the worst off class.[36]

Some, including Rawls himself, have suggested that there is an egalitarian element in the Rawlsian theory of justice.[37] That very well may be true. Nevertheless, DPped is clearly not equivalent to the corresponding form of egalitarianism, Eped. Imagine a situation in which there are low paid menial workers, moderately paid middle managers, and very well paid business owners. Suppose there is no feasible redistribution that would enhance the status of the low paid workers. The wealthy business owners are already taxed as much as possible. If taxes are increased, they will have to close their businesses and move away. Similarly, they cannot increase the wages of the low paid workers without pricing their products out of the market. In this case, there might be quite a lot of inequality with respect to political economic deserts; Eped might have to say that

[35] I recognize the need to explain what "feasible" means. This is not the place to try to do it.

[36] The problem concerning the delimiting of the worst-off class should be obvious here. Suppose there is one profoundly badly-off individual in some society. Suppose it would be possible but tremendously expensive to increase his supply of political economic goods. If we suppose that the "worst-off class" is the class consisting of just this one individual, then DPped implies that all efforts must be devoted to improving his situation. On the other hand, we might take the worst-off class to consist of thousands of individuals, most of whom are better off than this unfortunate one. If we understand DPped to be advocating that the average amount of political economic goods enjoyed by these people must be maximally increased, then achieving maximal distributive justice might be far less difficult and expensive. And it might leave the worst-off individual still in a very bad situation.

[37] Rawls discusses the connections between the difference principle and a principle of equality in section 17, "The Tendency to Equality."

there is a very low level of distributive justice. But DPped might declare the situation to be as just as it could possibly be.[38]

Here is something that I find interesting: Suppose you start with a robust form of political economic desertism like PED. Suppose you then modify this by saying that there is really only one political economic desert base, and that is *being in the lowest class with respect to political economic benefits and burdens.* Suppose you also say that having this desert base makes the person who has it deserve to have a boost with respect to political economic benefits and burdens sufficient to improve his allocation of political economic goods as much as is feasible. Then the severely restricted form of desertism would have implications that are interestingly similar to those of DPped.[39]

The difference principle is in one respect quite like sufficientism. Each of these theories, in its own way, seems to imply that the justice of a redistribution of goods depends essentially on its implications for the worse-off members of a society. Sufficientism identifies these people as the ones below the threshold; the difference principle identifies them as the ones in the worst-off class. As a result of this focus on the less well off, these theories seem to be relatively indifferent to the effects of redistributions on those in the upper classes. I tried to highlight this problem for sufficientism earlier in my argument concerning a society with Red, Blue, and Green ethnic groups. A similar problem arises in the case of the difference principle.

Suppose there is a society in which there is an entrepreneurial class, a middle class, and a lower working class. Suppose that those in the entrepreneurial class enjoy very high net levels of political economic goods, those in the middle class enjoy moderate levels of these goods, and those in the lower class are forced to get along with low levels. Imagine furthermore that half of the wealthy members of the upper class are Blue, and half are Green. Using some numbers for illustrative purposes, we might say that the Before situation looks like this:

	Receive
Upper Blue	+100
Upper Green	+100
Middle	+50
Lower	+24

The "Before" Situation

[38] Rawls discusses this point in some detail in section 13 "Democratic Equality." See especially the discussion of the situation in which the difference principle endorses inequalities in wealth between the "entrepreneurial class" and the "unskilled laborers" on p. 78.

[39] I am certainly not suggesting that Rawls was really a desertist with a strange view about what we deserve.

Suppose there are two different ways in which extra taxes could be imposed on the Upper class entrepreneurs. One way would tax all members of that class equally and only moderately. Perhaps there would be a 5 percent surcharge on their savings. Suppose the revenues could be redistributed to the Lower class unskilled laborers, thereby improving their status. In this case the After situation might look like this:

	Receive
Upper Blue	+95
Upper Green	+95
Middle	+50
Lower	+30

The First "After" Situation

Suppose that the second system for extra taxes would put the entire burden on the Upper Blues, while leaving the Upper Greens unaffected. In this case, the After situation might look like this:

	Receive
Upper Blue	+90
Upper Green	+100
Middle	+50
Lower	+30

The Second "After" Situation

Surely the Upper Blues might feel that there is something unfair about the second taxation scheme. After all, they are being required to foot the bill for the improvements to the condition of the lower class, while the Upper Greens are contributing nothing. If the Upper Blues and the Upper Greens had worked just as hard for their wealth, and had treated their employees equally well, and were otherwise alike with respect to all political economic desert bases, I would be inclined to say that the Upper Blues would have a legitimate complaint. But DPped can draw no distinction between the outcomes of the two taxation schemes. Since each scheme enhances the standing of the worst-off class just as much as the other, DPped would have to declare them to be equally just. If there is no other feasible redistribution that would enhance the standing of the workers even more, then DPped would declare not only that these outcomes are equally just, but that each of them is maximally just.

The example has been described incompletely. I have not stipulated much about the desert levels of the members of the various groups. Thus, there is not enough information to determine what PED would say about this case.

However, if we assume that the entrepreneurs are all equally deserving of their upper class status, it would seem to follow that the differential treatment illustrated by the second taxation scheme is less just than the equal treatment illustrated by the first taxation scheme. In such a case, PED would have more plausible implications.

The focus on the status of the members of the worst-off class in DPped in effect says that justice always requires that benefits be given to the worst off—as if all we have to know about some people is that they are in the lowest class with respect to political economic goods. The exclusive focus in effect says that justice always requires that the benefit that goes to the members of the worst-off class is always the same—a maximally feasible increase in political economic benefits. These restrictions seem to me to be far too narrow, leading to another obvious defect in DPped. Surely there are other desert bases; surely we deserve other things; surely there are other facts about a case that can override the desert resulting from membership in the lowest class. Here is a case that illustrates the problem:

Suppose there is a society with shares of political economic goods distributed like this:

	Worst Off	Middle Class	Rich
Status Quo	10	50	60
Pardons	20	45	55
Grants	40	45	50

Now let me tell you more about the situation. The Worst-Off people are all the prisoners in the supermax prisons. They are terrible people who have murdered and stolen and committed arson etc. They are living with small amounts of political economic goods because they are in solitary confinement. The Governor could give them pardons and just let them all go free. This would be good for the convicts, but bad for everyone else. The Governor could go further; he could give them pardons and then give them grants that would enable them to purchase guns and burglary tools and drugs. Since of all feasible distributions, this is the one that maximizes the political economic share of those with the minimum political economic shares, DPped implies that the most just distribution is Grants. That seems like a seriously implausible result.

Rawls (1971) restricted the application of his difference principle to cases involving "strict compliance"—that is, cases in which everyone complies with the laws, so this objection would not be applicable to what he actually said in *A Theory of Justice*. It seems to me that a theory of political economic distributive justice should yield judgments about the level of justice in countries in which there are widespread violations of law. The restriction to the ideal case seems to me to rob the theory of application to any country in the real world.[40]

My desertist theory has more plausible implications for this case. Since the innocent citizens of the society have desert bases stemming from their need for security, they deserve to have the convicts remain in prison. And since the convicts are indeed guilty, and have been found guilty in a duly authorized court of law, they deserve to serve out their sentences.[41] Of course, before we can determine precisely what PED implies for this case, we would have to know quite a bit more. We would have to know about the other political economic deserts of the members of the society. However, if we assume that they are typical law-abiding citizens, the theory implies that there is a high level of political economic distributive justice in Status Quo; a move toward Pardons or Grants would be a move toward a situation in which the level of political economic distributive justice is decreased.

5.5 Extreme Libertarianism

Earlier, in Chapter 1, I sketched a form of libertarianism. I put it this way:

> L': There is perfect distributive justice in a state, S, if and only if every holding owned by a citizen of S is such that either (a) he got it fairly from the state of nature, or (b) he got it in a fair transaction, or (c) he got it as a result of a fair rectification.

It is not clear that it makes any sense to compare L' with PED. The central problem is that these two theories seem to be theories about two different topics. Note that L' purports to give necessary and sufficient conditions for "perfect distributive justice" whereas PED purports to give necessary and sufficient conditions for "perfect political economic distributive justice." It is not clear that the theories can conflict, since they might be theories about different subject matters.

[40] Rawls explained his rationale for focusing on strict compliance on p. 8 of *A Theory of Justice*. He evidently thought that it would make more sense first to describe the ideal state. With that in hand, he hoped that he could later investigate different ways in which nonideal states approximate the ideal. He later discussed this issue at much greater length in section 39. He returned to the problem in later writings, but it is not clear that he ever provided a full account of the operations of the difference principle in conditions of partial compliance.

[41] I am assuming that the judicial system in the imagined country is in the deserved range. This would support the claim that the convicts deserve—as a matter of political economic justice—to stay in prison.

I propose to deal with this problem by constructing a new form of libertarianism. This is intended to have the same subject matter as PED, but to offer a different set of alleged necessary and sufficient conditions for that subject:

LDJ: There is perfect political economic distributive justice in a group, G, if and only if if a person, S, is a member of G, then S owns a holding if and only if either (a) S got it fairly from the state of nature, or (b) S got it in a fair transaction, or (c) S got it as a result of a fair rectification.[42]

Here is something that I find interesting: if you start with a robust form of political economic desertism, but then you say that there is really only one political economic desert base, and that is *having come into the possession of a holding via a fair initial acquisition, or a fair transaction, or a fair rectification*; and you also say that having this desert base makes the person deserving of the right to continue possessing the holding; then the severely restricted form of desertism would be equivalent to LDJ. Again, it would be presumptuous of me to suggest that Nozick or any other libertarian started out as a desertist and then came to believe in libertarianism as a result of thinking that the only thing we deserve is to retain our legitimately acquired holdings.

Some objections to LDJ emerge from its excessively narrow focus on rightful possession of holdings. This theory seems almost to amount to the idea that political economic distributive justice is simply a matter of ensuring that citizens retain ownership of all and only the holdings to which they are entitled—as if all that is required for perfect distributive justice is that everyone have possession of the items to which he or she is entitled. Yet we all think that there is much more to political economic distributive justice than this. Consider all the other deserts and desert bases that play a crucial role in PED but that are ignored on this theory. Although there are many examples that could be discussed here, I will focus on one that seems to me to be especially important.

I have claimed that our political economic deserts and desert bases are all linked in one way or another to the fact that we have community essential needs—in order to flourish as human beings, we need to be embedded in a community that recognizes that individuals need things that they cannot secure on their own, but that may be secured by collective action. Earlier I mentioned such things as security from marauders and natural disasters, provision of infrastructure,

[42] This view is modeled on Nozick (1974, ch. 7). For a nice discussion of Nozick's theory of justice, see Vallentyne (2011). I am not suggesting that Nozick endorsed, or even would endorse, LDJ. I leave it to the interested reader to determine whether the critical remarks that follow bear on what Nozick actually said.

defense of political rights, a system for compensation of losses. I would now like to focus on one of these: special assistance for innocent needy infants.

Earlier I described a case in which an abandoned infant is discovered on the front steps of Town Hall.[43] Imagine that the infant is malnourished and sickly. In addition to the ordinary sorts of nurturance—change of diapers, some baby formula, a warm place to sleep—the infant needs lots of special medical care. Without this help, the infant will suffer and die.

I have stipulated that at the time when she is discovered, the infant has virtually no holdings. Perhaps we can say that she owns the basket in which she is found, and the dirty diaper she is wearing. Other than that, she owns nothing. It would be quite easy to ensure that the infant continues to possess her meager collection of holdings. The authorities could just leave her in her basket until she dies. As a result, it appears to me that LDJ implies that merely leaving the infant to die would not adversely affect the level of political economic distributive justice in the community. If we assume that all other citizens are secure in their holdings, this sort of treatment of abandoned infants would have no effect on the level of distributive justice. If it were a perfectly just state before the death of the infant, it would be a perfectly just state afterward.

PED has dramatically different implications for this case. I have claimed that among our most fundamental desert bases are certain kinds of *community essential need*. These are needs that must be satisfied if we are to flourish as human beings; furthermore, they are needs that we cannot secure on our own—in the normal course of events we would need the assistance of a community in order to get the things that we need in this way. On this basis we deserve such things as *ready access to medical care if we need it*. I also mentioned that we deserve certain sorts of *opportunity*, such as opportunity for education. I claimed that these deserts and desert bases bear on the level of political economic distributive justice in our communities. We deserve to be embedded in a community that somehow ensures that members receive these things. If members fail to receive these deserts when they deserve them, then the community has failed. The level of political economic distributive justice has gone down.

The implications for the case of the abandoned infant should be clear: PED implies that it is the business of the government to ensure that the infant receives the medical care and nurturance she needs in order to flourish. If there is a government agency such as Child Protective Services, then presumably the responsibility would fall to it. If the government determines that there is a suitable church group or non-governmental agency that is taking care of the

[43] Near the end of section 5.1.

infant, then the government has fulfilled its responsibility. It has seen to it that the infant will receive the benefits that she deserves. But if no one takes on the job of nurturing the infant, and if the government merely stands aside and allows the infant to suffer and die, then this will be a serious black mark against that government according to PED. It will have allowed a member to go without some goods that she deserved to receive.

I think the implications of PED for this case and others like it are far more attractive than the implications of a view such as LDJ.

6

The Priority View

6.1 A Puzzle about Prioritarianism

Ever since the publication of Parfit's 1991 Lindley Lectures, critics and commentators have assumed that prioritarianism is intended to be a theory of distributive justice. Thus, for example, in his article on "Justice and Distribution" in the *Routledge Companion to Ethics* Matthew Clayton first mentions Rawls, Nozick, and some egalitarians; then he cites the Parfit article and says:

> This conception of justice [viz., prioritarianism] directs our concern to those who are less advantaged, not because they are worse off than others but simply because of their low absolute level of advantage. Public policy should be directed to the satisfaction of the needs of less advantaged individuals, on this view, and sometimes even when we can benefit them less than we can someone who is better off.[1]

In his *Stanford Encyclopedia of Philosophy* article on "Justice and Bad Luck" Kasper Lippert-Rasmussen starts out by listing some of the main theories of distributive justice. Among these he includes egalitarianism, sufficientism, the difference principle, and:

> Prioritarianism, given which we should maximize the sum of welfare that is weighted to ensure that benefits at lower levels of welfare have more weight than those at higher levels.[2]

Many others do the same thing—they list prioritarianism as a theory of justice.[3] Accordingly, the expected procedure for me here would involve first providing a

[1] Clayton (2010: 700–1).

[2] Kasper Lippert-Rasmussen, "Justice and Bad Luck," *The Stanford Encyclopedia of Philosophy* (Summer 2014 Edition), Edward N. Zalta (ed.): http://plato.stanford.edu/archives/sum2014/entries/justice-bad-luck.

[3] In Crisp (2003: 745–63) Roger Crisp begins by saying that in recent years there has been discussion of the idea that considerations of equality should give way to considerations of priority in "the best account of distribution or distributive justice." The remark strongly suggests that Crisp also understands prioritarianism to be a theory about distributive justice.

clear statement of the theory and then going on to compare the implications of prioritarianism with the implications of desertism.

The remarks quoted above are suggestive, but the actual content of prioritarianism is open to a variety of interpretations. I will first introduce an interpretation that is sometimes seen in the literature, though it seems to me that this is not a fair interpretation of Parfit's idea. Furthermore, it seems to me that when interpreted in this way, prioritarianism is seriously implausible. Then I will turn to a second interpretation that might be closer to what Parfit actually had in mind. I will try to show why, if interpreted in this somewhat more plausible way, prioritarianism is not a theory of justice at all.

6.2 An Interpretation of the Priority View

Near the beginning of "Equality or Priority?" Parfit says that he is engaged in a project concerning "the ethics of distribution."[4] When (later in the paper) he states the central thesis of what he there calls "the priority view," he puts it this way: "utility has diminishing marginal moral importance."[5] This statement of the central thesis of prioritarianism seems to make use of two evaluative concepts. The first of these is just the concept of *utility* itself, or welfare. We can assume that every person to be considered here is at some level of welfare; he or she is enjoying some amount of utility. For present purposes it will not be necessary to settle on any particular theory of welfare, so long as absolute levels of welfare can be plotted on a number line, with higher numbers representing higher levels of welfare. I do not assume that there is either a highest or a lowest possible level of welfare—though in this chapter I will focus on examples involving (I will suppose) typical levels of positive welfare between zero and 100.

The second evaluative idea is the idea of *moral importance*. The concept of moral importance is going to play a central role in the prioritarian theory of justice. A simple view would say that the moral importance of being at a welfare level of +10 is just +10 units. But this is precisely the point that the prioritarian wants to reject. Prioritarians want it to turn out that marginal units of welfare enjoyed by people at higher levels of welfare have smaller "moral importance." This may not be an entirely transparent notion. One way to understand it involves dividing a person's welfare at a time into "increments." We can then assign full moral importance to increments of that welfare that are at the lowest level, and lower moral importance to the increments of utility that are at higher levels. A sketch of one possible way to work this out may make the idea clearer.

[4] Parfit (1991: 82). [5] Parfit (1991: 105).

Suppose a person, P1, is at welfare level +50. We may imagine that P1 is receiving five bundles, or "increments" of welfare, each with an absolute value of +10. A utilitarian would want to say that each of these increments has a moral importance of +10 units, but the prioritarian wants to say that the first increment has full moral importance, whereas the second increment has slightly less moral importance; and the third increment has even less moral importance; and so on up the line until we reach the final +10 unit increment which has, in this example, the smallest degree of moral importance of the five we imagine P1 to be enjoying. In this way, welfare is seen as having diminishing marginal moral importance.

But this is all very programmatic. Any specific form of prioritarianism would make use of some systematic way of assigning degrees of moral importance to all these different increments of welfare. One way to do this would involve a "weighting function."[6] The weighting function assigns weighting factors that decrease as we reach higher levels of welfare.

Let us assume a simple model in which the welfare levels to be compared are always between 0 (a very low welfare level) and +100 (the highest welfare level achieved in the normal course of events). Obviously, this model is unrealistic, since there is no reason to suppose that there is an upper or lower limit to levels of welfare. Furthermore, this model does not contain information about negative welfare levels. But for present purposes the simpler model may be sufficient.

We can assume that the weighting factors are all numbers between zero and 1. At the lower end of the welfare spectrum the moral importance of each 10-unit increment of welfare is determined by multiplying its absolute value by a relatively large weighting factor, something approaching 1. But at the high end of the welfare spectrum the moral importance of a 10-unit increment of welfare is determined by multiplying its absolute value by a small weighting factor, something approaching zero. As we consider increments of welfare at higher and higher levels, weighting factors steadily decrease and eventually approach zero. Since the moral importance of an increment of welfare is the product of the weighting factor and the absolute value of the increment, this ensures that a given increment of welfare has diminishing moral importance depending upon where it fits in the spectrum of increments enjoyed by the recipient. So we need some

[6] I got the idea of using weighting factors from Crisp, who used them in a very similar way in Crisp (2003: 745–63). I should note that Crisp employed a somewhat more complicated incremental system for assigning adjusted values to benefits. For details, see his discussion on p. 753. Nothing I say in this chapter turns essentially on my choice of the simpler procedure.

weighting factors. Here is a chart that shows a possible set of weighting factors[7] for some welfare levels:

Welfare	Weighting factor
0	1
10	0.9
20	0.8
30	0.7
40	0.6
50	0.5
60	0.4
70	0.3
80	0.2
90	0.1
100	approaching 0

The prioritarian idea, then, is that we should not focus on the absolute amount of welfare that a person is enjoying. Instead, we should focus on the weighted values that we get when we split up his welfare into 10-unit increments, and then multiply the absolute value of each increment of welfare by the weighting factor determined by its place in the recipient's total collection of increments. The sum of these weighted values is the "morally more important" value that will figure prominently in the theory.[8]

This naturally leads to a systematic way to assign levels of moral importance to a collection of welfare levels being enjoyed by the members of a group: for each member of the group, determine the moral importance of his or her welfare level; the moral importance of the collection of welfare levels is the sum of these.[9] Here is a simple example to illustrate how this works:

Suppose a society has four members, P1–P4. Suppose their welfare levels are as shown in this chart:

[7] I have stated a few conditions that must be satisfied by a collection of proposed weighting factors. I think that there are in fact indefinitely many collections that satisfy the conditions I have stated. As a result, it turns out that there are indefinitely many forms of prioritarianism that differ from each other in the way that weights are assigned to welfare levels. I am inclined to think that my comments in this chapter are equally applicable to all these different versions of the theory.

[8] It is possible that Lippert-Rasmussen had this idea in mind when he said, in a passage quoted above, that prioritarianism involves the idea of "the sum of welfare that is weighted to ensure that benefits at lower levels of welfare have more weight than those at higher levels."

[9] Crisp initially states a form of prioritarianism that makes use of this idea of summing adjusted values. Later, he considers a different version that introduces a discount rate for larger groups of recipients.

P1: 20
P2: 30
P3: 40
P4: 50

To find the morally important value of the welfare for each member, we divide the member's welfare into 10-unit increments and multiply the absolute value of each increment by the appropriate weighting factor. So, for example, just focusing on P4, we find these more important values:

Increment	Absolute Value	Weighting factor	Morally Impt. Value
1	10	1	10
2	10	0.9	9
3	10	0.8	8
4	10	0.7	7
5	10	0.6	6
Total Morally Important Value for P4: 40			

So, while P4 is enjoying 50 units of welfare, the theory is going to focus on +40, which is declared to be the morally more important value. This value is intended to capture the intuition that increments of welfare enjoyed at higher levels have smaller amounts of the morally important sort of value. It is as if we give P4 10 points for his first increment, 9 points for his second increment, 8 for his third, 7 for his fourth, and 6 for his fifth. This yields a total of 40 points for the whole collection.

To find the morally important value of the whole collection of welfare levels, we just do the same for each other member of the society and then sum the results. What we find in the example postulated above is that the morally important values of the welfare receipts of the other members are as follows:

P1: 19 (1 x 10) plus (0.9 x 10)
P2: 27 (1 x 10) plus (0.9 x 10) plus (0.8 x 10)
P3: 34 (1 x 10) plus (0.9 x 10) plus (0.8 x 10) plus (0.7 x 10)
P4: 40 (1 x 10) plus (0.9 x 10) plus (0.8 x 10) plus (0.7 x 10) plus (0.6 x 10)

As a result, the total morally important value for the society as a whole is 40 + 34 + 27 + 19 or 120.

On one interpretation, the claim is that the procedure outlined here gives us the prioritarian way of determining the level of distributive justice in a society. So, on this view, one society is more distributively just than another if and only if the total morally important value for the first society is greater than that for the second; and a given society has increased its level of distributive justice through time if and only if it has managed to increase the total amount of morally important value.

If so, the prioritarian principle would be:

> PR1: The level of distributive justice in a society, S1, at a time, t, is proportional to the total amount of morally important value enjoyed by the citizens of S1 at t.

PR1 is intended to have implications such as these: the level of distributive justice in a society, S1, at t is greater than the level of distributive justice in another society, S2, at the same time, t, if and only if the total amount of morally important value of S1 at t is greater than the total amount of morally important value of S2 at t; the level of distributive justice in S1 at t is greater than the level of distributive justice in S1 at a different time, t', if and only if the total amount of morally important value of S1 at t is greater than the total amount of morally important value of S1 at t'.

Principle PR1 gives us a way to make such comparisons of justice levels for one society at different times. It will also enable us to compare the relative degrees of justice that a society would enjoy under different assumptions about policy implementation. We merely need to calculate, for the society, the total amount of morally important value that its members would enjoy if the first policy were implemented, and then compare this value to the amount of the same sort of value that the members would enjoy if the other policy were implemented.[10] Thus PR1 may seem to be the prioritarian theory of distributive justice that has been widely discussed. However, there are problems.

As I see it, a desideratum of a theory of justice is that it should enable us to say what would make for perfect distributive justice in a society. Yet if there is no upper limit to the amount of welfare that a person can enjoy, PR1 implies that there is no upper limit to the amount of justice that a society can enjoy. Of course, as we reach higher and higher levels of welfare, the morally important value of each increment of that welfare decreases. As a result, we have something like diminishing marginal justice approaching but never reaching some limit. No society is perfectly just, but it may seem that it is possible for some to get close.

Another desideratum of a theory of justice is that it should enable us to compare the levels of justice in societies of different sizes. Thus, for example, we might want to appeal to a theory of justice to enable us to compare the current level of distributive justice in a somewhat more socialist democracy such as Sweden

[10] I write here as if it would be a straightforward practical matter simply to list the welfare levels for all the citizens in some country. Of course, that is preposterous. No one has the detailed empirical or evaluative information that would be needed to determine those values. Perhaps it would have been better for me to have said that *if we had relevant information about welfare levels and weighting factors* the calculation of justice levels would be a straightforward matter of simple arithmetic.

(population 9.5 million) with the current level of distributive justice in a somewhat more capitalist country such as the United States of America (population 320 million). Egalitarianism, sufficientism, desertism, and other familiar theories of justice seem to be able to provide such comparisons. Principle PR1, on the other hand, seems to be incapable of yielding useful comparisons in such cases.

A simplified example may help to highlight the problem. Suppose there are two societies, S1 and S2. Suppose welfare is distributed according to exactly the same pattern in the two countries, but suppose in addition that the population of S2 is exactly ten times the size of the population of S1. For every person at welfare level n in S1, there are ten people at n in S2. It follows from this that the total amount of welfare being enjoyed in S2 is ten times the total amount of welfare in S1.[11] It also follows that the total amount of the morally important value being enjoyed in S2 is ten times the total amount of morally important value being enjoyed in S1. PR1 then implies that the level of distributive justice in S2 is ten times the level of distributive justice in S1. That seems wrong to me; it seems to confuse a measure of total welfare with a measure of justice. Size clearly matters when we are trying to assess total amounts of welfare; size seems to me not to matter when we are trying to assess levels of justice.

PR1 has other implausible implications. Given that the population of the United States is so much greater than the population of Sweden, it could turn out that even though a very large percentage of Americans would have reasonable complaints on grounds of injustice about the way in which welfare levels are distributed in their country, still, because there are so many Americans and so many of them have positive welfare levels, the total amount of the morally important value in their country could be a huge number. At the same time, even if no one in Sweden has any reason to complain about injustice in the way welfare levels are distributed in their country, the total amount of the morally important value in Sweden could be much smaller since there are not very many people in Sweden. A straightforward comparison of morally important values such as is proposed by PR1 would yield the implausible result that the level of distributive justice is higher in the United States than it is in Sweden, entirely because there are so many more people in the United States.[12]

A closely related point is analogous to a point that Parfit made in another context concerning the repugnant conclusion.[13] Imagine a society—call it “A”—

[11] Assuming that everyone is at a positive level of welfare.

[12] Comparing average levels of morally important value will not work either. The problems with this idea are discussed a few paragraphs later.

[13] *Reasons and Persons*, chapters 17, 18 and 19.

of ten million people; imagine that each of them has a high welfare level; let the weighting factors be assigned so that the amount of morally important value for each citizen of A is somewhat smaller than the absolute amount of welfare each enjoys. Find the sum of the amounts of morally important value. That gives you the total amount of morally important value for A. Now it should be fairly obvious that there could be a society—call it "Z"—containing billions of people, each of whom is at a much lower welfare level. Assume that these people are barely scraping along. In each case, the amount of morally important value to be ascribed to each citizen will be a very small number (but close to the recipient's absolute welfare). If there are enough people in this huge low-welfare society, the total amount of morally important value that they are enjoying will be greater than the total amount of morally important value enjoyed by the citizens in the smaller world where everyone has much higher welfare.

I can readily grant that there is a way of thinking of utility according to which there is more utility going around in Z. But I have a hard time seeing any reason to say that the situation in Z is more just than the situation in A. Yet this is an implication of PR1.[14]

These examples show that on the proposed interpretation the prioritarian idea does not readily apply to cases involving comparisons of justice levels in countries of different sizes. The same problem would arise if we were to apply a PR1-like theory to a case in which the population of one society is larger at one time than it was at an earlier time. Even if everyone at the earlier time were at the same positive welfare level as everyone at the later time, the principle would imply that the level of justice has increased through time merely because the population has grown. That seems odd to me. It would seem even more odd in a case in which the earlier population was relevantly like the population of the A society in the earlier example, and the population at the later time was relevantly like the population of the Z society. I cannot see any reason to say that the move from A to Z in a case such as this would mark an increase in the level of justice in the society.

Perhaps it would make more sense to try to develop this as a theory of justice restricted to cases involving countries with populations of the same size. We can say:

[14] In Brown (2007: 325–61) Campbell Brown presents an argument designed to show that a form of prioritarianism that he formulates generates a version of the repugnant conclusion. His argument concerns cases involving only negative welfare values; he dubs the undesirable result "The Nauseating Conclusion" (340). Theron Pummer distinguishes among a couple of different ways in which forms of prioritarianism yield conclusions relevantly like the repugnant conclusion. See his currently unpublished "The Priority Monster" available at https://sites.google.com/site/tgpummer.

PR2: If there are two societies, S1 and S2, and the populations of S1 and S2 are equal at some time, t, then the level of distributive justice in S1 at t is greater than the level of distributive justice in S2 at the same time, t, if and only if the total amount of morally important value in S1 at t is greater than the total amount of morally important value in S2 at t.

PR2 has no implications concerning the relative degrees of distributive justice in societies of different sizes, nor would an obvious extension to PR2 have implications concerning the relative degrees of justice in a single society at two different times if the size of the population at the later time were different from the size of the population at the earlier time. So PR2 or its natural extension cannot tell us whether the level of justice in Sweden is greater than or less than the level of justice in the United States; it cannot tell us whether the level of justice in the United States now is greater than the level of justice in the United States a century ago; it cannot tell us whether a proposed policy change in a certain country would yield an outcome that would be more just than a different proposed policy change if the populations in the two imagined outcomes would be different.

But there are some cases to which PR2 applies. These are cases involving comparisons between arrays of welfare levels in same-sized groups.

It seems to me that PR2 yields some unwelcome results even in this narrowed range of cases. To make things simpler, imagine a little country with only four citizens. Suppose that as things now stand, some are slightly better off than others. But under a proposed new policy, the better-off citizens would be even more better off, and the worse-off citizens would be even more worse off. This would seem to violate the prioritarian idea of giving priority to the worse off. But if the numbers are chosen appropriately, PR2 will imply that it is more just to institute the new policy. Here is a chart to simplify consideration of the case. First consider the status quo:

Citizen	Welfare level	Morally important value
P1	60	45
P2	60	45
P3	50	40
P4	50	40

Status Quo in Society S1

The total amount of morally important value currently being enjoyed by citizens of S1 is +170. (Their total *absolute* welfare is much greater, but—using the chart "Welfare/Weighting factors" in section 6.2 above—we are weighting this value in order to give priority to increments of welfare at lower levels.) Now compare the status quo in S1 to what would happen if the new policy were implemented:

Citizen	Welfare level	Morally important value
P1	90	54[15]
P2	90	54
P3	40	34
P4	40	34

Society S1 with New Policy in Place

The total amount of morally important value that would be enjoyed in this case would be +176 and thus *greater than* the total amount of morally important value being enjoyed in the society under the status quo. The implication of principle PR2 would then be that the level of justice in S1 would *increase* if the new policy were implemented. That seems precisely the sort of result that defenders of prioritarianism want to avoid. They claim that justice requires that priority be given to the worse off; but principle P2 implies, in this example, and with the present system of weighting factors, that justice requires that the better off be made significantly more better off, and the worse off be made even more worse off. Surely, that is not a result to be welcomed by the prioritarian.

It may be interesting to note, in this example, that the average level of morally important value is greater (44 vs. 42.5) under the new policy than it is under the status quo. This shows that it would not help to revise PR2 by making it rank distributions by appeal to the average level of morally important value. Reflection should reveal that the move to average levels of morally important value would only serve to blur the factor that prioritarians presumably want to emphasize—the alleged importance of giving benefits to the worse off rather than to the better off.

6.3 A Different Approach to Prioritarianism

I suspect that no defender of prioritarianism would have any interest in defending a principle like PR1 or PR2. Those are simply non-starters. I think it is also important to recognize that in virtually all of his discussions of prioritarianism, Parfit seemed not to be thinking of a theory that would evaluate standing, or static arrays of welfare in the way that these principles do. Rather, he seemed to be

[15] I get the value of 54 by adding together 10 (for the first +10 increment where the weighting factor is 1) and then 9, 8, 7, 6, 5, 4, 3, and 2 for the remaining increments in order. The final increment in this case has a dramatically decreased morally important value of only 2 points. This is intended to illustrate the idea that welfare has diminishing marginal morally important value.

thinking of a theory that would evaluate *new benefits or burdens* that would be going to people already at welfare baselines. That may be why he so often gave the prioritarian motto in this form: "Benefiting people matters more the worse off these people are."[16] Sometimes he referred to these benefits as *increases or decreases* of welfare. I am inclined to think that his theory was intended to evaluate these new benefits or burdens, not the standing arrays of baseline welfare levels.

Let us attempt to formulate a theory of justice that is more closely connected to the things Parfit actually said. The theory will not evaluate societies for levels of justice. Rather, it will evaluate *new distributions* of welfare to people who are already assumed to be at baseline welfare levels. Roughly, the theory is intended to respect the idea that one possible new distribution is more just than another if and only if it gives greater priority to the recipients who are starting off at lower baseline welfare levels. It respects this idea by saying that the morally important value of a new bit of distributed welfare is not its absolute value, but is its priority adjusted value. Thus we adjust only the values of the added benefits or burdens, rather than the values of pre-existing standing baselines. In the present context, this is how we understand a slightly revised version of Parfit's motto: "benefiting people is *more just* the worse off these people are."

Understood in this way, the theory makes use of three evaluative concepts. The first of these, as before, is suggested by Parfit's mention of recipients who are *worse off*. Evidently, he is assuming that potential recipients have some level of "worse-offness" at the outset. We can put this by saying that people start off at what we may call "baseline welfare levels." I will assume that a person's baseline welfare level (perhaps like his net worth) remains relatively steady through time unless something happens to perturb it (perhaps like a receipt or an expenditure). As before, it will not be essential to choose among theories about what makes for welfare. We just need to agree that there are baseline welfare levels, and that these baseline levels are subject to interpersonal comparison on a suitable number line. I understand Parfit's talk of "worse-off" recipients simply to mean recipients who are at lower baseline levels of welfare.[17]

On the proposed interpretation, the prioritarian thesis also involves a second evaluative concept; this is the idea of *benefits* that will be going to some potential recipients. We can assume that these benefits are temporary increases in levels of welfare. Thus, if a person receives a benefit, his welfare will increase from his

[16] As he did, for example, when he stated the priority view in Parfit (1991: 101).

[17] I suspect that Parfit would not be keen on the idea that everyone's welfare level can be represented by a number; I suspect that he would insist that welfare levels should be more like ranges, or vaguely defined areas.

baseline to some higher level for a while and then, unless some other benefit or burden intervenes, it will revert to the baseline. The absolute magnitude of the benefit will just be the difference between his pre-benefit level and his welfare level while receiving the benefit. If as a general rule you are at welfare level 100, and you get a benefit that puts you at welfare level 110 for a short time, then the benefit you have received has an absolute magnitude of +10.

The third evaluative idea is the idea of *mattering more* or *moral importance.* The prioritarian, under this new interpretation, wants to say that a benefit of a given absolute size is morally more important or matters more if it goes to someone whose baseline is lower. So the same +10 unit benefit would have greater moral importance if it were to go to someone whose baseline is low, but it would have smaller moral importance if it were to go to someone whose baseline is high. In order to state a version of this view clearly, we can again make use of a list of weighting factors that will enable us to calculate the moral importance of benefits going to people at different baseline welfare levels. The weighting factors will decrease as the baseline welfare levels increase.

Here is a chart that shows a possible set of weighting factors for some welfare baselines:

Welfare baseline level	Weighting factor
0	1
10	0.9
20	0.8
30	0.7
40	0.6
50	0.5
60	0.4
70	0.3
80	0.2
90	0.1
100	approaching 0

The prioritarian idea, on this second interpretation, is that we should not focus on the absolute values of the benefits that recipients are to receive. Nor should we divide the recipient's standing welfare into incremental bundles and weight the bundles for morally important value. Instead, we should focus on the numbers that we get when we multiply the absolute values of the new benefits by the weighting factors determined by the recipient's baseline welfare level. To avoid confusion with the idea that I discussed in section 6.2, I will use the term "priority adjusted value" to refer to this "more important" value—the product of the absolute value of the new benefit, multiplied by the weighting factor associated with the recipient's baseline welfare level. The aim is to make it come out that a benefit of a fixed size will have a greater priority adjusted value if it goes to a recipient who is worse off. Thus, for example, suppose we have an opportunity to give out a benefit with an absolute value of +10. Suppose it can go either to a recipient with baseline of 20 or to a recipient with a baseline of 80. If it goes to the former, not very well-off recipient, the priority adjusted value of the benefit is +10 x 0.8, or +8. If it goes to the latter, considerably better-off recipient, the priority adjusted value of the benefit is +10 x 0.2, or +2.

This naturally leads to a systematic way to assign a priority adjusted value to a collection of benefits that would go to the members of a group: for each member of the group, determine the priority adjusted value of the benefit that would go to him or her; the priority adjusted value of the collection of benefits is the sum of these priority adjusted values.[18] Here is a simple example to illustrate how this works:

Suppose we have a small group consisting of four individuals, P1–P4. Suppose P1 and P2 are at baseline welfare level +10, whereas P3 and P4 are at baseline welfare level +20. Suppose we have the opportunity to distribute one benefit with an absolute value of +10 points. We can give this benefit to any member of the group, but it cannot be divided. First consider what would happen if we were to give the benefit to P1:

Person	Base welfare level	Abs. benefit	Adjusted value of benefit
P1	10	+10	+9
P2	10	0	0
P3	20	0	0
P4	20	0	0

The priority adjusted value of the benefit to P1 is +9 because P1's baseline welfare level was 10, and the weighting chart says that the absolute value of a benefit going to a person with baseline 10 should be multiplied by the weighting factor of 0.9 to find the priority adjusted value.

And now what would happen if we were to give it to P3:

Person	Base welfare level	Abs. Benefit	Adjusted Value of benefit
P1	10	0	0
P2	10	0	0
P3	20	+10	+8
P4	20	0	0

[18] Crisp (2003) initially states a form of prioritarianism that makes use of this idea of summing adjusted values. Later, he considers a different version that introduces a discount rate for larger groups of recipients.

A benefit with a value of +10 has an adjusted value of +9 if it goes to a person whose baseline is 10; but the same benefit has the slightly smaller adjusted value of +8 if it goes to a person whose baseline is 20. A benefit of a given size has greater adjusted value if it goes to a person with a lower baseline welfare level. This is an illustration of my interpretation of Parfit's idea that benefits "matter more if they go to people who are worse off."

If we focus on the sum of the priority adjusted values of the benefits, we see that we manage to distribute more priority adjusted value if we give the +10 pt. benefit to one of the worse off recipients. This can be extended to a wide variety of cases. One striking example involves a case in which recipients start with unequal welfare baselines and we can give out some benefits that will either yield welfare equality or will lead to even greater welfare inequality. Imagine that we have the opportunity to distribute two +10 pt. benefits. We have several options. Two options are as follows:

Person	Base welfare level	Abs. benefit	Adjusted value of benefit
P1	10	0	0
P2	10	0	0
P3	20	+10	+8
P4	20	+10	+8

Distribution A

In Distribution A, the benefits go to the better-off recipients. There was already an inequality in welfare at the outset; we make the inequality even more extreme by giving the benefits to P3 and P4. We can compare A to B:

Person	Base welfare level	Abs. benefit	Adjusted value of benefit
P1	10	+10	+9
P2	10	+10	+9
P3	20	0	0
P4	20	0	0

Distribution B

If we choose Distribution B, we give the benefits to the worse off people (P1 and P2), thereby eliminating the inequality, at least for the period of time during which P1 and P2 go on enjoying the benefits. In that case, the sum of the priority adjusted values of those benefits is +18 pts. If we choose Distribution A, we give the benefits to the two better-off people (P3 and P4). In that case, the sum of the priority adjusted values of the benefits is only +16 pts. An egalitarian might say that what makes Distribution B better than Distribution A is that B is a move toward equality, whereas A is a move away from equality. The prioritarian has a different explanation. As he sees it, B is better than A because the sum of the priority adjusted values is greater in B than it is in A.

Here is a simple way to express this thought:

> PR3: If there is a group of people who are already at some baseline welfare levels, and there are some possible ways, D1 and D2, of distributing welfare increases and decreases to these people, then distribution D1 is more distributively just than distribution D2 if and only if the priority adjusted value of D1 is greater than the priority adjusted value of D2.

It is important to see that PR3 is not just a variant of PR1 or PR2. Those theories purport to assess the level of distributive justice in standing situations in societies. They allow us to compare the level of justice in one society to the level of justice in another. They are silent on questions about the justice or otherwise of new distributions. But PR3 purports to assess only these new distributions. It is silent on questions concerning the relative degrees of distributive justice in standing arrays of welfare. Thus, it has nothing to say about whether the current situation in Sweden is more just than the current situation in the United States. Nor does it have anything to say about such simpler matters as whether a situation in which people are at standing welfare levels of 50, 50, 50, 50 is more or less just than a situation in which people are at standing welfare levels of 60, 60, 40, and 40.

In cases in which people remain fixed at some level of welfare, PR3 is inapplicable. It does not evaluate arrays of standing welfare. Rather, it evaluates new collections of benefits going to people already at welfare baselines.

But PR3 has yet more limitations. It does not evaluate new distributions if these go to different groups, or even to a single group at different times. It cannot tell us whether the level of justice of a certain distribution in Sweden is greater than or less than the level of justice in a distribution in the United States; it cannot tell us whether the level of justice of a distribution in the United States now is greater than the level of justice in some distribution in the United States a century ago; it cannot tell us whether a proposed distribution to a certain group would be more just than a proposed distribution to a different group. But, if there are several different ways of distributing benefits and burdens to the members of a group at a time, PR3 will have implications concerning which of these is the more just.

However, PR3 yields some surprising results even in this very narrow range of cases. Imagine a little country with only four citizens. Suppose two of these citizens are at a relatively high welfare baseline of 70 and two are at a relatively low welfare baseline of only 30. Suppose we have the opportunity to distribute some welfare benefits to these people. Here is a chart showing the first possible distribution:

Citizen	Baseline	Weighting factor	Size of benefit	Adjusted value
P1	30	0.7	10	+7
P2	30	0.7	10	+7
P3	70	0.3	0	0
P4	70	0.3	0	0

Distribution C

In Distribution C the two benefits go to the two worse-off citizens, P1 and P2. The total priority adjusted value of Distribution C is +14. But suppose the second possible distribution would give larger benefits to the better off:

Citizen	Baseline	Weighting factor	Size of benefit	Adjusted value
P1	30	0.7	0	0
P2	30	0.7	0	0
P3	70	0.3	50	+15
P4	70	0.3	50	+15

Distribution D

The total priority adjusted value of Distribution D is +30. PR3 implies that Distribution D is considerably more just than Distribution C. But this seems contrary to the fundamental prioritarian intent. Distribution D gives significant benefits to the better off and nothing to the worse off, whereas Distribution C gives (admittedly modest) benefits to the worse off and nothing to the better off. I cannot imagine why (in the absence of further unexpected information) anyone—especially a prioritarian—would want to say that Distribution D is *more just*.[19] I am happy to acknowledge that there are ways of thinking of utility according to which Distribution D has higher *utility*. After all, 100 units of welfare have been distributed in the second distribution rather than merely 20 as in the first distribution. But to focus on this in the present context seems to me to confuse questions of total utility with questions of justice.[20,21]

[19] Crisp's *pain relief/chocolates* argument on p. 754 of Crisp (2003) seems to turn on relevantly similar considerations, though his example involves further complexities—in his example there are many more people at the higher baseline.

[20] The example also shows that it would be pointless to revise PR4 so that it focuses on *average amounts of adjusted welfare* in the distribution. Since the population is fixed at 4, the average amount of adjusted welfare in the second distribution is much greater than the average amount in the first (7.5 vs. 3.5).

[21] In a passage that I quoted at the beginning of this chapter, Matthew Clayton mentions that prioritarianism sometimes favors giving a smaller benefit to a worse-off citizen, rather than a larger

It is possible to avoid this difficulty if we restrict the prioritarian idea to an even narrower range of cases. These would be cases involving only one country, with a fixed population starting out from a single fixed set of baselines, and furthermore cases in which we have some options for distributing some benefits *with a fixed total absolute value*. That is, no option would allow us to distribute benefits with a greater total absolute value than any other option. We can then compare different possible distributions of this fixed collection of benefits that might start from this baseline. We can say that one way of distributing *that collection of benefits and burdens, from that baseline, in that country* is more just than another way of distributing *that same collection of benefits and burdens, from that same baseline, in that same country* if and only if the former distribution has greater total priority adjusted value than the latter. In other words, we can try:

PR4: If there is a group of people who are already at some baseline welfare levels, and there are some possible ways, D1 and D2, of distributing a collection of welfare increases and decreases with fixed total absolute value to these people, then distribution D1 is more distributively just than distribution D2 if and only if the total priority adjusted value of D1 is greater than the total adjusted value of D2.

The principle would then yield judgments of the relative degrees of distributive justice in an even more limited class of distributions. These would be cases in which we start with a baseline distribution in a certain group of people and then have our choice of different ways of distributing a package of welfare benefits and burdens with a fixed total absolute value to the people involved. It would yield conclusions about the relative amounts of distributive justice in these distributions.

If understood in this way, PR4 is of limited application, since it does not enable us to make any assessments of the level of justice in a society at a time. If all the citizens are at some specified baselines, and they are getting no new benefits or burdens, PR4 has nothing to say about the level of justice in that society. Associated with this is the fact that PR4 has nothing to say about intersocietal comparisons. It is silent on questions such as the question whether there is greater justice in Sweden or in the United States. Furthermore, the theory does not permit us to compare the level of justice in a single country at a given time to the level of justice in that same country (even assuming that the population

benefit to a better-off citizen. PR3 has that feature. But it also has this feature: if the benefit to the better-off citizen is sufficiently great, it declares it to be more just to give that larger benefit to the better-off citizen rather than to give the smaller benefit to the worse off citizen.

remains fixed) at another time. That is because the citizens may have different baselines at different times. Thus, if we want to know whether the situation in the United States has improved from the perspective of justice in the years since Jim Crow laws were eliminated, PR4 will be of no help. Furthermore (contrary to what Clayton says about prioritarianism in the passage quoted at the outset), this theory would have no relevance to cases in which we have options involving different-sized collections of benefits and burdens. Thus it could not imply in such a case that it would be more just to give smaller benefits to worse-off people than larger benefits to better-off people. It applies only in cases in which the total amounts of benefits being distributed are equal in the compared cases. Additionally, it should be noted that PR4 says nothing about *perfect* distributive justice. In light of this limited application, I would be inclined to say that PR4 is really not a theory of distributive justice at all—though it might be considered a component of such a theory.[22]

Nevertheless, it is still possible to compare the implications of this form of prioritarianism with the implications of other theories of distributive justice in the limited class of cases I have identified. For egalitarianism and sufficientism and desertism and other similar theories of distributive justice also have implications concerning cases in which we start with a collection of people at some baseline welfare levels and have some options for distribution of a package of benefits and burdens with fixed total value. Those theories also yield results concerning the relative degrees of distributive justice in the various available distributions in this limited type of case.

6.4 Desertism and Prioritarianism Compared

In my view, PR4 generates implausible results even in the narrow range of cases to which it applies. This is a result of PR4's failure to take account of differential amounts of desert in that narrow range of cases. As I see it, the theory generates counterintuitive results in cases where the worse-off people actually deserve to be worse off. In any such case, my form of desertism generates more attractive results.

Imagine a little society containing, in addition to a large number of regular people, two lazy bums and two hard-working, generous people who devote a lot

[22] In Chapter 1 I quoted a remark from Richard Arneson (2007: 262) in which he seemed to place comparable restrictions on a form of egalitarianism. In my view, in light of its limited application, that form of egalitarianism would also be a mere shred, or fragment, of a theory of distributive justice.

of time to their work as volunteers in a hospital. Suppose that as a result of their unproductive ways, the bums have a relatively low baseline welfare level. They just manage to survive on the modest welfare benefits that they receive from the government. Suppose the energetic volunteers are at a slightly higher baseline welfare level. They could make much more money if they were to work full time at their day jobs, but they prefer to devote themselves more energetically to their unpaid but valuable work at the hospital. Suppose now that it is possible to distribute some fixed total amount of benefits to members of this society. One option, D1, would involve giving some modest benefits to the two bums. The other option, D2, would involve giving similar benefits to the two volunteers.

PR4 focuses exclusively on the baseline welfare levels of the potential recipients. Since the bums are at lower baselines, PR4 implies that it would be more distributively just to give them the benefits. Desertism has no such implication. The bums have been lazy and unproductive; they have done nothing for their fellow citizens. Some would say they already have higher welfare than they deserve. Since the volunteers have done so much good for their fellow citizens and have received no compensation for their efforts, it may seem that they deserve some sort of reward or benefit. They deserve to be at a higher welfare level. Given natural assumptions about desert, a suitable form of desertism implies that it would be more distributively just to give the benefits to the volunteers.[23]

Prioritarianism in all the forms considered here can be viewed as being based on the assumption that there is really only one thing that makes it more just to give some benefit to a certain person rather than to another person—and that is that the first person's baseline welfare level is lower than the second person's. The lower the baseline, the more distributively just it would be to give him the benefit. But that seems to give far too much importance to just one factor that might influence the justice of a distribution. Surely there are other factors that might help to make it more just to give a certain benefit to a certain person. In my example, the bums have been lazy and unproductive; they have accepted welfare assistance from the state while giving nothing in return; as a result, they deserve to be at their low level of welfare. The volunteers have engaged in generous, helpful, thoughtful behavior; as a result, they deserve to receive some sort of prize or award that would place them at a higher level of welfare. As it evaluates the situation to determine to whom new benefits are to be given, prioritarianism ignores all of this potentially relevant information, focusing only on baseline

[23] I leave it to the interested reader to fill in the numerical details of the case in such a way as to generate the conclusions I have specified. I have tried it; it is a bit tedious but it can be done.

welfare levels. So I think that in this case—and in others that illustrate the same point—desertism yields more attractive results than prioritarianism.

The reader may be surprised to discover that this example and my remarks about desert have no relevance to the theory that Parfit actually presented. That is because Parfit said:[24]

> These objections we can set aside. We can assume that, in the cases we are considering, no one deserves to be better off than anyone else; nor does anyone have special claims to whatever we are distributing. Since there are *some* cases of this kind, we have a subject. If we can reach conclusions, we can then consider how widely these apply. Like Rawls and others, I believe that, at the fundamental level, most cases are of this kind.[25]

This means (as I understand it) that the theory Parfit had in mind is intended to apply to a distribution of benefits and burdens to a group only if all members of that group are equally deserving. In my example involving the bums and volunteers, the potential recipients are not equally deserving. I described the case in such a way as to make it plausible that the volunteers are more deserving than the bums. So Parfit could say that my example is not relevant to his theory. If we take the Parfittian comment seriously, and we want to take account of it in our formulation of prioritarianism as part of a theory of distributive justice, we need to revise our statement of the view. We need to say something more like this:

PR4': If there is a group of people who are already at some baseline welfare levels, *and all of these people are equally deserving of an increase in welfare* and there are some possible ways, D1 and D2, of distributing a collection of welfare increases and decreases with fixed total absolute value to these people, then distribution D1 is more distributively just than distribution D2 if and only if the total priority adjusted value of D1 is greater than the total priority adjusted value of D2.

If the prioritarian view is really PR4' instead of PR4, then there is a straightforward reply to my objection: the reply is that the theory is not intended to have any application to cases such as the one described. The case I described is one in which the potential recipients are not all equally deserving.

But then there is an even more troubling question about PR4' Suppose the theory applies only in cases in which all potential recipients are equally deserving of some new benefits; and suppose the theory says that in such cases it is more

[24] Parfit (1991: 82).

[25] It is interesting to note that at the beginning of Crisp (2003), when presenting his first introductory example of a pair of distributions for comparison, Roger Crisp similarly stipulates that considerations of desert will not be relevant to his discussion. More exactly, he says "there are no questions of desert at issue" (Crisp 2003: 746). My comments on Parfit's view will therefore apply also to Crisp's.

distributively just to give benefits to the worse off. The troubling question then is this: if all recipients are equally deserving of these benefits, why would it be more just for the worse off to get priority? Clearly if they are equally deserving of these benefits, the better off deserve these benefits just as much as the worse off. And in that case the notion that it would be more just to give those benefits to the worse off seems inexplicable.

Maybe Parfit was thinking that his view would apply to cases in which all potential recipients are equally deserving *except for the desert that arises from having a low baseline welfare level.* Maybe he was thinking that in this severely restricted sort of case, *having a low baseline* would be the sole remaining basis for saying that worse-off people deserve more. The view then would look like this:

> PR4'': If there is a group of people who are already at some baseline welfare levels, *and all of these people are equally deserving of an increase in welfare except for the desert that arises from having a low baseline welfare level* and there are some possible ways, D1 and D2, of distributing a collection of welfare increases and decreases with fixed total absolute value to these people, then distribution D1 is more distributively just than distribution D2 if and only if the total priority adjusted value of D1 is greater than the total priority adjusted value of D2.

PR4'' has very limited application. It has no implications for the justice or otherwise of distributions of benefits to people who have unequal deserts for reasons other than those arising from their baselines; it has no implications for cases involving comparisons of distributions of benefits that do not have equal fixed total value; it has no implications concerning the relative levels of justice in societies of different sizes, or in a given society at different times; it has no implications concerning perfect distributive justice. It is therefore at best a mere shred of a theory of distributive justice.[26]

Here is something I find interesting: If we make one assumption about desert, we can construct a variant form of desertism whose implications about the justice of distributions mirror those of PR4'. To arrive at this variant, assume that facts about a person's baseline welfare level are the only desert bases—none of the factors that I described in Chapter 4 are allowed. More specifically, assume that the lower a person's baseline welfare level, the greater his or her desert of a benefit. The worse off you are, the more you deserve a benefit. Vulnerability to

[26] I am inclined to think that it would be more reasonable to reconstrue PR4' as a theory about right action. So interpreted, it would say that if you face a situation in which you have a fixed package of benefits to distribute to some people, you ought to distribute those benefits in such a way as to maximize priority adjusted value. I discuss this form of prioritarianism in Appendix B, "Two Helpings of Desert."

attack, need for opportunity, entitlement, etc. are all now irrelevant. Given this assumption, desertism implies that it would be more just in cases in which we have to give out a fixed package of benefits to give greater priority to people with lower baseline welfare levels (because in every case such people would have greater desert). And in that case, the implications of the variant of my form of desertism would be the same as the implications of PR4"[27]

How could someone come to believe in PR4"? Someone might start by thinking that justice is a matter of receipt in accord with desert; he might furthermore think that the only reason why one person deserves more than another is that the one person has a lower baseline welfare level than the other. He might assume that nothing else could make anyone deserve more or less than anyone else. And he might then conclude that an adequate theory of distributive justice would be one that simply said that justice requires that when distributing benefits, it is always more important to give priority to people with lower baselines.

As I see it, that line of reasoning would involve a serious and implausible restriction on the desert bases that bear on distributive justice. Surely there are many other desert bases that also must be taken into account. And so I would say that if a philosopher arrived at PR4' via the reasoning described, he had settled via a bad argument on a form of desertism that has very limited application.[28]

6.5 Is Prioritarianism Intended to be a Theory of Justice?

It may be interesting in this context to recall some things that Parfit says about prioritarianism. At the beginning of "Equality or Priority?" Parfit says that he is engaged in a project concerning "the ethics of distribution."[29] When (later in the paper) he states the central thesis of what he there calls "the priority view," he puts it this way: "Benefiting people matters more the worse off these people are."[30] In the same context he comments:

[27] It would be interesting to compare the reasoning of this paragraph with the reasoning presented by Matthew Rendall in Rendall (2013: 939–51). I have in mind such remarks as these: "Distributive justice depends on the extent to which competing claims are satisfied—the extent to which people receive their just deserts. Claims modify the moral value of welfare. People don't deserve to be worse-off through no fault of their own, and if we have a benefit to distribute, those who are worse-off have, *ceteris paribus*, stronger claims. This makes it better to give them benefits of a given size" Rendall (2013: 950).

[28] I hope it is clear that I am not suggesting that Parfit arrived at PR4" or any other form of prioritarianism via a line of reasoning like the one suggested here. So far as I know, Parfit never arrived at PR4" at all.

[29] Parfit (1991: 82). [30] Parfit (1991: 101).

Like the belief in equality, the Priority View can take either Telic or Deontic forms. It can be a view about which outcomes would be better, or a view that is only about what we ought to do. But, for most of my discussion, this difference does not matter.

So Parfit suggests two main forms of prioritarianism. In its "Telic form" the idea seems to entail this: If some extra benefit can be distributed to some possible recipients, and one way of distributing it would involve giving it to the worse-off recipients, whereas another way of distributing it would involve giving it to the better-off recipients, then the first distribution is *better*. That seems to be a thesis in axiology, or the theory of value.

In the Deontic form, the thesis concerns what we ought to do. Presumably, the idea here seems to entail something like this: If you have the opportunity to distribute some benefit to some possible recipients, and one way of distributing it would involve giving it to the worse-off recipients, whereas another way of distributing it would involve giving it to the better-off recipients, *you ought to distribute it in the first way*. This seems to be a thesis in the normative ethics of behavior.

The surprising fact about these two options is that neither of them explicitly says anything about justice.

It should be clear that Telic Prioritarianism is not a theory about distributive justice. It is a theory in axiology. It gives a systematic account of the value (the relevant sort of value is here identified as "priority adjusted value") of a distribution of benefits and burdens to the members of some group. It says that the intrinsic value of a distribution of benefits is equal to this value. The direct competitors to Telic Prioritarianism would be such things as "absolute value totalism" (which says that the value of such a distribution is just the sum of the absolute values of the benefits and burdens distributed) and "absolute value averagism" (which just divides the total absolute value by the number of people in the group). Another view (which I find interesting) would say that the value of such a distribution is found by adjusting the value of each benefit or burden by a number that represents the extent to which the recipient deserves to get that benefit or burden. These are all theories about the intrinsic value of a distribution of benefits and burdens to the members of a group. None of them explicitly says anything about justice.

It should also be clear that Deontic Prioritarianism is not a theory about distributive justice either. Rather, it is a theory in the normative ethics of behavior. Its direct competitors would be such things as a form of consequentialism that says that you ought behave in such a way as to maximize total absolute value; another competitor would be a form of consequentialism that says that you ought to maximize average absolute value; and yet another competitor would be Desert Adjusted Consequentialism, which says that you ought to choose an alternative that maximizes the sum of desert adjusted values in all affected.[31] None of these is a theory of justice. Each is a theory in the normative ethics of behavior.

So it appears that Parfit has given us hints of two forms of prioritarianism. The Telic form is not a theory of distributive justice; it is a theory in axiology. The Deontic form is not a theory of distributive justice; it is a theory in the normative ethics of behavior. Each is interesting, but neither is the theory of distributive justice that we might have expected to find here. Neither of them yields conclusions about what makes for perfect justice in a group, and neither of them has immediate implications for the comparative levels of distributive justice in a given society at different times or in different societies. In these respects, Parfit's prioritarianism in either of the two forms he specifies is different from all the various forms of egalitarianism, sufficientism, and libertarianism that I discussed in earlier chapters. It is also different in this way from my desertist theory of distributive justice.[32]

As I understand it, a theory of distributive justice is intended to give an account of the conditions under which the distribution of the currency of justice in a society is perfectly just; such a theory is also intended to give an account of the conditions that would make such a distribution in one society more just than the distribution in some other society. In itself, such a theory would not have direct implications about what we morally ought to do, or about the levels of intrinsic value in various arrangements. I think that if we take a theory of justice to have the aims I have specified, then it remains possible that prioritarianism was never intended to be a theory of justice in the first place. Perhaps, when Parfit said that he was engaged in a project concerning "the ethics of distribution," he had something different in mind.[33]

[31] This is the view that I defended in "Adjusting Utility for Justice." See Appendix B "Two Helpings of Desert" for further discussion.

[32] The comparison to the difference principle is far more complicated. If we take the difference principle as a stand-alone principle of distributive justice, it will confront difficulties comparable to the ones I describe for the prioritarian principle. It is doubtful that Rawls intended for his principle to be understood in this way.

[33] Earlier I quoted a remark from the Preface to the first edition of Moore's *Principia Ethica*. Moore emphasized the importance of being clear on the question you mean to answer before setting out to answer it. I think the present case might be an example of the sort of thing Moore was warning against.

7

Rawls Against Desertism

7.1 Some Rawlsian Remarks about Desertism

In earlier chapters, I presented my desertist theory of political economic distributive justice and tried to show that it generates more attractive results than competing theories of justice. According to my theory, there is perfect political economic distributive justice in a country if and only if the citizens of that country receive their political economic deserts from their government (or suitable agencies overseen by the government), and they receive these political economic deserts on the basis of their possession of appropriate political economic desert bases. So far as I know, precisely this form of desertism has not previously been discussed in the literature. Thus, so far as I know, no one has attempted to refute it.

However, Rawls discusses desertism about distributive justice in a couple of places in *A Theory of Justice*.[1] He presents an array of objections. It is not clear that Rawls would have used these arguments against my form of desertism if he had been aware of it. Nevertheless, in virtue of the remarkable impact that Rawls's discussion has had, and in virtue of the fact that some of these arguments have not been widely discussed in the critical literature, it may be a good idea to review them. One aim here is to determine whether these Rawlsian arguments constitute sound objections to desertism in general; another aim is to determine whether they refute the form of desertism that Rawls explicitly attacks. But my main aim is to determine whether anything in any of these Rawlsian arguments presents a serious objection to the form of desertism that I mean to defend.

There are two main passages in *A Theory of Justice* in which Rawls presents his objections to desertism. The earlier passage is in section 17. According to some commentators, Rawls claims in this passage that desertism fails because it

[1] He returns to this topic in corresponding passages in *Justice as Fairness* and *Political Liberalism*.

conflicts with the "deserve to deserve" principle.[2] In a widely quoted remark, Rawls says "It seems to be one of the fixed points of our considered judgments that no one deserves his place in the distribution of native endowments, any more than one deserves one's initial starting place in society."[3] Our moral virtues "flow" at least in part from these native endowments. Since we did not deserve to have these native endowments in the first place, we cannot deserve any benefits as a result of having the moral virtues that flow from those endowments. And thus desertism—which as Rawls sees it is committed to this claim—must be wrong.

Because it makes essential use of the principle that if you deserve something in virtue of having some property, P, then you must have deserved to have P in the first place, I will refer to this as the "Deserve to Deserve Argument."

In section 48—"Legitimate Expectations and Moral Desert"—Rawls presents several further objections to desertism. Although others might organize this material differently, I think I see three main lines of argument in this passage. I also see hints of two other minor or subsidiary arguments. I will discuss what I take to be the main arguments.

As the title of the section suggests, Rawls distinguishes between "legitimate expectations" and "moral desert." One of his arguments turns on this distinction. Suppose you live in a well-ordered society where the institutional framework is just. Suppose that according to the applicable institutional rules, you are entitled to some benefit such as a refund on your income tax, or a discount on your tuition bill at the state university. Then you have a legitimate expectation.

In one thread of this argument, Rawls seems to be thinking that desertism implies that if a society were well-ordered, then the institutional rules would be set up in such a way as to ensure that citizens receive benefits and burdens proportional to their moral desert. But Rawls claims that in fact the distributive rules of a well-ordered society would not be set up in this way. He acknowledges that if the rules are set up in such a way as to allocate certain benefits to certain citizens, then those citizens are legitimately entitled to the things in question, "but what they are entitled to is not proportional to nor dependent upon their [moral] worth."[4] Rawls goes on to imagine an example to illustrate this. Suppose there is a just state in which "everyone is of equal moral worth." Still, contrary to what desertism implies, the citizens might receive unequal shares of social benefits and burdens. This inequality would not necessarily indicate any injustice. This is one version of "The Equal Worth/Unequal Shares Argument."

Apparently in an attempt to bolster the Equal Worth/Unequal Shares Argument, Rawls makes some claims about the "common sense precepts of justice."

[2] I allude here to Zaitchik. [3] Rawls (1971: 104). [4] Rawls (1971: 311).

One of these is the precept of contribution: other things being equal, justice requires that a person who makes a bigger contribution gets a larger reward. But Rawls points out that (for example) as a singer's ability to sing deteriorates and is less in demand, justice permits him to start receiving a smaller reward for his performances. This could happen even if the singer maintained a constant level of moral worth. Hence the familiar common sense precept justifies distributions that are not based on moral worth. Rawls generalizes, saying that "none of the precepts of justice aims at rewarding virtue." I view this "Precepts of Justice Argument" as subsidiary to the Equal Worth/Unequal Shares Argument. I will not have much to say about it.

Another line of argument emerges in section 48. Rawls seems to think that desertism involves a sort of conceptual circularity. On the one hand, as he sees it, desertists want to define justice by appeal to the concept of moral worth. Yet on the other hand, the concept of moral worth is defined by appeal to the concept of justice. Rawls sometimes expresses this argument by appeal to some claims about conceptual priority. Desertists want to say that the concept of moral worth is prior to the concept of justice; and yet they also have to acknowledge that the concept of justice is prior to the concept of moral worth. I call this "The Circularity Argument."[5]

And finally there is a line of argument that is mentioned only briefly in *A Theory of Justice*, but that becomes more prominent in later writings. This is an argument based on the idea that desertism would be "impracticable."

Let us first look more closely at the passages in which Rawls presents the Equal Worth/Unequal Shares Argument.

7.2 The Equal Worth/Unequal Shares Argument

Rawls suggests that it is easy to see that desertism is false. He says:

> We have only to consider a well-ordered society, that is, a society in which institutions are just and this fact is publicly recognized. Its members also have a strong sense of justice, an effective desire to comply with the existing rules and to give one another that to which they are entitled. In this case we may assume that everyone is of equal moral worth. We have now defined this notion in terms of the sense of justice, the desire to act in

[5] Rawls makes some brief remarks that suggest some further arguments. One of these turns on the claim that desertism would not be chosen by the participants in the original position (310). It is not clear to me that Rawls intended this to be an independent argument against desertism. In any case, I will not discuss the argument beyond saying that it seems to presuppose that whether a theory of justice is true depends upon whether it would be chosen in the original position. That seems to me to be a dubious presupposition.

accordance with the principles that would be chosen in the original position (§72). But it is evident that understood in this way, the equal worth of persons does not entail that distributive shares are equal. Each is to receive what the principles of justice say he is entitled to, and these do not require equality.[6]

Rawls makes a variety of claims in this passage; some of them are not directly relevant to what I take to be the central argument. I will highlight the core of the argument by appeal to an example. Let us stipulate that S is a "well-ordered" society. When Rawls describes the society as "well-ordered," he means to indicate that it is a just society. Since it would be question-begging to appeal to any particular theory of justice to support this, let us assume that no one has any complaints from the perspective of justice with the institutions in S. Presumably we are to imagine that the people in S go about their business in conformity with the rules of S, and nobody is angry or dismayed; nobody feels that he is being treated unfairly by the system. Each person is content with the way the shares are being distributed, feeling that this is distributively just. We can characterize this aspect of the situation in S by saying that it is "intuitively just."

Furthermore, the citizens of S are of "equal moral worth." Rawls expands on this by saying three things about them: (a) each has a strong sense of justice; (b) each wants to abide by the rules; (c) each wants to give others that to which they are entitled by the just institutional rules that are in place in S. This suggests that Rawls identifies being of moral worth with accepting and being motivated to act upon a certain set of institutional rules concerning distribution. However, this characterization of moral worth seems too narrow. The concept of moral worth must extend beyond this. Surely it includes the possession of compassion, generosity, loyalty, benevolence, courage, and other such moral virtues. Perhaps it would be sufficient for present purposes for us simply to agree in the abstract that the citizens of S are equally and very highly morally worthy. We can understand moral worthiness in whatever way we preanalytically like.

In some passages Rawls points out that it is consistent with these assumptions that the citizens of S could end up with different sized shares of the social good. In other passages he makes what seems to be essentially the same point by saying that the citizens of S could end up with different amounts of happiness. Maybe he was thinking that a person's level of happiness is determined by his or her share of the social good. I will develop the argument in the "happiness" form, though most of what I say here would carry over directly to the "shares of social good" form.

Rawls gives an example involving what he takes to be one of the "precepts of justice." Suppose that one of the precepts of justice is the Precept of Contribution:

[6] Rawls (1971: 312).

Other things being equal, as the value of a person's contribution to society decreases, so should the wage he or she receives. Now imagine a singer who lives in this intuitively just society; imagine that as he gets older, his voice deteriorates and his performances yield less value to the society.[7] According to the Precept of Contribution, he is no longer entitled to the large wage that he could command in his prime. There is no injustice here, even though the singer may have maintained a perfectly uniform level of moral worthiness throughout his career. This illustrates one way in which the standard (and presumably acceptable) precepts of justice function; clearly, they are not intended to reward moral virtue. The singer may no longer enjoy his former high level of happiness as his voice deteriorates and his wages go down, but he has no basis for saying that he has been treated unjustly.

We have imagined that our intuitively just society is composed of people in one way like this singer: they are all of outstanding and equal moral worth. It is consistent with this that they are not equally happy. Some, like the singer, are no longer making as much money as they formerly made, and are less happy. Perhaps others founded successful companies, or came up with useful inventions. They are now making more money and enjoying greater happiness. Others may have squandered their funds on ill-conceived ventures. So different members enjoy different levels of happiness. But no citizen of this society has any basis for claiming that the system is unjust. This shows that a just distribution is not necessarily one that matches levels of happiness to levels of virtue.[8]

This thought experiment is intended to show that desertism as Rawls conceives it is false. The point is that if desertism were true, and there were perfect distributive justice in S, then the equally morally worthy people in S would have to be equally happy. And in the Rawlsian example, though justice reigns, the equally worthy citizens are not equally happy. So desertism must be false. We can formulate the argument as follows:

Equal Worth/Unequal Shares Argument

1. It is possible for there to be a country in which (a) there is a very high level of intuitive justice, (b) the citizens are all equally morally worthy, and (c) the citizens enjoy unequal levels of happiness.

[7] Rawls (1971: 311).

[8] It is interesting to note that the overall structure of this argument is similar to the structure of Nozick's Wilt Chamberlain argument (Nozick 1974: 161–4). That is, we start by stipulating that some society is perfectly just, then we allow various innocent things to happen, and then we see that the society is still perfectly just *even though it no longer satisfies the conditions required by the theory we are interested in refuting.*

2. If it is possible for there to be a country in which (a) there is a very high level of intuitive justice, (b) the citizens are all equally morally worthy, and (c) the citizens enjoy unequal levels of happiness, then desertism is false.
3. Therefore, desertism is false.

I think that while the argument might refute some forms of desertism, it does not refute the form of desertism that I mean to defend in this book. In order to explain this point, it may be helpful to highlight the distinction between two importantly different forms of desertism. Each of these theories maintains that justice obtains when people get what they deserve in virtue of their possession of the appropriate desert bases. The theories differ on the nature of the things deserved and the desert bases.

In an important footnote (fn. 38, p. 310) Rawls quotes a passage from Leibniz's "On the Ultimate Origin of Things." In that passage, Leibniz states a form of desertism. Leibniz mentions "the law of justice" which, according to him:

> Declares that each one participate in the perfection of the universe and in a happiness of his own in proportion to his own virtue and to the good will he entertains toward the common good.

The Rawlsian argument may be seen as an attack on something like this Leibnizian view. As I mentioned in Chapter 3, following Leibniz, Rawls seems to be thinking of a form of desertism whose motto is "justice is happiness according to virtue."[9] The view differs from the Leibnizian version in two important ways: first, the happiness in question is to be enjoyed here on earth during the recipient's life, rather than in an afterlife in heaven; and second, the distributor of this happiness is the government of the recipient's country rather than God. Earlier I formulated the absolute version of this view in this way:

MDa: There is perfect moral distributive justice in a society if and only if in every case in which a citizen of that society deserves a level of happiness or unhappiness in virtue of having a moral desert base, he or she receives that level of happiness from his or her country.

As before, I assume that associated with this principle about absolute justice there is a principle concerning relative degrees of imperfect justice. One society enjoys a greater level of moral distributive justice than another if the distribution of happiness in accord with virtue in the one more closely approximates the perfect fit as described by MDa than does the other.

[9] Rawls (1971: 310).

On this view, there is only one desert base—moral virtue. And there is one main desert—an appropriate level of happiness. I refer to this theory as "earthly moral desertism."

Perhaps the argument points up a difficulty in earthly moral desertism. For it does seem that it is possible for there to be an intuitively just country in which happiness is not distributed in proportion to moral virtue.[10] Maybe some good people do not get all their deserved happiness. Maybe they made some unfortunate investments; maybe they were unlucky in love. Maybe some bad people are happier than they deserve to be. Maybe they made better investments; maybe their love lives were more rewarding. Surely it is still possible that the government was doing its work in a completely just way.

However, the form of desertism that interests me differs from this moral desertist form in two important ways. First, it differs with respect to the relevant desert bases. On my theory, a person's level of moral virtue or vice does not count as a desert base. Instead, the theory identifies a class of political economic desert bases. These include such things as the need for security, the need for economic, educational, and healthcare opportunity, the fact of having been unfairly harmed, being disabled, etc. I have informally characterized these desert bases by saying that they are the features such that it is the business of a community to take note of them when distributing the socially distributable benefits and burdens at its disposal. More generally: these are the features such that everyone deserves to live in a country where the government makes its distributional choices in such a way as to requite them. As I claimed earlier in Chapter 4, I think every one of these desert bases can be explained ultimately by appeal to the notion of community essential needs.

The second main difference between my form of desertism and moral desertism concerns the deserved things. According to moral desertism there is only one deserved thing and that is an appropriate level of happiness. But on my theory we focus instead on what I have called "political economic deserts." These include such things as the right to vote; the right to be protected by a police force or a military; the opportunity to have access to roads, schools, hospitals, and other items of community infrastructure. More generally, I have characterized these as the items such that it is the business of a community to see to it that citizens

[10] Although of course a diehard Leibnizian might say that if the distributive rules of some country make it possible for people of equal moral worth to enjoy different levels of happiness, then there is something wrong with those rules. Perhaps the Leibnizian would insist that truly just rules would do a better job of making happiness track virtue. I am not keen on pursuing this line of thought here.

receive their fair share of them. Again, I think these deserts can be explained ultimately by appeal to the notion of community essential needs.

With these alterations in place, my desertist theory of political economic distributive justice is as follows:

PEDa: There is perfect political economic distributive justice in a country if and only if in every case in which a citizen of that country deserves some political economic desert in virtue of having a certain political economic desert base, he or she receives that desert from the government of his or her country.

The motto of this form of desertism may be taken to be: "justice is receipt of political economic deserts according to political economic desert bases." It is important to recognize that distributions of political economic deserts do not automatically translate into distributions of happiness, or of shares of the social good. The government might see to it that every citizen receives the political economic items that he or she deserves, but as a result of naturally occurring psychological tendencies toward cheerfulness or its opposite, or because of bad luck or laziness or mistakes some citizens might still end up less happy than others, and with smaller shares of the social good.

Let us first consider what happens when we view Rawls's argument as an argument against PED. On this interpretation, the argument looks like this:

Equal Worth/Unequal Shares Argument (first revision)

1. It is possible for there to be a country in which (a) there is a very high level of intuitive justice, (b) the citizens are all equally morally worthy, and (c) the citizens enjoy unequal levels of happiness.
2. If it is possible for there to be a country in which (a) there is a very high level of intuitive justice, (b) the citizens are all equally morally worthy, and (c) the citizens enjoy unequal levels of happiness, then PED is false.
3. Therefore, PED is false.

So interpreted, the argument is unsound. There is nothing to be said for premise (2). There is nothing in PED to suggest that equally morally worthy citizens are to receive equal portions of happiness. PED is silent on moral worth as a desert base; it is silent on happiness as a desert. It focuses on political economic deserts and political economic desert bases. So the thought experiment that provides the basis for premise (1) has no relevance to PED.

In another interpretation, we can revise the thought experiment so that it bears directly on factors that are deemed relevant by my theory of justice. On this interpretation, the argument looks like this:

Equal Worth/Unequal Shares Argument (second revision)

1. It is possible for there to be a country in which (a) there is a very high level of political economic distributive justice, (b) the citizens all have equal collections of political economic desert bases, and (c) the citizens enjoy unequal levels of political economic deserts.
2. If it is possible for there to be a country in which (a) there is a very high level of political economic distributive justice, (b) the citizens all have equal collections of political economic desert bases, and (c) the citizens enjoy unequal levels of political economic deserts, then PED is false.
3. Therefore, PED is false.

Premise (2) of this version is far more plausible. If it is possible for there to be a just society where people deserve to have equal political economic deserts, but do not get them, then PED would be in trouble. However, the argument still fails. On this interpretation, the problem is in the first premise. As I see it, if there is a high level of political economic justice in some country, then the citizens of that country must be getting the political economic deserts that they deserve on the basis of their political economic desert bases. So this version of the argument is also unsound.

My verdict on the Equal Worth/Unequal Shares Argument should be clear: it might reveal a difficulty for moral desertism, but it constitutes no difficulty for my form of political economic desertism.

7.3 The Circularity/Priority Argument

In several places in *A Theory of Justice*, Rawls hints that desertism goes wrong because it involves a kind of circularity. He seems to think that desertists accept a definition of justice that makes use of the concept of moral worth, but at the same time they also accept a definition of moral worth that makes use of the concept of justice. In other places, the argument seems to turn on some claims about priority. In these passages, Rawls seems to be saying that desertists make the concept of moral worth prior to the concept of justice, but at the same time they make the concept of justice prior to the concept of moral worth.

Here is a passage in which these two lines of argument seem to be mingled:

> The essential point is that the concept of moral worth does not provide a first principle of distributive justice. This is because it cannot be introduced until after the principles of justice and of natural duty and obligation have been acknowledged. Once these are on hand, moral worth can be defined as having a sense of justice; and... the virtues can be

characterized as desires or tendencies to act upon the corresponding principles. Thus the concept of moral worth is secondary to those of right and justice, and it plays no role in the substantive definition of distributive shares.[11]

Rawls alludes to a couple of definitions here, and so it is reasonable to suppose that he thinks the problem arises because of them. The suggestion, then, is that he thinks that if you assume that desertism is true, then you will be stuck with a kind of definitional circularity. Moral worth will be defined in terms of justice; justice will be defined in terms of moral worth. If Rawls is right about this, it would be bad news for desertism. I must acknowledge that the remarks in the quoted passage are not entirely clear. Rawls sometimes focuses on definitions, but he also talks about introductions, acknowledgments, and characterizations; and he hints at some definitions but does not state them. So I recognize that the argument I am going to discuss might not be one that Rawls meant to present.

To see how this argument might work, let us consider an analogy. Suppose someone proposed a view in normative ethics that included these two definitions:

D1: An act, *a*, is *morally right* = df. the ideal observer would approve of *a*.
D2: S is the *ideal observer* = df. S approves of an action if and only if it is morally right.

It is clear that there is a definitional circularity here. Each definition makes essential use of a term defined in the other. "Ideal observer" appears in the definition of "morally right," and "morally right" appears in the definition of "ideal observer." The combination of D1 and D2 is unacceptable as a result. If these two definitions were both accepted, then we would have to say that each of these two concepts "contains" the other; and that is impossible. The point can be recast in terms of one sort of priority: if we endorse both of these definitions, then in order to understand the concept of moral rightness, you must first understand the concept of the ideal observer; but in order to understand the concept of the ideal observer, you must first understand the concept of moral rightness. That would be equally unacceptable.

Under the interpretation now under consideration, Rawls was claiming that this sort of problem arises in the case of desertism. In this case, half of the problem is that the concept of moral worth would be defined by appeal to the concept of justice. Rawls says "moral worth can be defined as having a sense of justice"; this suggests this definition:

D3: S has *moral worth* = df. S has a sense of justice.

11 Rawls (1971: 312–13).

The other half of the problem apparently involves a proposed definition of justice in terms of moral worth. Rawls suggests that desertists will want to define justice by appeal to moral worth. He alludes to the "substantive definition of distributive shares." Perhaps he is thinking of something like this:

D4: The situation in society S is *distributively just* = df. members of S receive distributive shares in proportion to their moral worth.

Then the argument might be this:

The Circularity/Priority/Containment Argument

1. If desertism is true, then the concept of moral worth is defined by appeal to the concept of justice and the concept of justice is defined by appeal to the concept of moral worth.
2. If the concept of moral worth is defined by appeal to the concept of justice and the concept of justice is defined by appeal to the concept of moral worth, then the concept of moral worth contains the concept of distributive justice and the concept of distributive justice contains the concept of moral worth.
3. It is impossible for the concept of moral worth to contain the concept of distributive justice and the concept of distributive justice to contain the concept of moral worth.
4. Therefore, it is not the case that desertism is true.[12]

If we understand desertism to be the moral desertism that I formulated above as MDa, some elements of the argument might have some plausibility. For moral desertism does attempt to explain distributive justice by appeal to the concept of moral worth. As a result, there might be some support for premise (1)—or at least for the part of premise (1) that claims that if desertism is true, then the concept of justice is "defined" by appeal to the concept of moral worth.

Nevertheless, even under this interpretation, the argument fails. Premise (1) is false. Someone who accepts moral desertism would not have to define moral worth in the manner suggested by Rawls as "having a sense of justice." The

[12] A slight variant of the argument would replace talk of "containment" with talk of "priority". Instead of (2), we would have:

2'. If the concept of moral worth is defined by appeal to the concept of justice and the concept of justice is defined by appeal to the concept of moral worth, then the concept of moral worth is conceptually prior to the concept of distributive justice and the concept of distributive justice is conceptually prior to the concept of moral worth.

Corresponding changes would then be made in (3). My critical comments apply just as well to this version of the argument.

definition D3 is implausible and clearly not an essential component of any recognized form of desertism. The definition is implausible in part because it seems to identify moral worthiness with the possession of just one of the moral virtues—justice. What about all the other virtues? Surely they too are components of moral virtue. It would be more reasonable to define moral worth by saying that a person is morally worthy to the extent that he or she has the moral virtues, whatever they may turn out to be.[13]

There is another reason for rejecting (1). A person could accept moral desertism without taking its central principle to be a *definition* of justice. We might take it simply as a substantive principle about distributive justice. We might leave the concept of distributive justice undefined; or we might define it in terms of desert without mentioning moral worthiness.

But the argument confronts an even deeper difficulty. It seems to be designed as an attack on only certain forms of desertism—the forms of *moral* desertism. In these forms desertism does attempt to explain justice by appeal to the concept of moral virtue. But my preferred form of desertism—PED—purports to explain justice in a different way. It does not claim that justice requires receipt of the currency of justice according to moral virtue. Rather, it claims that justice requires receipt of that currency according to possession of political economic desert bases. Moral virtue is not one of these desert bases.

So my verdict on this argument is a bit more harsh. As I see it, the argument does not present a serious difficulty for any recognized form of desertism, even desertism of the "justice is happiness according to virtue" form. It is even less effective against the form of desertism that I prefer. I reject premise (1) of the circularity argument. I would say that according to my form of desertism we do not explain justice by appeal to moral virtue, and we do not explain moral virtue by appeal to justice. The argument, whether Rawlsian or not, reveals no defect in PED.

7.4 The Deserve to Deserve Argument

In section 17 of *A Theory of Justice*, Rawls is discussing the difference principle, according to which:

> the higher expectations of those better situated are just if and only if they work as part of a scheme which improves the expectations of the least advantaged members of society. The intuitive idea is that the social order is not to establish and secure the more attractive prospects of those better off unless doing so is to the advantage of those less fortunate.[14]

[13] William Galston points out this defect in the Rawlsian argument in Galston (1992: 171).

[14] Rawls (1971: 75).

Rawls turns to the question whether reasonable citizens would consent to having their society operate under the difference principle. It is fairly easy to see why the least advantaged member of a society would agree to an arrangement under which the institutions of his society would be governed by the difference principle. After all, no other way of organizing his society could be as beneficial to him as one based on the difference principle. But then Rawls tries to explain why the most advantaged members of the society would also agree to have those institutions governed by the difference principle. The explanation here is not so straightforward. The most advantaged members would be asked to give up some of their advantage so that the worst off will be doing as well as they possibly can do. As critics of the difference principle have pointed out, in some cases this might require very large sacrifices of advantage on the part of these advantaged citizens. What could motivate them to agree to this? Or, as Rawls asks, "Now what can be said to the more favored man?"[15]

Rawls replies that the more favored man should realize that "the well-being of each depends on a scheme of social cooperation without which no one could have a satisfactory life." This sounds a bit like blackmail—as if the worst-off man is threatening: "if you do not agree to live under the difference principle, then we will have no institutional structure at all, and then you will be back in the state of nature—and your life will be poor, nasty, brutish and short." Rawls also says, "we can ask for the willing cooperation of everyone only if the terms of the scheme are reasonable."

But of course the more advantaged man might not be moved by these thoughts. He might insist that he deserves to keep his greater advantages whether others benefit or not. And here Rawls says that "At this point it is necessary to be clear about the notion of desert."[16] He grants that if an advantaged man has followed the established rules of his well-ordered society, and has thereby come to be entitled to some benefit, then he has a "claim" on that benefit, or a "legitimate expectation" that he will receive it. But Rawls goes on to distinguish between this sort of desert (which, to avoid confusion, I have tried to consistently call *entitlement*), and desert of another sort (which is sometimes called preinstitutional desert). A person preinstitutionally deserves something if he deserves it, but his desert of it is independent of his satisfaction of the conditions of any system of rules that has been established in his community.

Suppose someone claims that the more advantaged man deserves—in this preinstitutional way—to have the added assets because he achieved them as a result of having "superior natural endowments." These superior natural

[15] Rawls (1971: 103). [16] Rawls (1971: 103).

endowments, it might be claimed, make the advantaged man "more worthy" and his extra worthiness makes him deserve to have a greater share of the social product. But Rawls vigorously rejects this claim about preinstitutional desert. "This view," he says, "is surely incorrect."[17] There follows the well-known, widely quoted passage:

> No one deserves his place in the distribution of native endowments, any more than one deserves one's initial starting place in society. The assertion that a man deserves the superior character that enables him to make the effort to cultivate his abilities is equally problematic; for his character depends in large part upon fortunate family and social circumstances for which he can claim no credit. The notion of desert seems not to apply in these cases. Thus the more advantaged representative man cannot say that he deserves and therefore has a right to a scheme of cooperation in which he is permitted to acquire benefits in ways that do not contribute to the welfare of others. There is no basis for making this claim.[18]

Some apparently think they see in these remarks an argument against desertism as a theory of justice. Alan Zaitchik, for example, saw it that way; and he cited Nagel and Nozick as others who saw it that way.[19] I grant, of course, that hints of some elements of an argument against desertism might be found in the passage. However, Rawls himself did not mention any desertist theory of justice in this passage. His focus was much narrower; he was just trying to rebut the claim that the more advantaged man deserves the advantages that he has gained as a result of his superior natural endowments.

Whether Rawls presented this argument or not, we can consider an argument that Zaitchik extracts from the passage. Zaitchik first introduces the Deserve-to-Deserve Principle (which he calls "thesis I") in this passage:

> If someone claims to deserve something in virtue of a ground that just "happens to be true of him", says Rawls, then his claim must be false, for the fact that it is true of him will now be "arbitrary from a moral point of view." The man who deserves something must be able to claim credit, as Rawls puts it, for the ground's being true of him. But this means that he must deserve to have done or been, or must deserve to be the kind of person able to do or be, whatever is specified in the ground.
>
> In sum, we have thesis I: X deserves Y in virtue of having Z only if X deserves to have Z.[20]

Zaitchik points out that thesis I implies that if anyone ever deserved anything, the person would instantiate an infinite regress of deserved desert bases. Since an

[17] Rawls (1971: 104). [18] Rawls (1971: 104).

[19] See Zaitchik (1977: 370–88). There are suggestions that Nagel, Nozick, and perhaps others endorsed something like this line of reasoning. For a useful review of the literature, see Abad (2007).

[20] Zaitchik (1977: 372).

infinite series of this sort is impossible, no one ever deserves anything. And from this it follows that no form of desertism is true. The argument is presented in this passage:

> Suppose that Jones claims to deserve something in virtue of ground Z. By I he must deserve to have Z. He can deserve this only in virtue of some new ground for deserving Z'. This will require yet another ground Z'' and so on ad infinitum. Obviously, these conditions on deserving are never satisfied by anyone. Since the argument is perfectly general, we can state its conclusion as "no one ever deserves anything." Thus no desert theory could possibly be true, no matter what kinds of desert it sees as relevant to distributive justice.[21]

In one form, the argument looks like this:

The Deserve-to-Deserve Argument

1. If desertism is true, then sometimes people deserve things.
2. If sometimes people deserve things, then there are infinite regresses of deserved desert bases.
3. There are no infinite regresses of deserved desert bases.
4. Therefore, desertism is not true.

Zaitchik does not offer any explanation of premise (1), but it seems reasonable. Desertist theories of justice purport to explain the different levels of justice in different societies by appeal to facts about the different extents to which members of those societies receive the things they deserve. Since there obviously are cases in which different societies have different degrees of justice, it follows that if desertism is true, then people must deserve things. If no one ever deserves anything, then desertism would be forced to say—absurdly—that it is never the case that the level of justice in one society is different from the level of justice in any other society. The desertist might have to say that justice levels are "undefined" in every case.

Premise (2) is an immediate implication of thesis I, or the "Deserve to Deserve Principle."[22] If thesis I is true, then for every desert, there is a deserved desert base. If you deserve to have desert D, then you must have some desert base DB1 and you must deserve to have DB1; and if you deserve to have DB1, you must have some other desert base DB2, and you must deserve to have DB2; and so on ad infinitum. Thus, if anyone ever deserved anything, the chain of deserved desert bases could never end.

[21] Zaitchik (1977: 373).

[22] I assume that Zaitchik assumed that the regress of deserved desert bases could not be avoided by appeal to any sort of circularity in these desert bases.

I am not entirely clear on premise (3). Zaitchik does not say much about it. Let us simply agree that there would be something implausible about an infinite regress of deserved desert bases.

Zaitchik rejects the Deserve-to-Deserve Argument. He raises several objections to thesis I. He suggests that a defender of a form of desertism could interpret the argument as a reductio of thesis I. The suggestion here is that there is a sort of stand-off between thesis I and desertism. However, I think we can say something much stronger against thesis I.

Rawls insists that justice should not depend upon factors that are morally arbitrary; that no one should gain an advantage as a result of factors for which he can claim no credit, or which came to him simply as a matter of luck. And so, if someone deserves something on some basis, he must have deserved to have that basis. When so stated, the idea may seem somewhat plausible and it would lend support to the Deserve-to-Deserve principle. However, the idea will not bear scrutiny. This is especially obvious in cases in which people deserve sympathy and support in virtue of having suffered—arbitrarily and simply as a matter of bad luck—some natural disaster.

Suppose for example that a virulent strain of influenza randomly strikes some children but not others. Suppose no one is responsible for being stricken; no one deserves to be stricken. It is not as if the illness strikes certain children because they have been naughty. The illness struck some children and not others—and it did this in a morally arbitrary way. Yet in spite of this the stricken children deserve sympathy and perhaps medical attention, and they deserve these things in virtue of the fact that they have gotten sick. Surely the sick children deserve more sympathy than the children who fortunately were bypassed by the virus. So here we have a case in which someone deserves something (the sick children deserve sympathy and medical attention), and they deserve these things because they have a certain desert base (they came down with influenza), and they did not deserve to have that desert base (no child deserved to come down with influenza). This shows that the generalized form of the Deserve-to-Deserve Principle is false; thus the argument based upon it fails at premise (2).

I advocate a form of desertism about political economic distributive justice. I have formulated this theory as:

> PEDa: There is perfect political-economic distributive justice in a country if and only if in every case in which a citizen of that country deserves some political economic desert in virtue of having a certain political economic desert base, he or she receives that desert from the government of his or her country.

In Chapter 4 I listed what I take to be some of the most important political economic desert bases. The most fundamental of these is the possession of what

I called "community essential needs." Following Aristotle, I said that we are neither gods nor beasts; if we are to flourish as human beings, we need certain things that in the normal course of events individuals cannot procure on their own. We need to be embedded in a community that, by collective effort, may be able to supply them. Among the things that we need are such things as security from attack, opportunity for healthcare and education, the presence of an accessible legal system for the adjudication of disputes, a chance to participate in the affairs of our society. We need these things because we have a certain sort of vulnerability or inability to procure these things if left to our own devices. These are some of the desert bases that must be honored if our society is to have a high level of political economic distributive justice.

Let us focus on my need for security. In the absence of an organized and effective police force, I would be unable to protect my home and my family. Even if I had a rifle, I would still be vulnerable to attack or theft. This is an example of one form of community essential need. If I gather together with my neighbors and we agree to establish a police force, we will be able to diminish our vulnerability. If we do not come to any such agreement, we will find ourselves in something like the state of nature. So in my view, my need for this sort of security is a political economic desert base; it makes me deserve to live in a community where there is a properly organized police force.

The Deserve-to-Deserve Principle implies that if I deserve to live in a community that has a police force, and I deserve it on the basis of the fact that I am unable on my own to protect my family and possessions, then I must deserve to be unable on my own to protect my family and my possessions. But this is surely incorrect. I cannot imagine why anyone would think that normal citizens *deserve to need a police force*. The fact that I have this need is, as Rawls would put it, "simply a natural fact"—something that I did not deserve to have, but something that, at the same time, makes me deserve to live in a community where there is a police force.

Since, on my view, very many of my political economic desert bases are like the need for security, I conclude that the Deserve-to-Deserve Principle is false. Accordingly, the argument against desertism based on that principle is to be rejected. As I said earlier, I see no evidence that Rawls ever presented that argument; maybe Zaitchik invented it. But whatever its provenance, it is an unpersuasive argument. It cannot be used to refute any form of desertism.

7.5 The Impracticality Argument

As we have seen, one of the Rawlsian arguments against desertism is based on the idea that none of the traditional precepts of justice is designed to reward moral virtue. In passing, while discussing this argument, Rawls mentions the precept that says that people who exert greater conscientious effort are to receive greater compensation.[23] This, he acknowledges, at least comes close to suggesting that people who have greater moral worth are to receive greater compensation—and that would be an idea that might prove congenial to some desertists.

But then Rawls briefly mentions a possible difficulty for this view:

> It seems clear that the effort a person is willing to make is influenced by his natural abilities and skills and the alternatives open to him. The better endowed are more likely, other things equal, to strive conscientiously, and there seems to be no way to discount for their greater good fortune. The idea of rewarding desert is impracticable.[24]

One point that Rawls seems to be making in that passage is that it would be difficult in practice to distinguish between the part of a person's striving that is due to his moral virtue, and the part that is due simply to his good fortune in native endowment and training. If these things cannot be separated, then it will be difficult to determine the benefits he is to receive according to desertism. Rawls immediately repeats his claim that the precepts of justice do not—even "behind the scenes"—try to ensure that moral worth is rewarded. The claim about impracticality is so brief, and the point so enigmatic, that the reader might take it to be no more than a merely tossed-off remark in passing.

However, in *Justice as Fairness* Rawls gives a slightly expanded statement of the argument. In the later book he says again that desertism runs into trouble because of its impracticality. In that passage, after distinguishing strict moral desert from some related concepts, Rawls says:

> A conception of moral desert as moral worth of character and actions cannot be incorporated into a political conception of justice in view of the fact of reasonable pluralism. Having conflicting conceptions of the good, citizens cannot agree on a comprehensive doctrine to specify an idea of moral desert for political purposes. In any case, moral worth would be utterly impracticable as a criterion when applied to questions of distributive justice. We might say: Only God could make those judgments.[25]

Rawls also discusses this line of thought at some length in *Political Liberalism*.[26] As I understand it, Rawls was attempting to develop a conception of political distributive justice that could be adopted and endorsed by governments and citizens. Perhaps he was thinking that it would be a conception of justice that could be taught to children in their civics classes. Perhaps he was thinking that legislators could appeal to it when working on legislation. Thoughtful citizens

[23] Rawls (1971: 312). [24] Rawls (1971: 312). [25] Rawls (2001: 73).

[26] For an extended discussion of this and some related points, see Rawls (1993: xv–xxi).

could presuppose this conception of justice when discussing current political controversies.

The Rawlsian project apparently had an even narrower target. The conception of justice that he was trying to articulate would have to be suitable for use in a modern, relatively stable, liberal democracy. This would be a country in some ways like the United States—culturally diverse, with a multitude of religions and moral ideals, but bound together by a common commitment to living together under a single constitution.

It would be important for this project for Rawls to come up with a conception of political distributive justice that would be "practicable." In other words, he was seeking a conception of justice that could be used in practice by citizens as they confront practical political problems. In the passages I have mentioned, Rawls seems to be pointing out that a form of moral desertism would not be suitable in this context. Since different citizens in a pluralistic democracy would have different conceptions of moral virtue, different citizens would come to different conclusions about the moral deservingness of their fellows. So, if they believed in moral desertism, they would come to different conclusions about what justice requires. Their differences would be deeply rooted in their moral views, and so would be irresolvable. As Rawls suggests, only God would be able to determine who deserves what. This seems to be the core of the objection to desertism that Rawls had in mind in the passages in question.

Assuming that this rough characterization is correct, an argument based on these Rawlsian points might look like this:

The Impracticality Argument

1. Moral desertism would not be practicable in a modern pluralistic democracy.
2. If moral desertism would not be practicable in a modern pluralistic democracy, then moral desertism is not an acceptable theory of distributive justice.
3. Therefore, moral desertism is not an acceptable theory of distributive justice.

The first premise of this argument seems to me to be plausible. However, it is important to keep in mind that the Rawlsian claim applies here just to moral desertism. Thus, even if otherwise entirely successful, the argument would have no direct relevance to the sort of political economic desertism that I have been defending in this book.

But the second premise of the argument highlights a deep difference in approach between Rawls on the one hand, and many other contributors to the debate about distributive justice on the other. I think there is a profoundly important distinction between the Rawlsian project (as I have sketched it) and the project many others have pursued—and the project I mean to be pursuing in this book.

The Rawlsian project seems to be the project of articulating a conception of distributive justice that would be suitable for practical use in a pluralistic democracy. That is an interesting project, but it is not the one I mean to be pursuing here. My project is the more purely philosophical project of articulating a conception of distributive justice that is true.[27] I would like to give an account of what makes for distributive justice. Clearly, a theory could be an acceptable solution to the problem I find interesting even if it were not an acceptable solution to the problem Rawls found interesting. Thus, I reject premise (2).

As I see it, once we know what actually makes for distributive justice, we can turn to the less purely philosophical task of articulating a conception of distributive justice that would be practicable in a pluralistic democracy. First we have to figure out what makes for distributive justice. Then, with that solution in hand, we can attempt to figure out what would be the most effective way of working out the practical implementation of the theory.[28,29]

7.6 Conclusion on Rawls against Desertism

Nothing that Rawls actually said, and nothing that has been attributed to him, casts any doubt on my desertist theory of distributive justice.

[27] Or at least a conception of distributive justice that is plausible enough so that it is possible for thoughtful and intelligent philosophers to maintain it, together with their best intuitions about particular cases, while in reflective equilibrium. For more on this topic, see Appendix A.

[28] For a discussion of the relation between the truthfulness of a moral theory and the usefulness of that theory, see my "True and Useful: On the Structure of a Two-Level Moral Theory." The analogy to political theory should be fairly obvious.

[29] See also Mason (2012: 525–45).

8

Feinberg on Comparative and Noncomparative Justice

8.1 Feinberg's Distinction and its Implications for PED

In a highly influential paper[1,2] as well as in a book[3] about justice, Joel Feinberg has drawn attention to a distinction between two different ways in which claims of injustice can arise. In each case, a person may legitimately feel aggrieved—he may feel that he has been the victim of injustice. But the explanations or accounts of what has gone wrong differ in an interesting way.

In one sort of case, the aggrieved person can fully explain his grievance without mentioning anything about how others have been treated. An example may help. Suppose a student has written an excellent paper for a course. Suppose the paper was outstanding in every relevant respect and clearly deserving of a very high grade. But suppose the instructor assigns the paper a grade of D. The student may be aggrieved. He may feel that he has suffered an injustice. If he were to voice his concern, he might say that the paper was excellent and deserved a very high grade. He would not have to mention anything about the quality of work of other students in the class; nor would he have to say anything about the grades they received. He might explain his complaint in this way: "Justice requires that people get what they deserve; I deserved an A and I did not get it. So I have been treated unjustly."

In the second sort of case, an aggrieved person could not fully explain his grievance without saying something about what has happened to others. Suppose a different student has written a good paper for a course. Suppose he got a B for the paper. Suppose he knows quite a bit about the papers that were written by his

[1] My understanding of Feinberg's views has benefitted from discussions with several friends, especially Bob Gruber and Owen McLeod.

[2] "Noncomparative Justice," *The Philosophical Review* 83, 3 (July, 1974): 297–338.

[3] *Social Philosophy*, Englewood Cliffs, NJ, 1973.

classmates. Among other things, he knows that other students wrote papers that were on a par with his paper, but that each of them got an A. This student may also feel that he has suffered an injustice, but the explanation of his grievance turns essentially on facts about the quality of work and the grades received by his classmates. His complaint is that his work was just as worthy as theirs, but his grade was lower. If this student were to voice his complaint, he might say: "Justice requires that relevantly similar people be treated similarly. Although my work was relevantly similar to the work of my fellow students, I was not treated as well as they were. So I have been treated unjustly."

Sometimes Feinberg puts this point epistemically—in terms of what we would have to know in order to understand the grievance. In the first sort of case:

> It is not necessary for us to know what is due others in order to know what is due the person with whom we are dealing. *His* rights-or-deserts alone determine what is due him; and once we have come to a judgment of *his* due, that judgment cannot be logically affected by subsequent knowledge of the condition of other parties.[4]

But in the second sort of case, the person's grievance would be unintelligible in the absence of information about what others deserved or received. Feinberg illustrates this sort of case by appeal to the example of a prize in some sort of contest. Suppose we want to know which of the contestants deserves the blue ribbon. In this sort of case, since the whole purpose of the prize is to give recognition to the best in some competition, there is no way to tell whether the prize has been justly awarded to a given person without information about the credentials of the other contestants.[5]

Feinberg introduced some terminology to mark this distinction. He says, "I shall refer to contexts, criteria, and principles of the former kind as *noncomparative*, and those of the latter sort as *comparative*."[6] Feinberg announced his aim in the paper by saying that it was "to clarify the contrast between comparative and noncomparative justice, and also to investigate that which they might have in common, and in virtue of which the name of justice has come to apply to both."[7]

Note that Feinberg talks explicitly about two kinds of *justice*. He goes so far as to suggest that there is something of a puzzle about how these two different things fall under the same name—"justice." Some commentators take this talk of "two kinds of justice" quite seriously. They think that Feinberg's point was that there really are two different conceptions of justice ambiguously hiding behind a single term.

[4] Feinberg (1974: 300).
[5] Feinberg (1974: 299).
[6] Feinberg (1974: 298).
[7] Feinberg (1974: 298).

Joshua Hoffman[8] and Phillip Montague[9] have understood Feinberg in this way. They think Feinberg was claiming that there are two fundamental kinds of justice—comparative and noncomparative. Furthermore, Hoffman and Montague attribute to Feinberg the view that there is a most basic principle of justice for each. In the case of noncomparative justice, the basic principle is something like this:

> NCBPJ: Noncomparative Basic Principle of Justice: Justice requires that each person gets the benefits and burdens that he deserves.[10]

Whereas in the case of comparative justice, the principle is something like this:

> CBPJ: Comparative Basic Principle of Justice: Justice requires that relevantly similar people be given relevantly similar benefits and burdens [and relevantly dissimilar people be given relevantly dissimilar benefits and burdens.][11]

Hoffman and Montague seem to agree on the main point: Feinberg thought that these principles are independent and that each of them is a fundamental principle for a distinct kind of justice. There is support for this interpretation. Some of Feinberg's examples were apparently designed to illustrate the independence of these conceptions of justice. Of course, sometimes the implications of the two principles agree, as for example when someone deserves a grade of A because (a) his work was excellent and deserving of an A, and (b) others who did work of similar quality got As. The noncomparative principle asks us to focus on the quality of the student's work and to see what he deserves in light of that. His work was excellent and deserving of an A. If he gets it, noncomparative justice will be done regardless of what happens to his classmates. The comparative principle asks us to focus on the ways in which this student's work and grade compare to the work and grades of his fellow students. In this case, the other students did

[8] Hoffman (1993: 165–83). [9] Montague (1980: 131–40).

[10] Hoffman formulates the noncomparative principle as follows: "each person should be treated according to his rights and deserts." Montague puts it this way: "Justice requires that individuals be treated in accordance with their rights and deserts." Aristotle apparently had something like this in mind when, in Book V of the *Nicomachean Ethics*, he said: "everyone agrees that a distribution is just if and only if it distributes to each what he deserves, but they disagree about the basis for desert; supporters of democracy say it is free citizenship, some supporters of oligarchy say it is wealth, others good birth, while supporters of aristocracy say it is virtue."

[11] Hoffman, quoting Feinberg, formulates the comparative principle in this way: "The basic principle of comparative justice is that like cases are to be treated alike and different cases to be treated differently." Montague phrases it a bit differently: "Justice requires the similar treatment of relevantly similar cases and the dissimilar treatment of relevantly dissimilar cases" (132). Aristotle seems to have had something like this in mind in the *Politics* III, where he said "justice is . . . equality, not however, for all, but only for equals. And inequality is thought to be, and is, justice; neither is this for all, but only for unequals."

work of similar quality and got As; so comparative justice requires that he get an A as well.

But Feinberg points out that the implications of these conceptions of justice sometimes do not agree. These cause "stupefaction."[12] When we reflect on cases like these, we become confused. "Justice and injustice seem alternately to flit in and out of focus like the pictures in an optical illusion, . . . "[13] They make us feel that justice is pulling in two directions at once. He gives a couple of examples. One involves a system of criminal law in which everyone found guilty of a certain sort of crime is given a penalty that is much too harsh.[14] In this case, since equally guilty malefactors receive equally harsh penalties, the penalties conform to the requirements of CBPJ, and it appears that justice has been done. But since none of the malefactors deserves such a harsh penalty, the same penalties violate the requirements of NCBPJ and it appears that justice has not been done. It is also illustrated by the example of the coach who treats all his athletes like dogs. His treatment might be just according to CBPJ but unjust according to NCBPJ.

The fundamental principle that I have been defending throughout this book is PED which says that political economic distributive justice requires that people get the political economic benefits and burdens that they deserve in virtue of their political economic desert bases. Thus my principle is a version of the noncomparative principle, NCBPJ. Throughout the previous chapters of the book I have made no mention of the comparative principle, CBPJ, or of any version of that principle restricted to political economic deserts and bases. Thus it may seem that I have neglected to discuss an important element that would have to be incorporated somehow into any adequate theory of distributive justice. So we have our questions: is there really a fundamental distinction between comparative and noncomparative justice? And if so, does the existence of this distinction indicate that my theory (PED) needs to be supplemented by a complementary theory concerning comparative justice? A subsidiary, but also interesting question concerns the interpretation of Feinberg's paper. Did he really mean to claim that there are two independent and easily confused conceptions of justice?

8.2 Feinberg's Examples and What They Show

We need to check to see if we can find a case that illustrates the need for the addition of a comparative principle of political economic distributive justice. Our search might lead us to realize that the theory of justice that I have proposed will

[12] Feinberg (1974: 310).
[13] Feinberg (1974: 314).
[14] Feinberg (1974: 312).

not do all the work that needs to be done—that there are cases where our best justice-related intuitions tell us that justice requires that something be done or avoided, but that my theory—PED—has no way to account for our intuitions. Or, on the other hand, we may find that PED already contains everything required to explain the injustice that arises when relevantly similar cases are treated differently.

Feinberg presents (with some hesitation and sprinkled with disclaimers) a variety of examples apparently intended to show that we cannot get by with only a noncomparative principle. He seems to be claiming that we need in addition a comparative principle. The point seems to be that if we make use only of the noncomparative principle, we will have no way to explain why certain situations strike us as being unjust. I will focus on four examples that seem to me to be most interesting. The examples might reveal that I need to add a comparative principle as a supplement to PED.

8.2.1 God's infinite mercy

Suppose that no one, considered entirely on his own merits, deserves to be saved since everyone is by nature totally depraved.[15] But suppose that God decides to exercise "executive clemency" and arbitrarily permits some people to go to heaven. All the rest go to hell. It may appear in this case that a purely noncomparative principle cannot explain the intuition that an injustice has been done to those who go to hell. They are depraved; they have been consigned to hell. Where is the injustice? Feinberg explains:

> Yet if they think about their equally sinful but luckier comrades, they are likely to feel at least somewhat aggrieved at what they can only take to be unjust discrimination in plain contravention of comparative principles.[16]

If we focus on the complaints that might be made by the sinners who go to hell, we may agree with Feinberg: their complaints seem to be fundamentally comparative. They claim to be suffering an injustice since others who are just as guilty have been chosen for heaven. It may seem, then, that a purely noncomparative theory of justice would be left "stupefied" by this example.

Nevertheless, it seems to me that this example does not call for any additions to PED. In the first place, obviously, this example has no direct relevance to political economic distributive justice. The example concerns a matter of otherworldly theology. But a more troubling point concerns the intent of the example. What is it supposed to show? It would be relevant to my concerns if it illustrated the

[15] Feinberg (1974: 313). [16] Feinberg (1974: 314).

possibility that there could be an unjust situation whose injustice could not be explained by a noncomparative principle similar to PED.

In my view, this example does not illustrate that possibility. Note first of all that there are plenty of noncomparative injustices in the example. Consider all the sinners who deserve hell but who are going to heaven. Every such case is a clear violation of the principle that says that each person is to get the benefits and burdens that he or she deserves. The chosen sinners deserve the burden of hell but do not get it; they do not deserve the benefit of heaven but they do get it. So the example does not constitute a case in which we need to appeal to a comparative principle in order to explain the injustice. We can explain the intuition that something has gone wrong in the imagined world by appeal to a purely noncomparative principle.

There is a further question. My theory is a theory about the level of justice in a state. Feinberg had a different focus. He was talking about the justice or injustice of the way in which some individual is treated. Thus, instead of talking about the question whether an external justice review board would declare the situation in some country to be just, he talks about the grievances or complaints on grounds of injustice that would be made by individuals. So it may be important to ask about the individual grievances felt by the hell-bound sinners. Each of them feels that he or she has been treated unfairly. Can this complaint about the injustice suffered by an individual be explained on noncomparative grounds? Or will we need to make use of a comparative principle to account for the injustice that individuals seem to be suffering?

I acknowledge that this intuition of personal mistreatment has some plausibility. However, it seems to me that we can explain these grievances without appealing to a further principle of comparative justice. In light of the fact that God has arbitrarily allowed some sinners to go to heaven, there is something that hell-bound residents of the imagined possible world deserve to have but are not getting.[17] As I see it, they deserve to live in a world in which God allocates heavenly benefits and infernal burdens according to moral merit; and the hell-bound sinners are not getting this. Instead, they are getting to live in a world with an arbitrary and capricious deity who sometimes sends sinners to heaven for no good reason. So it seems that we can explain the personal grievances of the hell-bound sinners on noncomparative grounds. Each of them deserved something of huge importance; none of them got it.

There is an important similarity between the hell-bound sinners and the heaven-bound sinners: in each case, in my view, there is a disparity between

[17] My comment here presupposes the background theory about virtue and vice, heaven and hell.

desert and receipt. Everyone deserved to live in a world in which God metes out heavenly rewards in accord with virtue or vice. No one is getting this. So the heaven-bound sinners seem to be suffering from this same injustice. Yet they have no grievance. Only the hell-bound sinners, who are getting the punishment they deserve, have a grievance. Does this show that we need to introduce a comparative principle of justice?

As I see it, there is an important difference between the heaven-bound sinners and the hell-bound sinners. Every one of them is failing to get something he or she deserves; but the heaven-bound sinners benefit enormously from the failure of receipt/desert proportionality. It is no wonder that they are glad about the injustice of their world, for if it had been perfectly just, they would have gone to hell. On the other hand, the hell-bound sinners can find in God's injustice even further reason for complaint: if there is injustice in this world, and some sinners are going to heaven when they do not deserve it, why not me? Do not I deserve just as much to benefit from God's injustice?

So Feinberg's first example is (a) not directly relevant to my question about political economic distributive justice, and (b) incapable of showing the need for the addition of a comparative principle of justice even in the theological realm to which it is relevant.

8.2.2 Punishing one as a warning to others

Feinberg presents a pair of cases intended to illustrate a common pattern.

> When all the students in a class or all the soldiers in a barracks are equally guilty and only one is punished (as a threat to the others) or only one is left unpunished (out of favoritism) then the punished ones have no grievance on noncomparative grounds, since they are guilty after all, but they can complain against discriminatory treatment.[18]

Let us consider the case involving the soldiers in the barracks. In Feinberg's example, all the soldiers are equally deserving of punishment; only one gets it. The one who is punished has a comparative complaint. He might phrase it this way: "Why are you are punishing me, when all these others are just as guilty and are not being punished?" So it appears that the punishment of this one soldier is unjust according to a comparative principle, but just according to a noncomparative principle. Feinberg sums up by saying that the punished one has "no grievance on noncomparative grounds."

This example may seem to have greater relevance to my project in this book since the case involving the soldiers does seem to bear on political economic

[18] Feinberg (1974: 314).

distributive justice. We may assume that the soldiers are "employees" of the government and the one who is punished is receiving a penalty from a governmental agency. Nevertheless, it is not clear to me that Feinberg is right when he says that the punished one has "no grievance on noncomparative grounds." I think he does have such a grievance. We just have to be clear on the nature of his grievance.

If the punished soldier were to say that his punishment is unjust because he is not guilty, he would be obviously wrong. As the case has been described, he is guilty. So that cannot be his grievance on noncomparative grounds. But it seems to me that he has other noncomparative grounds for complaint. Suppose he were to claim that the noncomparative injustice inflicted upon him is this: as a member of the military, he deserved to live under a system of regulations and penalties that would be applied uniformly. Perhaps this was promised to him; perhaps it is written in the code of military conduct; perhaps it is just an unstated assumption that one is allowed to make when joining a highly regulated organization. Maybe he deserved this because without it he would be vulnerable to a sort of harmful treatment that he would be unable to defend himself against.[19] His complaint is that he has not received this benefit that he deserved. He finds himself living under a system in which the regulations and penalties are applied inconsistently and arbitrarily. So he has not gotten what he deserves. His complaint can be understood by appeal to the noncomparative principle that says that justice requires that people get what they deserve.

Additionally, it seems to me that the soldier would be justified in feeling that he is suffering yet another noncomparative injustice. He might point out that he has been selected to undergo punishment as an example to others; he might claim that while he does deserve the punishment, he does not deserve to undergo it as an example to others. Maybe his complaint is that he did nothing to deserve this special status as a warning to others. There is nothing in the code of military justice that says that from time to time a soldier will be required to undergo punishment in order to provide a warning to others.

Thus the existence of injustice in the unit, as well as this soldier's special grievance, can be explained by appeal to the noncomparative principle that says that justice is done when people get the benefits they deserve and do not get burdens that they deserve not to get.

[19] Thanks to Bob Gruber for helpful discussion of possible desert bases on which the soldier might deserve the benefit of living under a regime in which individuals are not required to be exposed to arbitrary selection for punishment as examples to others.

8.2.3 *Gratuitous benefaction*

Another of Feinberg's examples involves a "gratuitous benefactor."[20] In this example, there are ten beggars. None of them has any right to charity. A wealthy person chooses to give money to nine of the beggars but to give nothing to the tenth. Feinberg comments on the case as follows:

> The poor excluded beggar, his sense of justice confused, will feel aggrieved and unaggrieved in rapid alternation. There is no right to charity, or grace, or clemency, or any other form of gratuitous good treatment, and yet arbitrary inconsistency or favoritism in the distribution of these goods can seem unjust to those neglected or deprived of them.[21]

The example is intended to illustrate a case in which reliance on the noncomparative principle alone will be unable to account for the injustice. The tenth beggar's grievance can be explained only by appeal to the comparative principle of justice—or so it may seem.

Again it is important to see that the example does not concern political economic distributive justice. As Feinberg describes it, it is a case of private charity. Thus, even if it succeeds it cannot show that my desertist principle of political economic distributive justice needs supplementation with a comparative principle.

But in any case it does not seem to me that the example succeeds. As before, a purely noncomparative principle of justice would have no trouble finding things that have gone wrong in the situation: nine beggars who (according to Feinberg's description of the situation) do not deserve "any form of gratuitous good treatment" have received precisely this benefit that they do not deserve. So even if we stick exclusively to a noncomparative principle of justice, we can account for the sense that there is something unjust in the situation viewed as a whole.

Admittedly, this would not explain the idea that the tenth beggar's complaint is specifically a complaint about *justice*. But it is not clear to me that his complaint really is a complaint about injustice. Maybe it is simply an expression of disappointment. Maybe the beggar's grievance is just that there was money being distributed, he wanted some, and he did not get any. He might just be expressing disappointment about a missed chance for some free money.

Maybe the beggar would insist that it is the injustice of the case that is bothering him. I think his complaint still might be explicable on noncomparative grounds. Maybe his complaint would be that the gratuitous benefactor has

[20] Feinberg (1974: 314–15). [21] Feinberg (1974: 314–15).

treated him with undeserved disrespect.[22] Maybe he thinks that in spite of his low socio-economic status, he is still after all a human being; he has a certain amount of dignity. As a result, he deserves not to be treated with contempt and disrespect. Yet he has been singled out as someone who will receive no charity. So he has received some treatment (a snub) that he deserved not to get, and failed to receive some treatment (a modicum of respect) that he did deserve. Again, if we agree that the tenth beggar has suffered from unjust treatment, there is no need to introduce a new principle of comparative justice to explain this fact. An explanation purely in terms of noncomparative justice is available and suffices.

8.2.4 Unequal inheritances

Feinberg cites an example due to Woozley.[23] In this case, a rich person has two children who are alike with respect to "needs, deserts, and reasonable expectations." Feinberg goes further and says that the children are also alike with respect to such further and possibly irrelevant factors as "age, size, health, appearance, abilities, beliefs, and ideals." We are asked to imagine then that the father bequeaths enough money to each child to meet their needs. But he gives a million extra dollars to one of them simply because he likes that one better. Woozley apparently was not convinced that there is any injustice at all in this case, but Feinberg disagrees, saying that "comparative considerations might still properly agitate the sense of injustice (*pace* Woozley) of the 'deprived' son."[24]

Although the example is still a bit sketchy, I am inclined to agree with Woozley. It is not clear to me that there is any injustice here. But if there is an injustice, it is pretty clear that it is not a political economic injustice since the money is not being distributed by the state. Insofar as the state plays any role in the case, its role would be to establish and oversee the procedures by which parents bequeath their estates to their heirs. We may assume in this case that the state has discharged its duties. We may assume that the rules concerning inheritances are reasonable and have been followed. The state has no obligation to ensure that indiscernible sons receive indiscernible shares of their deceased father's estate.[25]

[22] In Avrahim and Statman (2013: 316–33), Ronen Avrahim and Daniel Statman propose a different account of the way in which disrespect can affect the justice of a distribution (in their case, a distribution of punishments). They offer a general theory—Respectarianism—in their account. It would be interesting to compare the Respectarian view to the view I propose here.

[23] Feinberg (1974: 315). The example comes from p. 313 of Woozley's (1973) "Injustice."

[24] Feinberg (1974: 315).

[25] Note that if the case occurs in a country in which the institution overseeing inheritance does have a rule requiring equal distributions in cases such as this, PED has no difficulty explaining the injustice. The deprived son is entitled to an equal share under the rules concerning inheritance in his

But if there is an injustice, it seems to me that it can be explained by appeal to the noncomparative principle. The father's decision to give all the extra wealth to the favored son may be seen as a gratuitous slap in the face to the short-changed son. We can imagine him complaining, "I did nothing to deserve this insult; I deserved to be treated with respect and generosity. And yet the old man decided for no good reason to treat me with utter disrespect. That is a pretty obnoxious way to treat a son!" Note that if this is the heart of the grievance of the short-changed son, and if it is a grievance about *justice*, then his grievance can be explained by appeal to the noncomparative principle. He is claiming that he deserved to be treated with respect and generosity but instead was handed a cold-hearted insult. He could make this complaint without ever mentioning the generous bequest to his brother. He could simply focus on the fact that his father had plenty of money and could have given him a nice inheritance but chose, for no good reason, not to give it to him.

It is not clear to me that there is any example in the Feinberg paper that convincingly illustrates the notion that there are some political economic distributive injustices that cannot be explained by appeal to a noncomparative principle. None of his examples demonstrates that in some cases, in order to explain the injustice, we need to turn in addition to a comparative principle. So we must attempt to construct a case that will illustrate the point that some have understood Feinberg to be making.

8.3 A New Example

We can construct a case involving distributions where the distributor is an agency of the government, and the recipients are citizens, and the thing deserved and the desert bases on which they deserve it all seem to be matters of political economic interest. If the injustice of this case is genuine and cannot be explained on noncomparative grounds, that will demonstrate the need for the addition of a comparative principle of political economic distributive justice.

Suppose Timm and Tomm are identical twins who are alike with respect to all political economic desert bases. Suppose they have worked equally hard and have earned the same amount of money over the course of a year. Suppose the IRS has withheld money from the paychecks of Timm and Tomm throughout the year. Now the tax year is over, and each twin has filed his return. Suppose each is now entitled to a $1000 refund. Suppose, however, that there is not enough money

country. Assuming that the institution is from the deserved range, this implies that the son deserves that share. His failure to get it therefore would be a noncomparative injustice.

in the treasury to give both of them the refunds they deserve. There is only $1000 in the kitty. The IRS has a variety of options:

1. Give one twin $1000 and the other twin nothing.
2. Give each twin $500
3. Give the twins some other combination of refunds—equal or not—totaling no more than $1000.
4. Give each twin nothing.

It seems clear that perfect justice is not an option here. Given the facts of the case, it is not going to be possible to give Timm precisely what he deserves and also to give Tomm precisely what he deserves. Perhaps it is here that the comparative principle becomes important. Perhaps the problem can be solved by appeal to CBPJ.

I have set up the case so that Timm and Tomm are relevantly similar. CBPJ then seems to imply that justice requires that they be treated similarly. One way of treating them similarly would be to give each $500. It may seem that in the example as described, that would be the most just resolution,[26] and this might seem to show that I need to supplement my noncomparative principle PED with a comparative principle such as CBPJ in order to deal with cases in which perfect noncomparative justice cannot be done.

I have two reasons for doubting that this is the ideal solution. First of all, it seems to me that CBPJ does not mandate the resolution in which each twin receives $500. Note that there are thousands of other resolutions that would involve treating these like cases alike. If the IRS were to give each twin nothing, they would be treating the twins similarly. And if they were to give each twin $1 they could appeal to CBPJ for justification in the same way. For any amount between $0 and $500, the IRS could give precisely that amount to each twin and thereby treat like cases alike. Yet some who consider this sort of example would apparently feel that there would be something unjust about refunding anything less than $500 to each twin. CBPJ provides no explanation of this fact.

It seems to me that my proposed theory of political economic distributive justice already provides a sufficiently good explanation of the attractiveness from the perspective of justice of the $500 refunds. If this is right, we have a second reason for doubting the need for a new principle. The old principle gives us the explanation we seek. The explanation works like this:

[26] But this assumption seems to me to be questionable. I explain my reservations in footnote 27 below.

Note that in the first place in any even moderately complex country with even a moderate level of political economic justice, there will have to be some institution in charge of taxation. Otherwise, it will be impossible for the community to finance the organizations and infrastructure that are deserved by citizens as matters of political economic justice. So there must be some institution in charge of the whole scheme of income taxation, withholdings, and refunds. In the United States, this job is done by a complex institution overseen by the IRS under regulations established by law. Since money has been withheld from Timm's and Tomm's paychecks, there must be some such institution in place in their country.

There are lots of different ways in which this institution can be organized. Some of these institutional arrangements will be better in various ways than others. Different sets of regulations for an IRS-like organization could have various advantages and disadvantages. One might produce more revenue than another; another might be simpler and make use of easier-to-understand forms; another might be more acceptable to the citizenry; another might have a better impact on the economy.

For any possible IRS-like institution, there is some extent to which the citizens deserve for it to be in place in their country. If the possible institutions are ranked according to this sort of desert, some will be up near the top of the list. We can say that each of those good institutions is in the "deserved range" for their country. I think it is reasonable to assume that there are quite a lot of significantly different IRS-like institutions that fall into this range for the United States. The same is true of the country where Timm and Tomm live.

Suppose some taxation institution is in place in the land of Timm and Tomm. Then, simply as a matter of law, Timm and Tomm will be entitled to whatever refunds are due to them under the law. Let us suppose the law says that in the first instance, if a citizen's tax liability is less than the amount that has been withheld, then he or she is entitled to receive as a refund whatever has been withheld in excess. We can assume that this explains why Timm and Tomm are legally entitled to $1000 apiece.

But what about desert? If the taxation scheme in place in their country is from the deserved range, then (in accord with the scheme I laid out in Chapter 4) Timm and Tomm have political economic desert of the refunds to which they are entitled. If it is impossible for the IRS to provide the deserved refunds, then it becomes necessary to consider the follow-up rules concerning what to do when there is not enough money to provide all the refunds.

Suppose that the IRS-like institution contains a rule that says that if there is not enough money to provide all the legally authorized refunds, then the IRS is to determine the largest percentage, *n*, such that it can refund *n* percent of the amount due to each taxpayer. In this case, application of the rule would result in Timm and Tomm receiving equal refunds.[27]

Let us assume that the actual taxation institution in Timm and Tomm's country is from the deserved range. Then, in the first place, Timm and Tomm will be legitimately entitled by these rules to full refunds. Since the institution is from the deserved range, they will deserve full refunds. Perfect justice would mandate it. But when lack of funds makes this impossible, each twin will be entitled to a refund in accord with the regulations. I have imagined that the regulations stipulate that each is to get the largest percentage refund consistent with equal refunds for all who are entitled to them. Thus, Timm and Tomm will be entitled to $500 each. Since the institution is from the deserved range, the brothers will deserve these refunds and, though perfect justice is not possible, the arrangement is more just than would be an arrangement in which one twin receives more than the other.

Thus, even though I have tried to set up the case in such a way as to make the requirement of equal treatment seem most pressing, there is still no need to appeal to a comparative principle of justice. My noncomparative principle of political economic distributive justice is sufficient to explain the intuition that justice requires that the twins receive equal and maximally large refunds.

8.4 Two Conceptions of Justice or Two Varieties of Desert?

The patient reader may be puzzled. It may appear that I have simply misunderstood Feinberg's main point. For in my defense of my noncomparative principle I have in several instances appealed to claims about desert that may seem to some readers to incorporate precisely the comparative notions that Feinberg was emphasizing. For example, in connection with the example involving the hell-bound sinners, I said that those sinners deserved to live in a world in which God

[27] I think it is interesting to note that there could be a system from the deserved range that mandated *unequal* refunds in a case like the one involving Timm and Tomm. For example, imagine a system according to which when there is not enough money to refund excess withholdings to all citizens, the size of the refunds should be calculated according to a progressive formula: taxpayers with lower incomes are to get a larger percentage share of the withholdings due to them. This would not affect Timm and Tomm in the example under consideration. But another regulation might: suppose the rule says that taxpayers who are due refunds should get them on a "first filed, first refunded" system until the money runs out. If Timm filed before Tomm, he might get a full refund while his brother gets no refund. It is not clear to me that this would be unjust, provided that the system for refunds was passed in legislation and announced to all taxpayers in a timely manner.

does not hand out heavenly rewards in an arbitrary and capricious way. In the example involving the soldiers in the barracks, I said that the singled-out soldier deserved to be serving in an institution in which the regulations governing punishment would be uniformly applied. So in spite of the fact that I am denying the need to introduce a comparative principle of justice, I am acknowledging the relevance of factors of the sort that would be essential to such a view.

This calls for some explanation. I think there is some considerable unclarity about the main point that Feinberg meant to make in his paper. Hoffman, Montague, and others attribute to him a view specifically about *justice*. The view in question may be approximately this:

2J: There are two independent conceptions of justice—the comparative and the noncomparative. Each has its own fundamental basic principle. For the comparative, it would be something like CBPJ saying that justice requires that similar cases be treated similarly; for the noncomparative it would be something like NCBPJ saying that justice requires receipt in accord with desert. Sometimes these conceptions of justice pull in opposite directions and cause stupefaction. What is just according to one of them is unjust according to the other.

But there are passages in Feinberg's paper where it seems that he means to defend a much less sweeping thesis. Near the beginning of the paper he says (in a remark that is surprisingly often overlooked):

> In all cases, of course, justice consists in giving a person his due, but in some cases one's due is determined independently of that of other people, while in other cases, a person's due is determinable *only* by reference to his relations to other persons.[28]

This remark is clearly the expression of an importantly different and far less dramatic thesis. According to this thesis, there is only one basic principle of justice. That is the noncomparative principle according to which justice obtains when people get what they deserve. What comes in two flavors is not justice, but *desert*.[29] The thesis of this passage may be put this way:

2D: There is only one fundamental conception of justice—justice obtains when people get what they deserve. But we can distinguish between two types of desert base—some desert bases are essentially comparative. To tell whether a person has one of these desert bases one would have to know something about how others in the relevant class of comparison are being treated. The

[28] Feinberg (1974: 298).

[29] Assuming that what a person is "due" is the same as what he deserves.

> other type of desert base is noncomparative. The question whether someone has one of these desert bases is independent of facts about what others deserve and receive. Sometimes a desert base of one sort pulls in one direction, while a desert base of the other sort pulls in the opposite direction. Justice requires that overall desert be calculated by adding them all together. There is no cause for stupefaction.

2J would constitute an important and controversial thesis in political philosophy. If it were true, there would be an irresolvable bifurcation in the field of justice. Indeed, talk of "the field of justice" would be in a way improper, since if 2J were true there would be two fields ambiguously going under the single name "justice." It would be more appropriate, if 2J were true, to banish the unadorned word "justice" from our vocabularies and instead to start talking in a new way of "comparative justice" and "noncomparative justice." There would be two essentially distinct phenomena that have hitherto been hiding behind a single name; sometimes these phenomena happen to evaluate things in the same way; sometimes they do not. We would then have to say that at least since the time of Plato and Aristotle, philosophers have failed to recognize that they were in fact talking about two different phenomena. No wonder there is so much confusion and disagreement; no wonder that "justice and injustice seem alternately to flit in and out of focus like the pictures in an optical illusion, ... " No wonder that we often are stupefied. Those who specialize in social and political philosophy would have to start afresh. The first step would be to tell us which concept of justice they have in mind when they present their views about "justice."

2D, on the other hand, would be a mere footnote to the theory of justice. If it were true, "justice" would be a term for a single attractive feature of states—receipt in accord with desert. Philosophers who think about such things have known all along that there are lots of different bases on which someone can deserve something. Some involve promises; some involve need; some involve the smooth operation of well-organized social institutions. If 2D were true, there would be yet another way to carve up the domain of desert bases. We would have to recognize that there are some cases in which a person's possession of a desert base is conceptually and epistemically independent of facts about the deserts and receipt of others; there are other cases in which this is not so. In these cases whether or not a person possesses some desert base intrinsically involves facts about the deserts and receipts of others. To reach a conclusion about a person's overall level of desert for some benefit, we would have to be sure to take note of all the applicable desert bases, comparative and noncomparative. In itself, this would be approximately as interesting as the fact that when determining a person's overall desert of some benefit, we have to be sure to take note of his possession of desert bases somehow involving social institutions as well as his possession of desert bases that do not involve social institutions. These two can "pull in opposite directions." And in this case as well, it would be a mistake to overlook a whole class of desert bases when trying to assess someone's desert of a benefit. There would be nothing in this that would create stupefaction. It would not be at all like two different concepts flitting in and out of focus like an optical illusion.

I do not think that 2J is true. I have seen nothing in Feinberg's paper or elsewhere that convinces me that we need to admit two distinct conceptions of justice. On the other hand, I think 2D is true. I take it to be a fairly trivial and completely innocuous point about one more way in which we can distinguish among desert bases.

Which thesis did Feinberg defend? Feinberg's title ("Noncomparative Justice") as well as many remarks scattered through the paper strongly suggest that he meant to be arguing for 2J. Commentators including Hoffman and Montague have plausibly interpreted him in this way. And yet other passages in Feinberg's paper just as strongly suggest that he was arguing merely for 2D. On balance, it seems to me that Feinberg did not clearly distinguish between these two views. In the more heated passages, he writes as if he means to be affirming something like 2J; in his calmer moments, it is merely 2D.[30]

For my purposes, however, the conclusion is relatively straightforward: there is nothing in the Feinberg paper that forces us to supplement the noncomparative principle PED with a comparative addition.

[30] Earlier, in Chapter 1, I quoted a warning from the Preface to G. E. Moore's *Principia Ethica*. He was emphasizing the importance of knowing precisely what question it is that you mean to answer before you set about to answer it. This is yet another instance in which Moore's remark seems apt.

9

Concluding Remarks

9.1 Some Things I Have Tried to Do

Perhaps it will be helpful, in this final chapter, to draw the reader's attention to what I take to be the most significant contributions I have made in this book.

1. In several places in the book I emphasized the importance of appreciating the difference between theories about distributive justice and theories about morally right action. I think theories about these matters belong in two different realms of philosophy. Theories about distributive justice belong in Social and Political Philosophy. Theories about morally right action belong in the Normative Ethics of Behavior. I think these realms differ in some important ways. Their aims, subject matters, terms of evaluation, etc. are all different. I also think that some of the most distinguished contributors to the recent literature about distributive justice often write in such a way as to suggest that their views can be seen simultaneously as theories of justice and as theories of right action. Maybe it is just a matter of formulation; or (more likely) it is due to the fact that these philosophers do not share my view that these are independent topics—that acceptance of a theory about one of them does not commit us to acceptance of any particular theory about the other. I have tried to illustrate the way in which these projects are often mingled and to explain the importance of keeping them apart. I discuss this point in several places in the book—the most extensive discussion is in Appendix B—"Two Helpings of Desert."

2. Critics of desertism often suggest that desertism comes in just one flavor—as if it is sufficient to say that desertism is the view that justice is receipt according to desert. Some of these critics seem to think that desert simply has to be *moral desert* or *moral merit.* Sometimes they seem to think that when we speak of "receipt" we simply have to be talking about *receipt of happiness* or *receipt of welfare.* Thus, those who share these assumptions seem to take desertism as the view that justice obtains when everyone's level of happiness (or welfare) is

properly aligned with his or her level of moral merit.[1] I tried to show (mostly in Chapter 3) that in fact there are many different forms of desertism. Some are more important than others; some are more plausible than others. There are objections that apply to some of these views but not to others. I tried to distinguish clearly among these different theories, and to point out various ways in which some forms are more worthy of study than others. One of my main aims was to show that my preferred form of desertism is different in important ways from this "justice is happiness in accord with virtue" view. I also attempted to show that certain critics of desertism have understood the doctrine in a narrow and implausible way. It is no wonder that they found reasons to reject it. I made this point especially in Chapter 7 where I was discussing some arguments due to Rawls.

3. Perhaps the most significant novelty here is the book's core doctrine—the proposed desertist theory of political economic distributive justice. Chapter 4 is devoted to an attempt to characterize this theory by explaining the items that it takes to be the most important political economic desert bases and deserts. In addition to merely describing these desert bases and deserts, I attempt to give an account of the feature that makes it appropriate to categorize them as the desert bases and deserts that bear on political economic distributive justice. My idea is that in each case these things are suitably related to what I have characterized (following an idea that I find in Aristotle) as "community essential need."

4. As I understand it, the main competitors to my proposed form of desertism are various forms of egalitarianism (including luck egalitarianism), sufficientism, Rawlsianism, libertarianism, and (perhaps) prioritarianism.[2] I devote what may

[1] In *The Geometry of Desert* Shelly Kagan steadily discusses what he calls "moral desert." He focuses throughout the book on cases in which what is deserved is happiness or welfare, and the basis on which it is deserved is virtue. So it may appear that Kagan thinks that desert is always moral desert of this sort. But Kagan makes it clear that this is not his view. At the beginning of the book he mentions that we make desert claims about all sorts of things including promotions, grades, and victories in athletic competitions. He emphasizes that he will not be discussing these other forms of desert; he suggests that some of the things he says about moral desert might also be relevant to these other forms of desert (4). Perhaps surprisingly, the form of desert that I have been discussing explicitly *excludes* moral virtue as a desert base, and explicitly *excludes* happiness as a desert. Another important difference is this: Kagan seems to be interested in the way in which the intrinsic value of a situation is affected by the quality of the fit between welfare and moral desert. I, on the hand, have steadfastly avoided questions about intrinsic value in this book. I have been talking about the way in which the level of political economic distributive justice of a situation is affected by the quality of the fit between political economic deserts received and political economic desert bases displayed.

[2] The reader may wonder if I forgot to mention utilitarianism and Marxism. Some take them to be among the most important theories of justice. I briefly discuss these ideas in Appendix B "Two Helpings of Desert." I did not forget them; I chose not to devote a lot of space to them.

seem to be a surprising amount of attention to what I take to be the proper formulation of these theories. I do that in part because I feel that it is essential to understand precisely what these theories imply. Along the way I try to show that several familiar formulations of these views require some revision before comparison with my view is possible. I recognize that in insisting on these reformulations I may have stepped on some distinguished toes. I am sorry about that, but in every case it seemed to me that the received versions of the views needed some revisions before critical discussion would be possible. In each case, after reaching what I take to be a sufficiently clear formulation of an opposing view, I attempted to show that cases that make trouble for these views are handled more effectively by the view I mean to defend.

The comparisons with egalitarianism, luck egalitarianism, sufficientism, the difference principle, and libertarianism were presented in Chapter 5. Chapter 6 was devoted to a discussion of prioritarianism.

5. Somewhat more defensively, I presented my interpretations of what I take to be some of the most important objections to desertism. I tried to show that my form of desertism is not refuted by any of these objections. I also tried to show that many of those objections seem to be based on a misunderstanding of what a reasonable form of desertism would imply. Some of these attacks misfire, as I see it, because they aim at the wrong target. Other attacks are simply duds and do not pose a threat to any form of desertism. The Rawlsian objections were discussed in Chapter 7. Something like an objection is discussed in Chapter 8.

6. Sometimes I think that everyone who writes about justice is, at bottom, a desertist. Some may be closet desertists. Others are not hiding their desertism; they do not realize that they are desertists at heart. Perhaps many of them would emphatically deny that there are any desertist thoughts behind what they have said. My idea here is that a suitably generic form of desertism can provide a kind of abstract structure that will be suitable for the formulation of any theory of justice. We get distinct theories of justice merely by imposing certain restrictions on the deserts and desert bases. Thus, for example, suppose we assume that the only things that a person can deserve are "holdings"—items that the person owns, or possesses. Suppose in addition that we think that the only bases on which someone could deserve a holding are such things as fair acquisition of the holding from the state of nature; or fair acquisition of the holding in a voluntary exchange with someone who already legitimately holds it. Suppose we say on this basis that distributive justice obtains when everyone in fact has every holding that he or she deserves to have, and has it on the basis of the above mentioned desert bases. Then we have a doubly restricted form of

desertism, but its implications for cases are exactly the same as the implications of a simplified form of libertarianism.

The patient reader may have noticed several passages in the book in which I started by saying "Here is something that I find interesting..." and in which I went on to sketch an argument intended to show that some seemingly anti-desertist theory is equivalent to some restricted form of desertism.[3] (I presented a much longer and more complicated argument in the case of prioritarianism, but in the end I reached a similar conclusion.) I sometimes expressed this point by saying that every other theory of justice can be seen as a restricted form of desertism. In each case we start with a generic form of desertism, and then add an appropriately narrowed doctrine about who deserves what and on what basis. The result is, in each case, a specific form of desertism equivalent to the non-desertist theory with which we started.

I think that desertism has a kind of priority over these other theories. Here is an example to illustrate why I think desertism has priority: Suppose a philosopher thinks that justice requires that inequalities of welfare should be eliminated in such a way that no one is worse off than others through no fault of his own. Suppose someone asks for a justification, or explanation, or basis for saying that this is what justice requires. A luck egalitarian might say that this is rock bottom; there is no further explanation. That is simply what justice requires.

But suppose we appeal to a generic form of desertism and say at a more foundational level that justice always requires that people get what they deserve. And suppose we go on to say that in the first instance people deserve to have shares of welfare equal to the shares that others have; and that in case someone—through no fault of his own but simply as a matter of bad luck—has a share smaller than the shares held by others, then he deserves compensation up to the point of equality with others. And suppose we say that that fact about desert explains why luck egalitarianism is true. Then we will have given a defense of a form of luck egalitarianism that presupposes the generic form of desertism together with a claim about what people deserve. This would show that the desertist claims are more fundamental than the luck egalitarian claims. We can attempt to justify the latter by appeal to the former.[4]

[3] The passages can be found in sections 5.1, 5.2, 5.3, 5.4, and 5.5. I make this claim with respect to egalitarianism, luck egalitarianism, sufficientism, the difference principle, libertarianism, and prioritarianism.

[4] An anonymous reader for Oxford University Press found my claims about the connections between desertism and other theories of justice to be seriously implausible. He or she said that it was a mistake for me to claim that philosophers have argued in the way I describe since in fact no one has ever done so. But it seems to me that the criticism misfires. First of all, my central claim here is not

I also think, and in several cases tried to show, that the restricted claims about deserts and desert bases are pretty implausible. I prefer to say that the sort of justice that has been the focus of attention among political philosophers depends upon the items that I have identified as the political economic deserts and desert bases. That is why I say that these other theories are linked to very limited forms of desertism; they employ unreasonably restricted views about what we deserve from our countries.

So those are some of the main "positive" contributions I hope to have made in this book. There are also a number of "negative" contributions. In several instances I said that received views are implausible and even suggested in some cases that the views are based on confusions. I fear that some will be offended. If so, then I am sorry. I do not mean to be offensive or disrespectful. I have been trying to present and defend the views about distributive justice that seem to me to be true. This inevitably involved trying to explain what I take to be defects in opposing views and arguments.

9.2 Remaining Unfinished Business

Distributive justice, as I conceive of it, is in general a matter of receipt in accord with desert. My topic in this book has been a historically important form of justice—political economic distributive justice. My claim has been that where this sort of justice is concerned, the relevant deserts are *political economic* deserts. I tried to describe these deserts by saying that they are things that we need in order to flourish as human beings, but at the same time things that in the ordinary course of events people are unable to secure on their own—we need to be embedded in a suitable community in order to get them. I used the phrase "community essential needs" to refer to things that are needed in this way.

that advocates of competing theories of justice are in fact desertists who have argued in the way I described. My point is more modest. I merely wanted to point out the interesting logical relations between desertism and these other theories. Furthermore, as I pointed out in footnotes 7 and 21 in Chapter 5, and footnote 27 in Chapter 6 there are passages in the literature that suggest that several contributors have seen things in approximately the way I suggest. Two of them (Persson and Christiano in essays they contributed to *Egalitarianism: New Essays on the Nature and Value of Equality*—a collection edited by Nils Holtug and Kasper Lippert-Rasmussen) strongly suggest that a form of egalitarianism could be founded upon a desertist basis, and Matthew Rendall in "Priority and Desert" strongly suggests that a form of prioritarianism could be based on a combination of desertism and the idea that those who have less have greater desert of a boost. Another (Arneson in "Luck Egalitarianism: A Primer") mentions that a form of luck egalitarianism could be based on a combination of desertism and the idea that those who are worse off through no fault of their own deserve compensation. I believe my point is correct and important. It points to a way in which desertism provides a more fundamental framework within which other theories of justice can be conceived.

In light of the fact that the concept of *human flourishing* figures essentially in my account of political economic deserts, and my account of political economic deserts figures essentially in my account of political economic distributive justice, the curious reader might naturally want a detailed explanation of precisely what I have in mind when I speak of human flourishing. So long as that explanation is missing, there is a certain amount of vagueness at the heart of my theory of justice. So it may seem that in order to complete the project at hand, I have to present my theory of human flourishing. Dealing with this possible complaint will be my first bit of unfinished business.

Community essential needs are ones that cannot be satisfied by individuals acting on their own. In the normal cases, in order for these needs to be satisfied, the individuals who have them must be embedded in suitable communities. Justice then requires the community to ensure that the needs are met. A second bit of unfinished business concerns a troubling question about the connection between the needy individual and the relevant community. Suppose we agree that a certain individual has a community essential need; suppose we agree that certain groups of people in the neighborhood constitute communities. Which among these communities (if any) bears the burden of ensuring that the individual's need is satisfied? Suppose the need goes unsatisfied. Which community thereby suffers a decrease in its level of political economic distributive justice? Which communities, on the other hand, can beg off, saying in effect, "we recognize that this individual has a community essential need for this desert; and we recognize that we are a community and we recognize that we have the power to provide what he needs; but it is not our problem; he is not a member of our community—he does not deserve this benefit *from us*"?

A third bit of unfinished business concerns a question about imperfect justice. Earlier I said that the degree of imperfect justice in a country is a matter of "approximation." One country has a higher level of distributive justice than another if the situation in the one *more closely approximates* perfect justice than does the situation in the other. I mentioned some factors that might be relevant when assessing approximation and I suggested that in actual cases their impacts would somehow have to be taken into account. Can we do better? Can we give a clearer account of what makes for a closer approximation to perfect distributive justice?

In this concluding section I say more about these questions. I should confess at the outset that I will not be offering a definitive answer in any case. The problems will remain *unfinished business.*[5]

[5] A reader for Oxford University Press suggested that I should attend to another bit of unfinished business. The reader thought that it would be important for me to defend some view about the

9.2.1 *Flourishing as a human being*

Several years ago, when I presented a preliminary version of my theory of distributive justice, the problem about human flourishing was brought vividly to my attention when someone raised a question.[6] The questioner agreed that we are social animals; he was concerned about the fact that we are also *sexual* animals. He wanted to know if, on my view, justice requires that the government ensure that everyone have the lover of his or her choice. Further discussion revealed that the questioner had in mind the notion that people cannot flourish as human beings without love; some of us are unable to secure suitable lovers without help; and so the possession of a suitable lover might have to be considered to be a community essential need. If this is so, then my view would imply that to the extent that people are left without lovers, the state apparently has failed in its duty and thus is declared to have an accordingly lower level of political economic distributive justice. The questioner wanted to know if that is really what I want to say. It apparently seemed implausible to him.

I do not have a definitive answer to the question. My conception of human flourishing is, as the questioner suggested, indeterminate on this point.[7] However, I feel that my inability to give a precise answer to this question does not reveal a serious defect in the view about justice that I mean to defend.

I see two main options here. According to the first, or Option A, a person cannot flourish as a human being unless he or she loves and is loved by a suitable

relative degree of justice of various forms of government. Surely, the reader thought, a theory of political economic distributive justice has to include a view about the most just form of government. In my view, however, no single answer will suffice. In different circumstances, different forms of government might be more just. For example, under some circumstances the most just form of government might be a somewhat tyrannical one that redistributed a lot of misbegotten wealth. In another set of circumstances, the best form of government might be highly democratic. The most just form of government would be whatever form would, given the contingencies of the particular case under consideration, best accomplish the end of ensuring that citizens receive the political economic deserts that they deserve.

[6] The presentation took place at a meeting of the Center for Human Values at Princeton University on December 12, 2012. The question was first presented by Eden Lin, and then discussed by others who were present at the talk. I thank Eden for raising the question and for discussing it with me in personal correspondence afterward.

[7] I should mention that I think that a person can have relatively high welfare while not flourishing as a human being. Perhaps this is because I think that welfare is fundamentally a matter of happiness, and I think that happiness is fundamentally a matter of taking a lot of pleasure in things that are worthy of having pleasure taken in them. I develop and defend this view in my 2010 book *What Is This Thing Called Happiness?* I think I can imagine a person who, perhaps as a result of injury or disability, is unable to flourish as a human being but who nevertheless takes a lot of innocent pleasure in worthwhile things. I am especially grateful to Kristian Olsen and Owen McLeod for helpful discussions of this point.

partner. Love, on this view, is as essential to human flourishing as security, education, and healthcare. Furthermore, according to this option, if individuals are required to look for love entirely on their own, many will fail to find someone to love. This inability, according to this view, is on a par with the individual's inability to defend himself against foreign invaders, or to build roads and bridges and sewer lines on his own. The need for love is, like these other needs, a community essential need. Anyone who sees it this way will have to go on to say that we deserve to live in countries that ensure that we have access to some institution that will function roughly like eHarmony, OKCupid, or Christian Mingle.[8] Such a person will also have to say that if a country fails to provide any such service, and some of its citizens suffer from a lack of love, then those countries have failed to provide a political economic benefit that they are called upon to provide. Accordingly, the level of political economic distributive justice in those countries is lower than it would have been if they had provided the necessary dating service.

Others may take a different view of things. This is Option B. Someone who adopts this view will say that while having a satisfying love life is certainly enjoyable and may enhance a person's welfare, it is not something people need in order to flourish as human beings. Those who take this option will say that people can flourish as human beings even if they have unsatisfying love lives, or no love lives at all. Furthermore, they may claim that it is possible for people to find love on their own—perhaps with a little help from their friends and family. The need for love, as these people see it, is not like the need for security against foreign invaders. It is reasonable to imagine that lots of people could manage to find love even while living in the state of nature. This suggests that one does not need to turn to the government as the dating service of last resort in order to find someone to love.

If we find Option B more plausible, then we will say that the level of political economic distributive justice in a country would not be adversely affected if a government failed to provide a dating service and if, as a result, some citizens suffered with unsatisfying love lives. I guess I am more inclined to adopt Option B, but I have to admit that I have no clear argument in support of this view.

I think this is a case in which intuitions will vary. Some will say that the need for love is a community essential need and that political economic justice requires each government to ensure that its citizens have the opportunity to be loved. Others will say that the need for love is not a community essential need and that it is possible for there to be a country with an outstanding score in political

[8] In section 5.2 I imagined that this might be dubbed "the Department of Romantic Affairs."

economic distributive justice but in which some people remain unloved. I will leave it to others to reach their own conclusions about this question. Perhaps someone will discover a convincing argument that will help us to see which view is correct. My theory of justice would remain viable no matter which of these views turns out to be correct.

A third possible option ("Option C"), however, is not compatible with my view. That is the combination of views according to which (a) people need satisfying love lives in order to flourish as human beings; (b) people need the help of the community in order to be assured of success in love, but at the same time (c) the level of political economic distributive justice in a state is not diminished when the government fails to ensure that citizens have the love they need. As I see it, this combination is ruled out since it makes success in love a community essential need but it does not require states to ensure that citizens receive this benefit. While I admit that I do not currently have a definitive view on whether the truth is closer to Option A or to Option B, I feel fairly confident that Option C can be rejected.

A more general point about the concept of human flourishing may be relevant here. When we say that an organism is flourishing, we seem to mean that it is growing and developing in accord with its nature.[9] Given natural assumptions about the nature of fruit trees, it would be reasonable to maintain that a pear tree is flourishing when it is vigorously moving along a path that will have it putting out blossoms and setting fruit according to schedule. Aristotle apparently would assume that the production of fruit in this way is the "function" of the pear tree.[10] But what about people? If we follow Aristotle here, we will have to say that a person is flourishing when he or she is fulfilling the human function. What is the human function?

In the case of a person, we might want to say that flourishing is somehow analogous to bearing flowers and fruit in the case of a pear tree. To flourish as a human being, on this view, is to fulfill the function that we are intended by nature

[9] Growth and development are obviously matters of degree; one organism can be developing more rapidly and more robustly than another. Analogously, flourishing is also a matter of degree. But still it makes sense to say that one organism is flourishing and another is not. In this respect the concept of flourishing is like the concept of being tall, or being overweight, or being smart. In each case there is a kind of measurement that is clearly a matter of degree (height, weight, intelligence). In each case as we move to higher and higher degrees of the measured item, we reach some vague range where it makes sense to attribute an unrelativized description—"she is tall," "he is overweight," "they are smart." The same is true of flourishing. It is a matter of degree, but when a person is flourishing to a sufficiently great extent, it makes sense simply to say that he or she is flourishing.

[10] I here allude to the "function argument" that seems to be present in Book I, Chapter 7 of the *Nicomachean Ethics.*

to fulfill. I have to admit that I am not sure what this function is. But, whatever our true function (if any) may be, some things would probably seem to be necessary conditions for our fulfilment of that function. Whatever precisely flourishing may be, it is reasonable to think that a person needs to be alive and conscious in order to flourish. Furthermore, since serious disability or illness would make it difficult or impossible to learn and grow, and since such development seems to be a component of flourishing, at least a modicum of health also seems necessary. Other conditions would probably be widely accepted: a person needs to have some freedom and opportunity in order to flourish. It is hard to flourish if your thoughts and actions are seriously constrained. Ignorance also presumably impedes flourishing. Accordingly, it seems that education is necessary for flourishing. But we run into debated territory if we try to go much beyond these platitudes.[11] Does a person need a lot of wealth in order to flourish? How about a car and a cell phone? I do not know the answers to these questions. These are problems for some other time—or, more likely, for some other philosopher.[12]

The reader may feel that I am being somewhat flippant about the concept of human flourishing. Perhaps it will seem that since my theory makes essential use of the concept, I have an obligation to say much more. But it is not clear to me that this is correct.

I do not assume that all readers will have the same view about what constitutes human flourishing. If a reader in fact has a view about human flourishing, then he or she is invited to make use of that view in the interpretation of my proposal about justice. If you are such a reader, then you are encouraged to proceed in this way: start with your own preferred view about human flourishing. Making use of that view, understand a community essential need as one that must be satisfied in order for a person to flourish (as you understand flourishing); but also as one whose satisfaction would normally require the cooperative efforts of a community. My view, as understood from your perspective, is the view that needs such as

[11] Aristotle says some surprising things about necessary conditions for flourishing. For example, he seems to say that you cannot flourish as a human being if you are poor or ugly, or if you have "lost good children . . . by death." (In Book I, Chapter 8 of the *Nicomachean Ethics*). I hope that Aristotle was mistaken about these things.

[12] For an outstanding collection of essays on human flourishing, see *Social Philosophy and Policy* 16, 1, Winter 1999, "Human Flourishing," ed. by Ellen Frankel Paul, Fred D. Miller, Jr, and Jeffrey Paul. This volume contains valuable contributions by Thomas Hurka, Richard Arneson, Thomas Hill, Stephen Darwall, Sarah Boadie, Richard Kraut, Thomas Pogge, and others. My own rough conception of flourishing seems to be closest to what Hurka identifies as the "first face" in his "The Three Faces of Flourishing."

these are the ones whose satisfaction is called for by the demands of political economic distributive justice.

I recognize that other readers, who come to the matter with different views about human flourishing, will reach different conclusions about which needs are community essential needs. Accordingly, they will also come to different conclusions about what is required by my theory about justice. My theory, as understood from their perspectives, becomes the view that these somewhat different needs are the ones whose satisfaction is called for by the demands of political economic justice.

Since I am not prepared to defend any detailed view about the concept of human flourishing, I am happy to accommodate a variety of views here. I encourage the reader to make use of his or her own conception of flourishing. I hope that, with the preferred conception of flourishing in place, the reader will be able to appreciate the resulting theory of justice.

There is yet another possibility that may be worth considering. Suppose that the reader, like me, is still a bit unclear about what makes for human flourishing. Then my theory of justice can be "reverse engineered" so as to suggest a view about flourishing. It works like this: start by imagining a country in which various benefits and burdens are being distributed to the citizens. Suppose that as you contemplate the situation in this country it strikes you that the level of political economic distributive justice is not as high as it might have been. Try to identify the source of the difficulty. Which citizens are suffering the injustice? Are there some identifiable needs that are going unsatisfied? Would the level of justice in the community be increased if the government ensured that such needs were met? If so, then these needs are—as you see things—community essential needs. Accordingly, you can conclude that these are needs that must be satisfied in order for a person to flourish as a human being. In this way, by implicit appeal to the proposed theory of justice, you may gain a deeper insight into your own conception of human flourishing.

9.2.2 Justice for all: or members only?

I turn now to a second bit of unfinished business.

Here is a letter that I found in a website[13] about immigration problems:

When I was a child, I didn't think we were different from anyone else. I didn't know I was illegal until I was 16 years old. I thought I had been born here. But my mother told me that I was born in Mexico and brought to the United States when I was about 11 months old. My mother told me this because I was graduating High School a year early and I was going

[13] Retrieved from http://myimmigrationstory.com/older-stories.

> to apply for college. She knew it was going to be a problem. It hurt me to know all my hard work was for nothing. I cannot get a driver's license or a Social Security Number. Basically I can't get anything. Now I am 26. I got caught driving without a license about 5 months ago. They took me to jail for three days. I thought they were going to deport me. But no instead I have a year to go back to Mexico. Which I know nothing about... I don't know anyone down there. Everyone I know is here in the United States. I don't know what I'm going to do. All my life all I've known is here. Please continue to fight for us illegal immigrants. Everyone deserves a chance right? *Lorena Fresno, California*

What should a desertist say about Lorena's case? Is she right? Does she deserve a chance to stay in the United States? Would she be suffering an injustice if she were sent back to Mexico? Could the United States deport her without thereby decreasing its level of political economic distributive justice?

When confronted with questions like these, some of us just crinkle up our foreheads and "see" that in virtue of having been raised here since infancy, Lorena deserves a chance to stay in the United States; she deserves to have the opportunity to get a driver's license and a social security number. Others crinkle up their foreheads and "see" that the fact that she was raised here does not make it the case that she deserves these things from the United States government. After all, she is not a citizen. The laws of the United States declare that since Lorena is not a citizen, she is not entitled to get from the government all the benefits that she would have gotten if she had been an otherwise similar citizen. Some may feel that the laws are approximately right in this matter. As they see it, the level of political economic justice in the United States is not affected by the treatment it affords to people like Lorena. Others may feel that Lorena deserves from the United States as much as any citizen; failing to ensure that people like her get what they deserve would lower the level of distributive justice in the United States significantly. It seems like a stand-off. The advocates of the different positions might then start talking about other matters, such as how painful it would be for Lorena to wander aimlessly around in Mexico, or how granting her citizenship would encourage other illegal immigrants to come to the United States. None of these considerations is (prima facie, anyway) relevant to the question that interests me here: is it the case that, in virtue of having been raised from early childhood here, Lorena deserves a chance to stay? And hence—for desertists, anyway—none of these other questions is relevant to the question whether political economic justice requires that Lorena be deported.

While some deep questions will have to go unanswered here, it is possible to say a few things about Lorena's case.

1. I think we can agree that Lorena is failing to get certain benefits that she needs in order to flourish as a human being. For example, she needs to live

in a country that will ensure that she has the opportunity to get a decent education and that she has access to healthcare. Lorena herself mentioned some things that seem to me to be pretty uncontroversial. She cannot get a secure job if she has no social security number and no driver's license. She needs to have the things that are necessary conditions for employment.

2. I think we can also agree that without the cooperation and help of suitable agencies of the government, Lorena will not be able to secure these benefits. She cannot give herself a social security number or a driver's license. She cannot give herself a decent education or healthcare. Just as she needs a government to construct roads and sewer lines, she needs a government to provide these benefits.
3. Thus, all of these things are community essential needs. They are things Lorena needs in order to flourish as a human being; they are things that require the cooperative efforts of a community. Her desert of these things therefore counts as political economic desert, and the benefits themselves count as political economic deserts.
4. Since Lorena is not getting these things that she deserves in this way, she is suffering a political economic injustice.
5. Since Lorena is evidently living in Fresno California, we can conclude that there is someone who is living in the United States and who deserves to live in a country that ensures that she receives certain benefits; but we can also conclude that this person is failing to receive the deserved benefits. This might suggest that the United States is guilty of imposing a political economic injustice; it might seem to be a black mark against our country. But there is a big difference between saying that Lorena deserves to live in a country that ensures that she gets certain benefits, and saying that since she lives in the United States, she deserves to get them *from the United States.* Maybe she deserves them, but not from the United States.

This leaves us with a puzzle. Surely many thoughtful people, when contemplating cases like Lorena's, will feel that the United States cannot simply walk away from these cases, even if the individuals involved are not citizens. Perhaps we can say this: on moral grounds (not strictly as a matter of distributive justice) the United States has an obligation to provide Lorena with an opportunity to become a citizen, or at least to become a legal resident. And then, if she takes advantage of that opportunity, in virtue of her citizenship or legal residency, and also partly in virtue of the regulations included in the institutions specifying how people in her category are to be treated, she would be entitled to the benefits specified by the law. And then, given that entitlement generates desert, she would deserve to receive what has been promised to her. In that case, if the United States decides to grant her citizenship, but then fails to ensure that she gets the things to which she is entitled, the United States will be guilty of a failure that adversely affects the level of political economic distributive justice here.

Another possible account might be worthy of consideration. Perhaps we can say that in virtue of the fact that she has lived in the United States for such a long time, Lorena deserves certain things from the country. Among these things, perhaps, is this: that the United States establish a set of regulations bearing on the circumstances of undocumented people living within its borders. For convenience, we can refer to such a set of regulations as an "immigration institution." There are many different ways in which such an institution could be organized. Among them, some are better in various ways than others. Following the pattern introduced earlier, we can say that some of these institutions fall into the deserved range; Lorena and others in similar circumstances deserve to have one of these immigration institutions set up here in the United States. Then, if the United States fails to set up one of these deserved institutions, this failure will serve to decrease the level of political economic distributive justice in the country. Similarly, if the institution is set up, but Lorena has no opportunity to make use of its provisions, the level of political economic distributive justice here will again be adversely affected.

I mention these alternatives merely as possibilities. I do not have a settled view about how best to explain what justice requires in the case of resident non-citizens.

Another closely related and troubling case involves people who want to come to the United States but who—unlike Lorena—are currently not here at all. Do such non-residents deserve an opportunity to come to the United States? If so, does their desert of this benefit count as political economic desert? And if the United States refuses to open its doors to them, does this serve to lower the level of political economic distributive justice here? These are difficult questions that I currently cannot answer.

There are still other deep and difficult questions concerning membership in benefit granting communities. One of these concerns global justice. Consider the entire population of the world as a whole. Although I do not have any analysis of the concept of a society, nevertheless I am uneasy about the notion that there is a "universal society" to which every human being on earth belongs. If there is such a society, and if people deserve certain political economic deserts from it, then my theory of justice applies just as well to it as it does to the United States or to Sweden. In this case, the level of global political economic justice could be understood to be the extent to which people receive the political economic deserts that they deserve from the world government.

On the other hand, if there is no such thing as the universal society, then there is no such state to be evaluated for political economic justice. Of course, we could still say that millions of people deserve millions of things. Among these things are many political economic deserts that people are not receiving. In that case, there is a huge injustice in the world. It is consistent with this to say that there is no nation, or society, or community that gets a black mark in virtue of those injustices.

When such widespread injustices take place, various governments may come to have moral obligations to try to offer aid. In my view, they would have these obligations if the desert adjusted utility of their so offering were greater than the desert adjusted utility of any alternative available to them. Other theories about morally right action would offer different accounts of the relevant moral obligations. But, as I have emphasized in several places already, there is a difference between saying that someone morally ought to do something and saying that some country gets a black mark in the column marked "political economic distributive justice" if they fail to do it. Even if some governments had moral obligations to offer aid to some non-citizens, it does not follow that failure to provide this aid would yield lower levels of political economic justice for those countries. They run that risk only if they fail to provide political economic deserts to those who deserve those deserts from them.

This hardly ends the catalog of puzzles about states, individuals, and justice. I have said nothing about intergenerational justice. Consider generations of citizens who will exist in the future; suppose those future people will have community essential needs; suppose our current government could do things today that would ensure that those future needs are met; but suppose, as seems likely in certain well publicized cases, that the current government behaves in such a way as to make it difficult or impossible for the needs of those future citizens to be met. Does that constitute a black mark against our current government? Must we say that the level of political economic distributive justice of our country now is adversely affected in virtue of the way future citizens fare as a result of its decisions?

This leads to an even deeper question: suppose the current government behaves in such a way as to prevent the existence of millions of people who might otherwise exist. Clearly, if a person never comes into existence, he or she does not flourish as a human being. I do not know whether it is correct to say that the community essential needs of such people are not being met; or whether, on the other hand, it would be correct to say that since these people do not exist, they have no needs. As a result, I do not know what to say about how the level of political economic distributive justice of our current government is affected by its behavior vis-à-vis these possible people. This is yet another bit of unfinished business.

9.2.3 *More on approximations to perfect justice*

In this book I have defended a view about distributive justice. In most cases I focused on a theory about perfect political economic distributive justice—PEDa. Where less-than-perfect distributive justice is concerned, I have committed myself to the idea that one situation is more just than another if the one "more closely approximates" perfect justice. This is the import of principle PEDc (where "c" stands for "comparative"):

> PEDc: There is greater political economic distributive justice in a group, G1, than there is in another group, G2, if and only if the situation in G1 more closely approximates perfect political economic distributive justice as measured by PEDa than does the situation in G2.

In section 3.2, when I introduced a comparative form of the principle about cosmic justice, I briefly mentioned a problem about *close approximation*. I explained why it would be a mistake to measure the relevant sort of proximity simply by appeal to what I there called "the receipt/desert ratio"—roughly the percentage of cases in which people get precisely what they deserve. Consider an example involving two cases. In the first, only a small percentage of the population is getting precisely what they deserve. In the second, a larger percentage of the population is getting precisely what they deserve. But in addition imagine that those in the first case who do not get precisely what they deserve are getting things *very close* to what they deserve, and at times *very close* to the times at which they deserve these things, etc. while in the second case those who fail to get precisely what they deserve instead do not get anything even slightly like the things they deserve. In cases like this, we may want to say that even though the percentage of cases in which people get precisely what they deserve is smaller in the first case, the overall level of justice there is higher.

Earlier I mentioned a variety of factors that might bear on the extent to which an imperfect distribution approximates a perfect one. Among these factors was *timing*. I suggested that, other things being equal, there is a closer approximation to perfect justice if people receive the things they deserve at moments closer in time to the moment at which they deserve to be getting them. Another factor was *amount*. In many cases (though clearly not in all) the deserved item is something that comes in measurable amounts. Money and happiness are two important examples. I suggested that, other things being equal, there is a closer approximation to perfect justice if people receive amounts of the deserved item that are closer to the amount that they deserve.

I also mentioned that some deserved items do not come in convenient measurable amounts. This is especially important in the case of political economic distributive justice. As I see it, we deserve a variety of things that are not open to easy measurement or comparison. For example, someone might deserve access to a judicial system that will provide him with a fair, speedy, and not too expensive trial if he is accused of having committed a crime. If we are given clear accounts of two significantly different less-than-perfect judicial systems, we may think we can see that one is closer to what we deserve than the other. But it is unlikely that such approximations to perfection can be measured on any objective scale. If another person claims not to see what we think we see, it may be difficult to show that our judgment is right and his wrong.

I suggested earlier that where imperfect distributive justice is concerned, we are somehow to take account of all of the considerations that bear on the extent to which some distribution departs from perfection. Then, taking account of all these departures, we are to find the overall extent to which a given distribution approximates perfect justice. I did not say much more and I admitted that the account was incomplete.

Now I need to make another admission: I am not able to provide a complete and detailed account of how these approximations are to be made or how they are to be combined so as to yield an overall level of less-than-perfect justice. This remains yet another bit of unfinished business.

In his book *The Geometry of Desert*, Shelly Kagan delves very deeply into a closely related question. He asks us to focus on a sort of moral desert. He assumes that what is deserved is always some measurable amount of welfare. He also assumes that the basis on which these bits of welfare are deserved is always a measurable amount of virtue and vice. He then proceeds to enquire into the general principles that bear on the intrinsic values of various levels of receipt given various levels of desert. Thus, for example, he asks us to imagine a case in which there are two people, one who rates very high with respect to virtue and the other who rates lower. Suppose now we are unable to ensure that either gets precisely what he deserves, but that we can give a boost to just one of them. Whichever we choose, he will get closer to the level of welfare that he deserves. Now Kagan asks whether it is intrinsically better to give the boost to the already better off person who starts at a higher level of virtue, or to give it to the already less well off person who starts at a lower level of virtue. This is a profoundly difficult question. But note that Kagan's questions are structurally much easier than the questions I am here trying to evade. For in Kagan's discussion there is the simplifying assumption that there is just one type of desert—welfare—and that this type of desert comes in convenient measurable doses. Also, in Kagan's discussion there is the further simplifying assumption that there is just one type of desert base—moral virtue—and that this too comes in convenient measurable doses. This makes it possible for Kagan to make use of ingenious and helpful graphs to illustrate geometric relations between desert, receipt, and intrinsic value. On the view I am discussing, on the other hand, there are many independent sorts of deserved treatment. Many of these do not come in readily measurable quantities; and even when two of them are measurable, there is no guarantee that they are measurable on the same scale. No convenient system of comparative weighting may be available. The same is true of the plurality of desert bases that I have described. It may be impossible to come up with an overall measure of a person's total level of political economic desert and it may be impossible to draw intelligible graphs to illustrate relations between political economic deserts, political economic desert bases, and justice. For all these reasons, the project that I am here trying to evade seems to me to be considerably less tractable than Kagan's project. Accordingly, I feel a bit less embarrassed by my inability to complete it.

Appendix A: A Note on Method

In the appendices I discuss some matters that are somewhat more personal than the matters discussed in the text of the book. Since, as I see it, it would be possible to understand the proposed theory of justice and its defense without delving into these topics, I have placed these discussions here rather than in the text. But perhaps some readers will find them interesting.

Here in Appendix A, I try to describe what I take to be a reasonable way of pursuing and defending a certain sort of philosophical view. This also serves to explain the sort of defense I take myself to have provided for my own view in this book. In Appendix B, I discuss an even more personal matter. In other work I have defended a desertist theory of moral obligation. In this book I defend a desertist theory of political economic distributive justice. A number of friends and colleagues have asked me to explain how, in my view, these theories are related. I give my answer in Appendix B.

The latter part of Appendix B is in some ways even more personal. I am inclined to think that different contributors to the literature on distributive justice have started out with importantly different conceptions of their target. That is, although different contributors sometimes tell us that they are going to give an account of "justice," in many cases it appears to me that they may have been attempting to give an account of a different subject. And, as I emphasized in earlier chapters, there are several cases in which commentators assume that a philosopher has presented a theory of distributive justice when—even after close scrutiny of the relevant texts—it remains unclear whether the philosopher was even attempting to discuss justice. Perhaps the philosopher was talking about some other topic. In the final paragraphs of Appendix B I discuss some cases that I find especially interesting.

In Appendix A I say a few words about how I have gone about my work in this book; I also comment on what I have hoped to accomplish by working in this way. Perhaps some would say that in doing this I am describing my "philosophical methodology" and its alleged product. I feel a bit uneasy about using such weighty terminology.

My target in this book has been something that I have characterized as *political economic distributive justice.* In Chapter 1 I attempted to identify this target. I did that by reminding the reader of some relatively uncontroversial things that many of us probably already believe about this sort of justice. For example, that it is a virtue of states; that it comes in degrees, so that one state might be more just in this way than another. I believe that citizens generally prefer that their own state be more just rather than less. Of course, there are other features that we hope our states will have, but among them this preference for justice ranks high. There is a great philosophical discussion apparently concerning this concept going back to Aristotle and Plato and coming up to the present.

The level of this sort of justice in a state is determined by the way in which certain benefits and burdens are distributed to the citizens of that state. In an effort to ensure that the reader would be focusing on this same target, I mentioned a bunch of theories concerning it. Among others, I mentioned egalitarianism, sufficientism, the difference principle, and libertarianism. Of course I also mentioned the view whose motto is "receipt in accord with desert." I mentioned these views in part because I thought that readers might be familiar with some of them, and that mentioning them would help to draw the reader's attention to the target I meant to be discussing. I wanted to say, roughly, that political economic distributive justice is the item such that each of these views is a proposed general principle about it.

We often talk about the level of justice in some society. We find nothing wrong with such talk and seem to understand it well enough for practical purposes. Thus, for example, we would not be mystified if someone were to say that there was a serious injustice in the United States during Jim Crow times, and that fortunately things now seem somewhat improved. Nor would we be mystified if someone were to say that as a matter of justice, same-sex couples who want to marry should not be forced to confront insurmountable legal barriers. When we hear about the legal restrictions on education, speech, travel, employment, and due process for women in certain foreign countries, we may say that women there are forced to live in a profoundly unjust system. Such remarks as these are common coin. Whether we agree in every case, we seem to understand what is meant by such remarks. We are familiar enough with the concept of justice for ordinary purposes. Nevertheless, if someone were to demand a deeper explanation, we might be nonplussed. We might not be able to say, in fully general terms, precisely why these arrangements are unjust. That is, we might not be able to say *what makes for injustice,* or explain why these unjust arrangements are unjust. Perhaps different speakers, familiar with different philosophical traditions, would be inclined to explain the injustices by appeal to different theories of justice. But on the other hand, some speakers would reject those theories or might not understand how they are supposed to explain the concept of justice. So the concept of political economic distributive justice is familiar and historically important, but at the same time controversial. It would be nice to have a clear account of what makes for this sort of justice.

I find that I have pretty clear intuitions about the level of justice in a variety of relatively uncontroversial cases. I described one such case in section 5.1 where I talked about a country in which there was thorough-going discrimination against women. In the imagined country, boys would get free public education, but girls would not be permitted to go to school. Girls would remain illiterate. Young men would be able to get drivers licenses but young women would not be permitted to drive. Opportunities to vote, to travel freely, to hold down jobs and other such things would also be subject to pervasive gender based discrimination. My intuition about this country is that the level of justice is low. I trust that the reader would agree.

I also sketched examples concerning comparisons between different countries. In one place I discussed two countries in which precisely the same distributional policies are in place so that the pattern of distribution of benefits and burdens is the same. But

I stipulated that one country had ten times the population of the other. My clear intuition in that case was that these countries would not differ in levels of justice, though they would differ in total levels of welfare or happiness or money. Again, I trust that the reader will share my intuition.

In some examples that I discussed, I imagined cases in which citizens do not enjoy equal levels of happiness. In one case[1] I stipulated that the laws and policies and procedures concerning the distribution of benefits and burdens in two countries are alike and are equally enforced. I went on to say that in one country the citizens naturally tend to be pretty glum, whereas in the other they naturally tend to be somewhat more chipper. I stipulated that though the citizens of the one country tend to be glum, their glumness is not a sign of any mental disorder. They are not clinically depressed. Similarly for the chipperness of the citizens of the other country. They are not manic; just a bit happier than the citizens of the first country.[2]

I said that when I try to evaluate these countries for political economic distributive justice, I find that this difference in happiness levels is in itself irrelevant. In my view, insofar as political economic distributive justice is concerned, it is not the business of a government to try to ensure that citizens are equally happy.[3] I imagined an "External Justice Review Board." As I see it, if there were such a board, and if it were called upon to evaluate the two countries I have imagined, the members of the board might be disappointed to find that the citizens of one country are less happy than the citizens of the other, but they would not allow this unfortunate fact by itself to affect their judgment about the levels of justice in the countries. They might want to look into the question whether the difference in happiness levels is due to a difference in levels of justice. But such a board could find the countries to be equally just.

A similar thing happens in cases in which citizens suffer injuries or insults that are of a purely private nature. For example, I imagined a case in which a neighbor is rude to me and refuses to offer a proper apology.[4] I said that as far as I can see, though I would fail to get something I deserve in this case, my failure to receive it would not adversely affect the level of political economic distributive justice in the country. It would be a private matter

[1] In section 5.1.

[2] There are of course popular stereotypes according to which the citizens of certain countries are happier than the citizens of other countries. Serious researchers have attempted to test these stereotypes empirically. For one of the most comprehensive attempts to evaluate countries for levels of happiness, see the World Happiness Report, which can be found at: http://unsdsn.org/resources/publications/world-happiness-report-2013.

[3] It is important in this context to see that my claim is restricted to the business of governments *insofar as political economic distributive justice is concerned.* I think it is fairly clear that governments may legitimately engage in all sorts of other activities. Perhaps in some circumstances a government could legitimately try to make its citizens happier. My point is that *insofar as justice is concerned*, that would not be a job for government. My thanks to Mark Walker for helping me to appreciate the importance of restricting the claim about the business of government to matters of justice.

[4] Section 3.2.

between my neighbor and me. It is not the business of government to ensure that we get all the apologies that are due to us from our neighbors.

There are, of course, plenty of examples in which my own intuitions are not quite so settled. Furthermore, I assume that there are plenty of examples in which the reader might not share my intuitions. These would be hard cases. They are put aside for the time being. I will come back to them in a moment.

Having identified the target of the enquiry, and having identified some clear intuitions about its application in some relatively clear cases, I moved on to my main project. My central aim in this book has been to provide an account of the necessary and sufficient conditions for perfect political economic distributive justice. I hope that the proposed conditions would not be merely accidentally associated with perfect justice; rather, the presence of these conditions should explain why the state is just; if a state is just, it should be just *in virtue of the fact that* these conditions obtain.[5]

My view makes use of some assumptions. First, I assume that there are certain types of benefit and burden such that states are called upon to distribute these to their citizens. Presumably Aristotle had these in mind when he said that there are certain benefits such that it "falls to the state" to distribute them. I called these "political economic deserts." I also assume that there are certain features of citizens, such that it is the business of states, when distributing these benefits and burdens, to try to distribute them in accord with these features, and to attempt to ensure that the benefits are properly matched to the features. I called these features "political economic desert bases." I tried to explain these deserts and desert bases by appeal to the concept of a community essential need. Something is a community essential need if it is something that people need in order to flourish as human beings, but cannot get on their own. They need the cooperative efforts of a community to secure these goods. My main claim is that there is perfect political economic distributive justice in a state when the state ensures that citizens receive the political economic deserts that they deserve in virtue of their possession of the relevant political economic desert bases.

Suppose we understand the concepts of political economic deserts, desert bases, and distributors. Then we will be able to understand the resulting theory of political economic distributive justice. We can then reflect on the implications of the theory of justice. When I do this, I find that my most firm and well thought out pre-theoretic intuitions about which situations are perfectly just are all ones that the theory declares to be perfectly just; I also find that my most firm and well thought out pre-theoretic intuitions about which situations are seriously unjust are all ones that the theory declares to be seriously unjust.[6]

[5] In a passage I quoted earlier, G. E. Moore highlights the importance of getting clear on our question before setting out to answer it. I hope I have not made the mistake against which Moore warned. I take my question here to be reasonably clear: what makes for political economic distributive justice in a state?

[6] When I speak of "intuitions" here, I do not mean to suggest the outputs of some powerful and mysterious epistemic faculty. Like so many other philosophers who have used the term, for me an intuition is just a statement that seems true even though it is not the product of straightforward

Furthermore, when a situation seems unjust, and I reflect on the features of the situation that seem to me to be the source of the injustice, I generally discover that those are precisely the features that the theory identifies as the ones that make for injustice.

Suppose I were to discover that the theory of justice had unacceptable implications for some class of cases. Suppose it turned out that my intuitions about those cases were in conflict with the implications of the theory. Then I would have several options. One option would be to reconsider my intuitions about the troubling cases in light of the theory. Maybe, upon seeing how the theory explains the justice of the situation, I would come to see that what I formerly took to be my final judgments about the cases were really open to revision. Upon further reflection, I might be prepared to let them go. Another option would be to discard my theory of justice. I could then attempt to come up with a new theory that would get the case right while continuing to adjudicate clear cases as before. Another option would be to retain the core principle of my theory of justice but to adjust my view about political economic deserts, or my view about political economic desert bases, or my view about community essential needs. Maybe I would have to reconsider my ideas about human flourishing. Perhaps with some slight "tweak" of one of these concepts, I would find a way to retain the core of the theory but to alter its implications enough so as to make it imply the judgments about cases that I find hard to resist. But suppose that after due reflection and tweaking, I find myself believing a general theory that entails the particular intuitions that seem right to me. The whole package seems stable. Then I am in reflective equilibrium with that theory of justice.

In fact I am now inclined to think that I am in reflective equilibrium with the proposed theory of political economic distributive justice based on the relevant claims about deserts and desert bases and community essential needs. The theory, so understood, seems to yield results consistent with my firm intuitions about cases. I am happy with the theory. (Of course, I recognize that some insightful critic very well may come up with a surprising case that upsets my equilibrium. Someone might remind me of a type of case about which the theory has implications that I cannot accept.)

Some philosophers have suggested that reflective equilibrium yields epistemic justification.[7] If this were true, then I would now be justified in believing my theory of justice,

perception or memory or merely a matter of introspection. From the fact that something is an intuition, nothing follows about its epistemic status. For all I know, many of my intuitions are false.

[7] Rawls discusses this question in section 87 "Remarks on Justification" in *A Theory of Justice*. He makes a number of remarks that suggest that he thinks that if we can get ourselves into reflective equilibrium with a theory of justice, then we will be justified in believing that theory to be true. For example, he says "I have not proceeded then as if first principles, or conditions thereon, or definitions either, have special features that permit them a peculiar place in justifying a moral doctrine. They are central elements and devices of theory, but justification rests upon the entire conception and how it fits in with and organizes our considered judgments in reflective equilibrium. As we have noted before, justification is a matter of the mutual support of many considerations, of everything fitting together into one coherent view" Rawls (1971: 507). I find remarks such as this inconclusive; but some commentators confidently affirm that Rawls thought that reflective equilibrium yields epistemic justification. See, for example, the article on "Reflective Equilibrium" by

together with the desert claims that I have associated with it. And if the theory is in fact true, then I would know it to be true.

But I am not claiming that reflective equilibrium yields epistemic justification. I think that it is possible for us to juggle completely unjustified theories and completely unjustified intuitions about cases in such a way as to get ourselves into completely unjustified reflective equilibrium with a theory that we have no business believing in the first place.[8] I acknowledge that this latest description may be true of me and my acceptance of my theory of political economic distributive justice.[9]

Even if it does not yield epistemic justification, I like being in reflective equilibrium. There are several nice things about it. When I am in reflective equilibrium concerning my theory of justice, then my intuitions about specific cases involving justice and my general theory about political economic distributive justice seem to fit together into one coherent whole. I find that each part seems plausible, and there seems to be no inconsistency among the parts. Certain components of the package seem to support or explain other parts. When, after thinking about some subject matter for a while, and considering various theories, I find that my beliefs about that subject matter have this sort of coherence, I feel good about it. I think then that there is a chance that the whole package might be true. It is different when I recognize that there are inconsistencies in my beliefs about some subject matter, for in that case I am pretty sure that at least some of my beliefs are wrong and need to be revised.

Furthermore, since I take myself to be in reflective equilibrium about distributive justice, I feel that I have a more clearly articulated understanding of the various concepts associated with desert, receipt, justice, the business of governments, etc. Each concept seems clearer when I see how it coheres with the other concepts in the vicinity. I can make use of this increased clarity. I can now propose a refinement of the ideas associated with the terminology that I used pre-theoretically to describe situations involving desert, receipt, justice, the business of governments, etc. I can say that I must have been using that terminology in a somewhat confused way to express vague ideas that can be explicated by the clearer ideas that figure in the coherent theory that I now accept. I can then think something like this: "now I see more clearly what I was confusedly trying to say previously."

Another nice feature of being in reflective equilibrium about distributive justice is that being in this state makes me feel that I have a deeper understanding of my reasons for thinking that certain arrangements are perfectly just and others are not. If, prior to

Norman Daniels in the *Stanford Encyclopedia of Philosophy*. Daniels says "The method of reflective equilibrium thus plays a role in both the construction and justification of Rawls's theory of justice."

[8] Hare (1973) and Brandt (1979, 1990) made this point. Hare approvingly quotes a remarkable passage from Plato: "If a man starts from something he knows not, and the end and middle of his argument are tangled together out of what he knows not, how can such a mere consensus ever turn into knowledge?" (Rep. 533 c).

[9] My view here is similar in important ways to the view defended by Michael DePaul in DePaul (1998: 293–310).

developing the theory, someone were to ask me why I think that a certain arrangement is more just than a certain other arrangement, I might have been baffled. Perhaps the best I could then say was that when I contemplate the two situations, it just seems to me that one is more just than the other. I then had no deeper explanation. But now if I should be asked the same question, I will be able to explain my reasons for holding that view, or at least I will know what sort of consideration ought to be relevant. I will not feel as if my thoughts about justice are just an unconnected bundle of arbitrary prejudices. (I admit that they might be a nicely coherent and mutually supporting bundle of prejudices.)

People disagree about justice. If I state my view about a case, someone may challenge me. Someone may ask me to defend my view. If I am in reflective equilibrium with a theory of justice, I will be able to offer responses to such challenges. I will be able to explain my general theory and I will be able to show that my particular judgment follows from the theory together with some background facts. I am not claiming that my defense would amount to irresistible proof; my interlocutor might simply reject my theory. But at least the original question would not utterly baffle me. I would have an answer—so far as it goes. If my interlocutor cannot refute my theory, and has no better theory of his own, my response may be sufficient as a reply to his objection.

Earlier I mentioned some hard cases. These are cases about which I had no settled pre-theoretical intuitions. I did not know what to say about these cases. But now that I take myself to be in reflective equilibrium with my theory of justice, I may be able to determine what the theory implies about these hard cases. If I can succeed at this, I will then see what I ought to believe about the case—ought to believe, that is, given my commitment to my theory. Thus, reflective equilibrium may shed light into dark corners.

It is easy to imagine that my pre-theoretic beliefs about the levels of justice in various cases might not have been entirely coherent. Perhaps I believed that there would be perfect justice in one imaginary state, but not in another. Perhaps the cases were so similar that it was hard for me to see why I did not come to the same conclusion about both. But now that I am in reflective equilibrium with a theory of justice, I may be able to understand what previously eluded me. Maybe now I can see that in spite of their superficial similarity, the cases were actually different with respect to some item that—according to the theory—bears on distributive justice. Or perhaps in light of my acceptance of the general theory, I will revise my view about one of the cases. Having the general theory at hand may enable me to refine my view so as to bring coherence to my beliefs where I previously was inclined to believe a collection of things that seemed to be in tension.

These are all nice things about being in reflective equilibrium with a theory of justice. But I want to emphasize that I am not claiming that this "niceness" shows that the theory is true. It goes a long way toward showing that it is coherent; it helps to clarify my thoughts and demonstrate their connections; it gives me suggestions about how to move from my clear intuitions about easy cases to views about harder cases about which I have no intuitions. It also suggests ways in which I can respond to challenges.

So I think I have a coherent collection of views about political economic desert and desert bases, the business of governments, community essential needs, and political economic distributive justice. I offer this collection of views to you as a package. I invite you to contemplate the views about political economic deserts and political economic desert bases; I invite you to contemplate the way the overall theory makes use of these ideas in the construction of a principle about political economic distributive justice; I invite you to consider the implications of the theory for cases; I invite you to reflect on the cases to see whether the implications of the theory coincide with your firm and well-considered intuitions. If you do this, and you also can get yourself into reflective equilibrium with the theory, then I invite you to do so. If some cases remain recalcitrant, I encourage you to see if you can tweak some part of the theory so as to make it yield the judgments that you cannot abandon. Perhaps you will be able to get yourself into reflective equilibrium with a theory that is a close relative to the one I have spelled out. I do not claim that this will give you further evidence that the theory is true, but it will give you something apparently coherent that you can believe about justice and the related concepts. You will also enjoy all the benefits that I have listed.

This seems to me to be a sensible way of doing philosophy. It does not involve any unrealistic views about the nature of "intuition." It does not involve any unrealistic views about the power of reflective equilibrium to serve as a gateway to truth or epistemic justification. It is modest. I think it is likely that, if they reflect with an open mind on their own practice, many other philosophers will realize that in at least some instances, when they have been struggling to develop a philosophical theory, they have been engaged in a project with roughly the same structure as the one I have described here.

Appendix B: Two Helpings of Desert

In papers and book chapters that I wrote over a period of quite a few years, I defended an idea that I (somewhat misleadingly) sometimes called "adjusting utility for justice."[1] In some of those papers I focused on a well-known category of objections to standard forms of act utilitarianism. Those forms of utilitarianism imply that there is a moral obligation to perform the alternative that yields the greatest amount of utility no matter how the utility is divided up among recipients. In familiar cases such as the Small Southern Town and the Organ Harvest, the implication is that morality may sometimes require us to impose huge undeserved harms on some individuals in order to give benefits to others. This implication strikes many (including me) as being very unattractive. I claimed that a revised form of utilitarianism would avoid these problems. Roughly, the idea was that we should adjust the value of each benefit so as to take account of the extent to which the recipient deserves that benefit. A benefit of a given absolute size would have greater adjusted value if it went to a recipient who deserves it; a benefit of the same absolute size would have a lower adjusted value if it went to a recipient who does not deserve it. According to the revised form of utilitarianism, we are not required to perform the act that maximizes absolute utility; instead we are required to perform the act that maximizes desert adjusted utility. I claimed that this revision would allow us to maintain a form of utilitarianism while evading the difficulty.

In this book I have again appealed to the concept of desert. I characterized desertist theories of justice as ones that conform, in one way or another, to the idea that justice is receipt in accord with desert. In Chapter 3 I distinguished among several different desertist theories of distributive justice. I singled out one of these for special attention. That is my theory of political economic distributive justice, formulated as the combination of PEDa and PEDc. According to that theory, there is perfect political economic distributive justice in a country if and only if in every case in which a citizen of that country deserves a political economic desert in virtue of having a political economic desert base, he or she receives that desert from the appropriate political economic distributor.

[1] I first sketched this idea in my 1992 *Confrontations with the Reaper* (182–90). There I called it "justicism." Then in my 2004 *Pleasure and the Good Life* (192–8) I presented a more complicated version of the axiological component that I called "Subject's Desert Adjusted Intrinsic Attitudinal Hedonism." Similar ideas were defended in "The Good Life: A Defense of Attitudinal Hedonism," *Philosophy and Phenomenological Research* LXV, 3 (November, 2002), pp. 604–28. The main idea was presented in "Adjusting Utility for Justice," *Philosophy and Phenomenological Research* LV, 3 (September, 1995), pp. 567–85. It might have been somewhat less misleading if I had dubbed it "adjusting utility for desert." A similar idea was put to use in my "Justice, Desert, and the Repugnant Conclusion," *Utilitas* 7, 2 (November, 1995), pp. 189–206. In light of criticism by Gustaf Arrhenius in "Feldman's Desert Adjusted Utilitarianism and Population Ethics," *Utilitas* xv, 225–36, I now realize that the main proposal of that paper needs reconsideration.

Thus I have made essential use of the concept of desert in two different contexts. First I used it in the formulation of my desert-adjusted form of act utilitarianism (or "DAU"), and then I used it again in the formulation of my desertist theory of distributive justice (or "PED"). The reader may be puzzled about how these two views are intended to be related. One possibility is that the new theory—PED—is just a reformulation of the old theory—DAU. A second possibility is that PED is intended to supersede DAU. It might appear that in light of criticism, or perhaps as a result of further reflection, I have come to see that the problems with DAU are insurmountable; perhaps I have concluded that the time has come to retire DAU; instead, I now want to advocate for PED. A third possibility is that DAU and PED are just two independent theories about two independent topics, in two different realms of philosophy. Maybe I want to retain DAU in its realm, and at the same time to embrace PED in its realm. But then there is a question about the connections between the theories. Does either entail the other? Does commitment to one naturally lead to commitment to the other? Are they parts of a "package deal"? Of course there is always the final possibility: maybe it is just a confused blur—two similar theories about two similar topics somehow uneasily crammed together.

My main aim in Appendix B is to explain how the theories are related.

I should start by saying something about what I take to be one of the central realms of moral philosophy. This is *normative ethics proper* or *the ethics of behavior.*[2] The central question in this realm of moral philosophy is a question about morally right actions: what makes morally right actions right? Ideally the answer to that question would come in the form of a criterion of moral rightness—something of the form illustrated by "an action is morally right if and only if it maximizes utility" or "an action is morally right if and only if it can be performed without violating any of God's commands."

Sometimes philosophers insist that a proposed criterion of right action be stated in a somewhat more complicated form. They say that the criterion of right action does not merely give necessary and sufficient conditions for moral rightness; they say that the criterion must furthermore specify that it is in virtue of having the cited feature that right acts are right. So they would prefer that the utilitarian principle be stated in this form: "an action is morally right if and only if *and in virtue of the fact that* it maximizes utility." They would say the same thing about the divine command theory and any other theory in the normative ethics of behavior.

My old theory of desert-adjusted act utilitarianism (DAU) is solidly in the normative ethics of behavior. It purports to give an account of the circumstances under which an action is morally right, or permitted, or "morally OK to do." The theory makes use of the idea that the value of each bit of utility is to be adjusted either upward if the recipient deserves to get it, or downward if the recipient deserves not to get it. Then the desert-adjusted utility of an action is the sum of the desert-adjusted values of all the episodes of

[2] Some other realms of moral philosophy: axiology or the theory of value; virtue/vice theory or the theory of good character; metaethics or the semantics and ontology of ethics; the epistemology of ethics; moral psychology; applied ethics; the history of ethics.

utility in its consequence. This concept of desert-adjusted utility is then used to give the proposed account of morally right action, as follows:

DAU: An action is morally right if and only if no alternative has greater desert-adjusted utility than it has.

If we assume that wrong actions are ones that are not right, we can make further use of DAU to give an account of morally wrong actions; they are ones that fail to maximize desert-adjusted utility. If an action is morally wrong then some alternative has greater desert-adjusted utility than it has. If we think that a morally obligatory action is one that would be wrong to fail to perform, then we again can use DAU. We can say that an action is morally obligatory if it has greater desert-adjusted utility than any alternative. It has this feature: if you fail to do it, you will end up doing something wrong.

DAU has many competitors in the normative ethics of behavior. Other forms of act utilitarianism are structurally like DAU, but give a different characterization of utility. Preference Act Utilitarianism says that we should maximize the net extent to which preferences are satisfied in the consequence; Ideal Act Utilitarianism says that we should maximize the balance of intrinsic good over intrinsic evil in the consequence. A form of rule utilitarianism would say that an action is morally right if and only if it is permitted by the code of rules whose general acceptance would maximize utility. A form of Rossianism makes use of the notions of prima facie rightness and prima facie wrongness. It would say that an action is morally right if and only if no alternative has a greater balance of prima facie rightness over prima facie wrongness. A form of Kantianism would say that the rightness of an action depends upon a certain feature of the maxim under which it would be performed. A maxim is universalizable if the agent who proposes to act on that maxim could consistently will that the universal form of the maxim should be a law of nature. The relevant form of Kantianism would say that an action is morally right if and only if its maxim is universalizable. There are, in addition, various forms of virtue ethics, social relativism, and the divine command theory. Though they give different answers, each of these theories purports to answer the same question: what makes morally right actions right? They are the competitors to DAU.

The theory that I have been defending in this book is not a theory in the normative ethics of behavior. It does not propose to tell us what makes right actions right. Instead, as a theory about distributive justice, it purports in part to tell us what makes for perfect distributive justice in a society. That part of the theory is this:

PEDa: There is perfect political economic distributive justice in a country if and only if in every case in which a citizen of that country deserves a political economic desert in virtue of having a political economic desert base, he or she receives that desert from the appropriate political economic distributor.[3]

[3] The name "PEDa" is supposed to indicate that it is a Desertist theory of Political Economic distributive justice—and that it is the "absolute" half of the theory—the half that gives conditions for perfect distributive justice.

The other part of the theory (PEDc) is a principle that says (in effect) that there is greater political economic distributive justice in one country than there is in another if the situation in the one more closely approximates perfect distributive justice than does the situation in the other. I use "PED" or "Political Economic Desertism" to refer to the combination of PEDa and PEDc.

PED is a view about what makes for distributive justice in a state. Accordingly, its competitors are other theories that purport to explain the same phenomenon. They are such theories as all the various forms of egalitarianism, sufficientism, the difference principle, libertarianism, Marxism, and (possibly) prioritarianism. As I have understood these theories, each of them offers an account of what makes for distributive justice in a society; none of them says anything about morally right action. Thus, just to take one simple example, an egalitarianism of wealth would say that a society is perfectly just if and only if every member has just as much wealth as every other member. For another simple example, a corresponding form of sufficientism would say that a society is perfectly just if and only if every member has at least a sufficient amount of wealth. Neither of these theories, on its own, gives us any directions about what we should do.

Thus I have defended a form of desertism about right action (DAU) and a form of desertism about justice (PED). Each is a normative theory; each makes use of the concept of desert. Beyond that, however, the theories have little in common. They differ in many important ways.

1. The theories are in different realms of philosophy. Desert-adjusted act utilitarianism is a theory in the normative ethics of behavior. The desertist theory of political economic distributive justice is a theory in a different realm of philosophy—sometimes known as "Social and Political Philosophy." The former theory purports to say what makes right acts right. It says nothing about justice. The latter theory purports to say what makes a state perfectly just and what makes one state more just than another. It says nothing about morally right action.
2. The theories have different subject matters. DAU is a normative theory designed to yield evaluative conclusions about *actions*, or bits of behavior. PED is a normative theory about *states*, or societies. It is designed to yield evaluative conclusions about which society is more just than which other one.
3. As they evaluate their respective subject matters, each of these theories considers what we may call a "class of comparison." DAU evaluates actions. When it does this, it focuses on these actions in certain important clusters. A relevant cluster would be the set of alternatives open to some agent at some time. DAU then segregates those alternatives into three main groups: the obligatory, the right, and the forbidden. It does not make any cross-agential comparisons. It does not say anything about what makes one act "righter" than another; nor does it say anything about a "perfectly right act." PED does not focus on acts at all. It focuses on states, or societies, or communities. The relevant class of comparison would consist of all other possible states or societies. These are not assumed to be alternatives for anyone; it does not

say anything about which one we morally ought to bring about. It does not segregate them into groups of obligatory, right, and forbidden. Instead, it says what it would take for a state to be perfectly just and it goes on to rank less-than-perfectly-just states according to degrees of political economic distributive justice.

4. The theories are intended to yield different sorts of evaluations. DAU yields evaluations of moral rightness, wrongness, and obligatoriness. It tells us (if I may speak loosely) what we should do. It does not yield any evaluations of degrees of justice. PED yields evaluations of relative degrees of justice. It tells us which society would be more just. It says nothing about obligation, permission, or forbiddenness. It does not tell us what we should do.
5. Although both theories make use of the concept of desert, they make use of different specific forms of desert. DAU makes use of a much wider class of desert bases especially including moral virtue and vice, past suffering, excess receipt, personal promises, family relationships, etc. When DAU asks us to adjust utility for desert, the relevant adjustment is to be made in light of all of these moral desert bases. PED does not make use of any of these specifically moral desert bases. Instead, it makes use only of political economic deserts and bases. I informally characterized political economic desert bases as the ones such that it is the business of a government to take them into account when distributing the various benefits and burdens that it is called upon to distribute. Chief among these are certain sorts of *vulnerability* such as vulnerability to violent attack, or to natural disaster, or to disease. Additionally, I mentioned the need for *opportunity* and I mentioned such things as the need for education, clean water, roads, a judicial system, a banking system. I also mentioned *legitimate entitlement*. As I see it, all such desert bases somehow derive from a community essential need—a need for something that people must have if they are to flourish as human beings, but something that in the normal course of events requires the cooperative efforts of a community to provide. There is not much overlap between the moral desert bases and the political economic desert bases.

It should be clear, then, that DAU and PED are two different theories, about two different subject matters, from two different realms of philosophy. They should not be seen as alternatives or competitors. Although I accept both, it is possible to accept either one without the other.

The difference between the aims and contents of these principles is perhaps most dramatically highlighted by reflection on the theories with which they compete. The theories have entirely different ranges of competitors. Here is a chart that lists, for each theory, some of its main competitors:

Competitors to Desert Adjusted Act Utilitarianism (DAU)

1. Other forms of act utilitarianism (for example, preferential, ideal, expected utility)
2. Forms of rule utilitarianism
3. The Kantian principle about universalizable maxims

4. The Kantian principle about treating people as ends in themselves
5. The Rossian principle about maximizing net prima facie rightness
6. Social relativism
7. The divine command theory
8. Ethical egoism
9. Certain forms of virtue ethics.

Competitors to Desertism about Political Economic Distributive Justice (PED)

1. Forms of egalitarianism (for example, of wealth, of welfare, of opportunity)
2. Forms of sufficientism (for example, of wealth, of welfare, of opportunity)
3. Forms of the difference principle
4. Forms of libertarianism
5. Marxism
6. Prioritarianism.

Earlier (in Chapter 1) I said that Rawls apparently assumed that utilitarianism is one of the main competitors to his own "justice as fairness" conception of distributive justice. (I said a similar thing about Rescher.) It may seem that I am simply rejecting Rawls's idea; that I am listing utilitarianism as a theory in the normative ethics of behavior rather than as a theory in social and political philosophy. Thus it may appear that I am committed to the view that Rawls was fundamentally confused about the nature of the theories he was discussing. This calls for some explanation.

In section 21 of *A Theory of Justice*, Rawls discusses what he takes to be the main alternatives to his own view about distributive justice. He does this by listing the theories of justice that would be up for debate in the Original Position. At the top of Rawls's list we find his own preferred principles—the liberty principle and the difference principle, components of a larger picture known as "Justice as Fairness" (A1, A2b). But just below that, listed among the main competitors to the Rawlsian principles, we find a very mixed bag of principles. First we find "The Principle of Average Utility" (B1) and "The Principle of Average Utility subject to the constraint that a certain social minimum be maintained" (B2a). I take B2 to be a hint of sufficientism. Then Rawls lists "The Classical Principle of Utility" (C1), followed by a principle that would somehow balance considerations of total utility with "a list of prima facie principles (as appropriate)" (D3). I take this to be a hint of Rossianism. The chart concludes by mentioning three forms of egoism[4] including "First-person dictatorship: Everyone is to serve my interests" (E1) and "General: Everyone is permitted to advance his interests as he pleases" (E3).

The thoughtful reader is sure to find Rawls's list puzzling. Recall the context. He is imagining a bunch of "representative men" behind a veil of ignorance trying to choose a conception of distributive justice that will be in place in the society they are to inhabit.

[4] Rawls later says that these forms of egoism should be disregarded.

Rawls offers this as a list of some of the most prominent ideas that would be debated by these choosers in the original position. Rawls's list is puzzling in part because the list seems to include several familiar principles from the normative ethics of behavior (for example, The Classical Principle of Utility[5], a form of Rossianism, and two forms of egoism). While anyone who has taught a course in ethical theory can easily imagine a bunch of people debating the relative merits of ethical egoism and the Rossian theory of prima facie duty, it is not quite so easy to see why the choosers in the original position, trying to find an acceptable principle of distributive justice, would want to spend a lot of time debating the merits of these theories. Surely one of the original choosers would interrupt the discussion; surely he would insist that they leave off this discussion of theories in the normative ethics of behavior and return to the main issue: what principle of distributive justice shall we choose for our society to come? Thus Rawls's list is puzzling because it includes theories that seem not to belong in a discussion of justice. Rawls's list is also puzzling in part because it does not include some of the most familiar and widely debated views about distributive justice (for example, egalitarianism of wealth, libertarianism, Marxism). And of course what puzzles me most is that Rawls does not list any form of desertism among the contending theories of justice. Surely if I were present at the original position, I would want an opportunity to say a few words in defense of such a view. And surely in any reasonably large collection of representative men from the twentieth century there would have to be at least one who would insist that they also discuss the theory behind the motto: "from each according to his ability; to each according to his need."

I have dwelled on these matters because I sometimes fear that there is an important confusion infecting the literature on distributive justice. The confusion in question would be a confusion about whether a theory of distributive justice is intended to give us an account of what makes our actions morally right, or whether on the other hand, it is intended to give us an account of what makes the situation in some society distributively just.[6] This sort of confusion is suggested when a philosopher, purporting to give an

[5] To be fair to Rawls, I should acknowledge that he understands the "Classical Principle of Utility" in what strikes me as an idiosyncratic way. After pointing out that there are many forms of utilitarianism, he says that he will follow Sidgwick in maintaining that the main idea behind utilitarianism is that "society is rightly ordered, and therefore just, when its major institutions are arranged so as to achieve the greatest net balance of satisfaction summed over all the individuals belonging to it" Rawls (1971: section 5). I have studied the relevant passages in Sidgwick; I do not agree with Rawls's interpretation. I think that Sidgwick was a desertist about justice—or at least about what he called "Ideal Justice." I think he optimistically hoped that the establishment of just institutions would probably lead to outcomes with higher utility.

[6] A reader for Oxford University Press suggested that it is impertinent or disrespectful to suggest that Rawls—universally acknowledged to be one of the greatest moral philosophers of recent times—could have confused questions of moral philosophy with questions of political philosophy. I think it is interesting to note that in the introduction to *Political Liberalism* Rawls himself seems to acknowledge that he was guilty of precisely that confusion. He explicitly says "Note that in my summary of the aims of [*A Theory of Justice*], the social contract tradition is seen as a part of moral philosophy and *no distinction is drawn between moral and political philosophy*. In [*A Theory of Justice*] a moral doctrine of justice general in scope is not distinguished from a strictly political

account of a principle about distributive justice, formulates that principle in the deontic style, saying something like: "We ought to see to it that benefits and burdens are distributed equally." Is the philosopher really talking about distributive justice? Or is he talking about what we morally ought to do?[7]

It might be interesting, in this connection, to recall the theory that Parfit identified as the "Deontic Form" of the priority view. As I pointed out at the beginning of Chapter 6, commentators assume that it was intended to be a theory about distributive justice. But note that Parfit indicated that in this form, the priority view is a view about "what we ought to do." If that is right, and his remark was intended seriously, and if the "ought" is intended to be a moral "ought," then the priority view is really not a view about distributive justice. It is really a view in the normative ethics of behavior. It is easy enough to state the view in such a way as to make this evident. Let us say that the priority adjusted welfare of an action is the sum, for all affected parties, of the welfare benefits and burdens they would receive in the consequence of the action, weighted for the recipient's baseline welfare level.[8] The resulting view could be stated in this form:

PRx: An act is morally right if and only if it maximizes priority adjusted welfare.

The natural competitor to this view would be something like this version of the difference principle:

DPx: An act is morally right if and only if it maximizes the welfare of the people in the worst off class.

Another competitor would be my desert-adjusted act utilitarianism.

At the outset of this Appendix, I mentioned that I have taken two helpings of desert. In earlier work I appealed to the concept of desert when I formulated my desert-adjusted act utilitarianism—a theory in the normative ethics of behavior. And then in this book I have appealed to the concept of desert in a different way as I have formulated my desertist theory of political economic distributive justice. I mentioned several questions about the connections between these two desertist views.

The first question was the question whether the view defended in this book is just a revised formulation of the old view. The answer is that it is not. They are two different theories, in different realms of philosophy, with different subject matters.

conception of justice. Nothing is made of the contrast between comprehensive philosophical and moral doctrines and conceptions limited to the domain of the political. In the lectures in this volume, however, these distinctions and related ideas are fundamental" (XV) (emphasis added, FF). This may serve to remind us of the relevance of the warning Moore gave about the importance of being clear about what question you mean to answer before you set about to answer it.

[7] In section 1.2.2, I cited several distinguished philosophers who sometimes state theories of justice in this "deontic" form. Many others do the same thing.

[8] The details concerning how this might be done were spelled out in section 6.2.

The second question is the question whether I am now proposing to toss out the old theory of desert adjusted act utilitarianism, and to advocate for this new desertist theory of political economic distributive justice instead. Again, the answer is "no." Aside from some awkwardness in the name ("adjusting utility for justice"), I still like the old theory.[9] I recognize that it may need some modification, but nothing I say in this book should be taken to suggest that I am giving up DAU in favor of PED. That would be a nonsensical move on my part—giving up a theory in one realm of philosophy in favor of a theory in another realm—as if the theories were in some sort of conflict. In this book I argue for PED; aside from a few brief remarks in this Appendix, I have said little about DAU here.

The third question concerned the connections between the two theories. Does commitment to one of them entail commitment to the other? Would it be a mistake to defend DAU but at the same time to reject PED? Or vice versa? In general, what are the logical relations between the two theories?

The short answer is that there are no such connections between the theories. From the fact that a possible state is perfectly just according to PED, nothing follows about what anyone morally ought to do according to DAU. From the fact that DAU implies that someone ought to do something, nothing follows about what PED implies would be just.

The reader may agree that since PED is not a theory about obligation, it has no immediate implications concerning what anyone ought to do. As a result, there is no way in which the obligations specified by DAU could conflict with those specified by PED: PED does not specify any obligations. But we can introduce an extended sense in which PED might be thought to involve a special sort of obligation; perhaps the reader would feel that more needs to be said concerning the relation between moral obligation and this special sort of obligation arising from considerations of justice. More precisely, the reader might want to know which sort of obligation has priority in cases of conflict.[10] In order to state the question clearly, we need to introduce a concept of obligation involving political economic distributive justice; and in order to do this we need to make some assumptions. Let us assume that whenever a person is about to act, he confronts a set of alternatives. Let us furthermore assume that each of these alternatives would lead to some consequence. And let us finally assume that each of these consequences can be evaluated in terms of political economic distributive justice for the agent's society. In other words, for each alternative available to the agent, there would be a definitive answer to the question "what would be the level of political economic distributive justice in the agent's society if he were to choose this alternative?" Let us say that a person's "justice-related" obligation is to perform the act that maximizes the level of political economic distributive justice in his society.

[9] I should mention that critical discussions by some colleagues have made me realize that I have not yet managed to state the theory in a sufficiently clear and convincing form. For critical discussion, see Carlson (1997); Persson (1997); Vallentyne (1995); Arrhenius (2003: 225–36); Arrhenius (2006), and Kagan (2006). For a reply to Kagan, see Skow (2012b).

[10] In fact, a reader for Oxford University Press raised precisely this question.

In typical circumstances, ordinary citizens have very little opportunity to affect the level of political economic distributive justice in their countries. No matter what I do this morning, the extent to which citizens of the United States receive their political economic deserts will remain pretty much unchanged. As a result, we can say that from the perspective of justice-related obligation, each of my alternatives is permissible. But when we look at the situation from the perspective of moral obligation, we find that my alternatives are not in this way uniformly permissible.

My moral obligation according to DAU depends on the desert adjusted utilities of my alternatives. These utilities, in turn, depend upon the extent to which the various recipients of pleasures and pains in the outcomes deserve to enjoy or suffer those pleasures and pains. The sort of desert that would be relevant in this case is importantly different from the sort of desert I have been discussing in this book—political economic desert. In the moral case, desert involves such factors as family relationships, promises that have been made, past suffering or excess enjoyment, moral virtue and vice . . . None of these factors bears on political economic desert. Someone can have great political economic desert of some benefit while having no moral desert of that same benefit. Suppose I face the choice of either (a1) giving a well-deserved gift to my long-suffering grandmother, or (a2) giving a gift of equal value to a stranger who has done nothing to deserve it, or (a3) wasting the money on a gift for myself from which I will gain no particular pleasure. If we assume that my grandmother deserves—in the morally relevant way—some happiness, and that receipt of the gift would make her happy, we may find that a1 maximizes desert adjusted utility. Let us assume that neither a2 nor a3 would yield as much desert adjusted utility.

Schematically the case looks like this: since a1 uniquely maximizes desert adjusted utility, it is morally obligatory according to DAU. But since none of my alternatives would have any effect on the extent to which my fellow citizens receive their political economic deserts, each of my alternatives is permissible from the perspective of justice related obligation. I do not have a justice related obligation to give the gift to my grandmother. That is a private matter.

To find a case in which moral obligations as determined by DAU really conflict with justice-related obligations as determined in the described way, we need to think of someone who has the opportunity to affect the extent to which political economic deserts are received by citizens in his country. An example involving a king might illustrate this.

Suppose a king finds himself in a situation in which his moral obligation is clear: according to DAU, he morally ought to perform some action, a4. Performing a4 would maximize the extent to which those affected would receive the happiness they deserve (in the ways relevant to moral obligation). But suppose that in the very same situation the king finds that, if outcomes are evaluated according to PED, his justice-related obligation is to perform some incompatible act, a5. We may understand the question about priority to be a question about what the king ought to do in this situation of conflict between moral obligation and justice-related obligation. Which obligation takes priority?

Before we can answer this question we have to be sure that we understand what it means to say that some form of obligation "takes priority" over another. It should be obvious that we cannot define priority by saying that when moral obligation conflicts with justice-related obligation, then what we morally ought to do is whatever we are called to do by moral obligation. That claim would be utterly trivial. Of course we morally ought to do whatever we morally ought to do. Similarly, we cannot define priority by saying that when someone's moral obligation conflicts with his justice-related obligation, then what he ought to do in terms of justice-related obligation is whatever he is called to do by justice-related obligation. That claim would be equally trivial.

To explain priority, we need to assume that there is some further, or "higher" kind of obligation that comes into play when lower forms of obligation conflict. We can call this "just plain obligation."[11] It cannot be identified either with moral obligation or with justice-related obligation. But appeal to it might help to clarify the current problem.

We can take the claim that one sort of obligation, O1, takes priority over another sort of obligation, O2, as meaning that when obligations of type O1 conflict with obligations of type O2, then the agent *just plain ought* to do the act required by the type O1 obligation. The application to the present question is clear: to say that moral obligation takes priority over justice related obligation is, therefore, just to say that when these sorts of obligation conflict, the agent's *just plain* obligation is to do what he is morally obligated to do rather than to do the incompatible thing that he is obligated to do by the demands of justice. Similarly, to say that justice-related obligation takes priority over moral obligation is just to say that when these sorts of obligation conflict, the agent's *just plain* obligation is to do what he is obligated to do by the demands of justice.

I see no reason to suppose that moral obligation always takes priority in this sense over justice related obligation (or vice versa). Perhaps in some of these "heterogeneous deontic dilemmas" the agent's just plain obligation coincides with his moral obligation; in other cases perhaps it coincides with his justice-related obligation. Perhaps, as Ross suggested in a different context, the determination of which sort of obligation has priority in a given case would depend on the precise details of that specific case. The example involving the king was sketched in such an abstract way that no decision can be reached.

There are lots of different kinds of normative evaluation: for example, aesthetic evaluation of works of art in terms of beauty; virtue/vice theoretical evaluation of people in terms of excellence of character; epistemic evaluation of propositions in terms of worthiness of belief; etc. These are types of evaluation that are studied in different realms of philosophy: aesthetics, the ethics of character, epistemology. They involve evaluation of different subject matters: works of art, persons, propositions. They yield evaluation in terms of different sorts of normativity: beauty and ugliness; virtue and vice; worthiness

[11] I discussed the concept of just plain obligation back in 1986 in Chapter 9 of *Doing the Best We Can*. My aim there was to explain the first "ought" that appears in the question whether we always ought to do what we morally ought to do. For an insightful extended discussion of the meaning and role of just plain obligation see McLeod (2001: 269–91). McLeod cites several other philosophers who have written on the topic. McLeod points out (274–7) that one reason to believe in just plain obligation is that appeals to just plain obligation would be useful in explaining what is meant by saying that one sort of obligation takes priority over another in a "heterogeneous deontic dilemma."

and unworthiness of belief. I see no reason to think that acceptance of a given theory in one of these realms commits someone to acceptance of another theory in another of these realms. Each theory must be evaluated in its own realm by comparison to its own competitors. The same is true of PED and DAU. I happen to believe both of them, but I view them as independent theories in different realms of philosophy. In this book, I have been concerned to defend PED as a theory about the evaluation of states for political economic distributive justice. I have not been offering it as a theory about what we morally ought to do. Elsewhere I have defended DAU as a theory about that.

Bibliography

Abad, D. (2007), *Keeping Balance: On Desert and Propriety* (Frankfurt: Walter de Gruyter).

Ake, C. (1975), "Justice as Equality." *Philosophy & Public Affairs*, 5, 1: 69–89.

Anderson, E. S. (1999), "What is the Point of Equality?" *Ethics*, 109, 2: 287–337.

Aristotle, *Nicomachean Ethics* (trans. W. D. Ross). Available from: http://classics.mit.edu/Aristotle/nicomachaen.html.

Aristotle, *Politics* (trans. B. Jowett), Available from: http://classics.mit.edu/Aristotle/politics.html.

Arneson, R. J. (1989), "Equality and Equal Opportunity for Welfare." *Philosophical Studies*, 56: 77–93.

Arneson, R. J. (2000a), "Luck Egalitarianism and Prioritarianism." *Ethics*, 110: 339–49.

Arneson, R. J. (2000b), "Welfare Should Be the Currency of Justice." *Canadian Journal of Philosophy*, 30, R. J. (4): 497–524.

Arneson, R. J. (2001), "Luck and Equality." *Proceedings of the Aristotelian Society*, Supplement, 75: 73–90.

Arneson, R. J. (2003), "The Smart Theory of Moral Responsibility," in S. Olsaretti, ed., *Desert and Justice*, (Oxford: Oxford University Press).

Arneson, R. J. (2007), "Desert and Equality," in N. Holtug and K. Lippert-Rasmussen, eds., *Egalitarianism: New Essays on the Nature and Value of Equality* (Oxford: Oxford University Press): 262–93.

Arneson, R. J. (2011), "Luck Egalitarianism: A Primer," in C. Knight and Z. Semplova, eds., *Responsibility and Distributive Justice* (Oxford: Oxford University Press): 24–50.

Arnold, N. S. (1987), "Why Profits are Deserved." *Ethics*, 97: 387–402.

Arrhenius, G. (2003), "Feldman's Desert-Adjusted Utilitarianism and Population Ethics." *Utilitas*, 15, 2: 225–36.

Arrhenius, G. (2006), "Desert as Fit: An Axiomatic Analysis," in R. Feldman, K. McDaniel, J. R. Raibley and M. J. Zimmerman, eds., *The Good, the Right, Life and Death: Essays in Honor of Fred Feldman* (Aldershot: Ashgate).

Arrhenius, G. (2007), "Meritarian Axiologies and Distributive Justice," in T. Rønnow-Rasmussen, B. Petersson, J. Josefsson and D. Egonsson, eds, *Hommage à Wlodek:. Philosophical Papers Dedicated to Wlodek Rabinowicz.* www.fil.lu.se/hommageawlodek.

Avrahim, R. and Daniel Statman (2013), "More on the Comparative Nature of Desert: Can a Deserved Punishment Be Unjust?" *Utilitas*, 25, 3: 316–33.

Brandt, R. (1979), *A Theory of the Good and the Right* (Oxford: Oxford University Press).

Brandt, R. (1990), "The Science of Man and Wide Reflective Equilibrium." *Ethics*, 100: 259–78.

Brown, C. (2005), "Priority or Sufficiency…or Both?." *Economics and Philosophy*, 21: 199–220.

Brown, C. (2007), "Prioritarianism for Variable Populations." *Philosophical Studies*, 134: 325–61.

Carlson, E. (1997), "Consequentialism, Distribution and Desert." *Utilitas*, 9, 3: 307–18.

Casal, P. (2007), "Why Sufficiency is Not Enough." *Ethics*, 117, 2: 296–326.

Chisholm, R. M. (1964), "The Ethics of Requirement." *American Philosophical Quarterly*, 1: 147–53.

Chisholm, R. M. (1974), "Practical Reason and the Logic of Requirement," in Stephan Korner, ed., *Practical Reason* (Oxford: Blackwell): 1–17.

Chisholm, R. M. (1986), *Brentano and Intrinsic Value* (Cambridge: Cambridge University Press).

Clayton, M. W. (2010), "Justice and Distribution," in J. Skorupski, ed., *Routledge Companion to Ethics* (New York: Routledge).

Cohen, G. A. (1989), "On the Currency of Egalitarian Justice." *Ethics*, 99: 906–44.

Crisp, R. (2003), "Equality, Priority, and Compassion." *Ethics*, 113, 4: 745–63.

Christiano, T. (2007), "A Foundation for Egalitarianism," pp. 41–82 in N. Holtug and Kaspar Lippert-Rasmussen, eds., *Egalitarianism: New Essays on the Nature and Value of Equality* (Oxford: Oxford University Press).

Cummiskey, D. (1987), "Desert and Entitlement: A Rawlsian Consequentialist Account." *Analysis*, 47: 15–19.

Cupit, G. (1996a), "Desert and Responsibility." *Canadian Journal of Philosophy*, 26: 83–100.

Cupit, G. (1996b), *Justice as Fittingness* (Oxford: Clarendon Press).

DePaul, M. (1998), "Why Bother with Reflective Equilibrium?," in Michael DePaul and William Ramsey, eds., *Rethinking Intuition: The Psychology of Intuition and its Role in Philosophical Inquiry* (Lanham, MD: Rowman & Littlefield).

Duncan-Jones, A. (1952), *Butler's Moral Philosophy* (Harmondsworth: Penguin Books).

Dworkin, R. (1981a), "What Is Equality? Part 1: Equality of Welfare." *Philosophy and Public Affairs*, 10: 185–246.

Dworkin, R. (1981b), "What is Equality? Part 2: Equality of Resources." *Philosophy and Public Affairs*, 10: 283–345.

Dworkin, R. (2000), *Sovereign Virtue: The Theory and Practice of Equality* (Cambridge, MA: Harvard University Press).

Feinberg, J. (1963), *Social Philosophy* (Englewood Cliffs, NJ: Prentice-Hall).

Feinberg, J. (1970), "Justice and Personal Desert," in J. Feinberg, *Doing and Deserving: Essays in the Theory of Responsibility* (Princeton, NJ: Princeton University Press): 55–94. [First published in *Nomos*, VI (1963), eds. C. J. Friedrich and John W. Chapman (NY: Atherton), pp. 63–97; reprinted in L. P. Pojman and O.McLeod, eds. (1999), *What do we Deserve? A Reader on Desert and Justice* (NY: Oxford University Press): 70–83.]

Feinberg, J. (1974), "Noncomparative Justice. " *Philosophical Review*, 83: 297–338.

Feldman, F. (1987), *Doing the Best We Can: An Essay in Informal Deontic Logic* (Dordrecht, Reidel).

Feldman, F. (1992), *Confrontations With the Reaper* (Oxford: Oxford University Press).

Feldman, F. (1995a), "Adjusting Utility for Justice: A Consequentialist Reply to the Objection from Justice." *Philosophy and Phenomenological Research*, 55: 567–85.

Feldman, F. (1995b), "Desert: Reconsideration of Some Received Wisdom." *Mind*, 104: 63–77.

Feldman, F. (1995c), "Justice, Desert, and the Repugnant Conclusion." *Utilitas*, 7: 189–206.

Feldman, F. (1996), "Responsibility as a Condition for Desert." *Mind*, 105: 165–8.

Feldman, F. (1997), *Utilitarianism, Hedonism, and Desert* (Cambridge: Cambridge University Press).

Feldman, F. (2010), *What Is This Thing Called Happiness?* (Oxford: Oxford University Press).

Frankfurt, H. (1987), "Equality as a Moral Ideal." *Ethics*, 98: 21–43.

Franfurt, H. (2015), *On Inequality* (Princeton: Princeton University Press).

Freeman, S., ed. (2003), *The Cambridge Companion to Rawls* (Cambridge: Cambridge University Press).

Fried, B. H. (2014), "The Unwritten Theory of Justice: Rawlsian Liberalism versus Libertarianism," in Jon Mandle and David A. Reidy, eds., *A Companion to Rawls* (Malden, MA: John Wiley and Sons, Inc.): 430–49.

Galston, W. (1992), *Justice and the Human Good* (Chicago, IL: University of Chicago Press).

Hare, R.M. (1973), "Rawls' Theory of Justice." *Philosophical Quarterly*, 23: 144–55; 241–51.

Hobbes, *Leviathan*, modernized by Jonathan Bennett found at: http://www.woldww.net/classes/General_Philosophy/Hobbes_on_the_state_of_nature.htm.

Hoffman, J. (1993), "A New Theory of Comparative and Noncomparative Justice." *Philosophical Studies*, 70: 165–83.

Holtug, N. and Kaspar Lippert-Rasmussen (2007), *Egalitarianism: New Essays on the Nature and Value of Equality* (Oxford: Oxford University Press).

Holtug, N. (2007), "Prioritarianism," in N. Holtug and K. Lippert-Rasmussen, eds., *Egalitarianism: New Essays on the Nature and Value of Equality* (Oxford: Oxford University Press): 125–56.

Holmgren, M. (1986), "Justifying Desert Claims: Desert and Opportunity." *Journal of Value Inquiry*, 20: 265–78.

Hospers, J. (1961), *Human Conduct* (1st ed.) (New York: Harcourt, Brace & World).

Hurka, T. (1999), "The Three Faces of Flourishing," in Ellen Frankel Paul, Fred D. Miller, Jr, and Jeffrey Paul, eds., *Social Philosophy and Policy*, 16, 1 (Winter 1999), "Human Flourishing."

Hurka, T. (2001), "The Common Structure of Virtue and Desert." *Ethics*, 112: 6–31.

Hurka, T. (2003), "Desert: Individualistic and Holistic," in S. Olsaretti, ed., *Desert and Justice* (Oxford: Oxford University Press): 45–68.

Hurley, S. (2001), "Luck and Equality." *Proceedings of the Aristotelian Society*, 75: 51–72.

Huseby, R. (2010), "Sufficiency: Restated and Defended." *Journal of Political Philosophy*, 118, 2: 178–97.

Kagan, S. (1999), "Equality and Desert," in L. Pojman and O. McLeod, eds., *What Do We Deserve?* (New York: Oxford University Press): 298–314.

Kagan, S. (2003), "Comparative Desert," in S. Olsaretti, ed., *Desert and Justice* (Oxford: Oxford University Press).

Kagan, S. (2006), "Indeterminate Desert," in K. McDaniel, J. Raibley, R. Feldman and M. Zimmerman, eds., *The Good, the Right, Life and Death: Essays in Honor of Fred Feldman* (Aldershot: Ashgate).

Kagan, S. (2013), *The Geometry of Desert* (Oxford: Oxford University Press).

Kleinig, J. (1971), "The Concept of Desert." *American Philosophical Quarterly,* 8: 71–8.

Knight, C. (2006), "The Metaphysical Case for Luck Egalitarianism." *Social Theory and Practice,* 32:173–89.

Knight, C. (2009), *Luck Egalitarianism: Equality, Responsibility, and Justice* (Edinburgh: Edinburgh University Press).

Knight, C. and Z. Semplova, eds. (2011), *Responsibility and Distributive Justice* (Oxford: Oxford University Press).

Lake, C. (2001), *Equality and Responsibility* (Oxford: Oxford University Press).

Lamont, J. (1994), "The Concept of Desert in Distributive Justice." *The Philosophical Quarterly,* 44: 45–64.

Lamont, J. and Favor, C. (2008), "Distributive Justice," in E. N. Zalta, ed., *Stanford Encyclopedia of Philosophy* (Fall 2008 ed.). Retrieved from: http://plato.stanford.edu/archives/fall2008/entries/justice-distributive.

Leibniz, G. W. (2007 [1697]), "On the Ultimate Origination of the Universe," trans. Jonathan Bennett: http://www.earlymoderntexts.com/authors/leibniz.

Lippert-Rasmussen, Kasper (2014), "Justice and Bad Luck," in E. N. Zalta, ed., *Stanford Encyclopedia of Philosophy.* Retrieved from: http://plato.stanford.edu/entries/justice-bad-luck.

Mandle, Jon, and David A. Reidy, eds. (2014), *A Companion to Rawls* (Malden, MA: John Wiley and Sons, Inc.)

Marx, Karl (1875), "Critique of the Gotha Program", pp. 112–32 in Lewis S. Feuer, ed., *Marx & Engels: Basic Writings on Politics & Philosophy* (NY, Garden City: Anchor Books 1959).

Mason, A. (2012), "What Is the Point of Justice?" *Utilitas,* 24, 4: 525–45.

McLeod, O. (1995), *On Being Deserving* (dissertation submitted at the University of Massachusetts at Amherst).

McLeod, O. (1996), "Desert and Wages." *Utilitas,* 8: 205–21.

McLeod, O. (1999a), "Desert and Institutions," in L. J. Pojman and O. McLeod, eds., *What Do We Deserve?: A Reader on Desert and Justice* (New York: Oxford University Press): 186–95.

McLeod, O. (1999b), "Contemporary Interpretations of Desert," in L. J. Pojman and O. McLeod, eds., *What Do We Deserve?: A Reader on Desert and Justice* (New York: Oxford University Press): 61–9

McLeod, O. (2001), "Just Plain 'Ought'." *The Journal of Ethics,* 5, 4: 269–91.

McLeod, O. (2003), "On the Comparative Element in Justice," in S. Olsaretti, ed., *Desert and Justice* (Oxford: Oxford University Press).

McLeod, O (2006), "Adjusting Utility for Justice: A Reexamination of the Connections between Desert and Intrinsic Value," in K. McDaniel, J. Raibley, R. Feldman and M. Zimmerman, eds., *The Good, the Right, Life and Death: Essays in Honor of Fred Feldman* (Aldershot: Ashgate).

McLeod, O. (2008), "Desert," in E. N. Zalta, ed., *Stanford Encyclopedia of Philosophy* (Winter 2008 ed.). Retrieved from: http://plato.stanford.edu/archives/win2008/entries/desert.

Mill, J. S. (1998) [1861], *Utilitarianism*, ed. R. Crisp (Oxford: Oxford University Press).

Miller, D. (1976), *Social Justice* (Oxford: Oxford University Press).

Montague, P. (1980), "Comparative and Noncomparative Justice." *Philosophical Quarterly*, 30: 131–40.

Moore, G. E. (1903), *Principia Ethica* (Cambridge: Cambridge University Press), [original edition].

Moore, G. E. (1993), *Principia Ethica: Revised Edition*, ed. and Introd. Thomas Baldwin (Cambridge: Cambridge University Press).

Nagel, T. (1973), "Equal Treatment and Compensatory Discrimination." *Philosophy and Public Affairs*, 2: 348–63.

Nagel, T. (1991), *Equality and Partiality* (Oxford and New York: Oxford University Press).

Nielsen, K. (1981a), "A Rationale for Egalitarianism." *Social Research*, 48, 2: 260–76.

Nielsen, K. (1981b), "Impediments to Radical Egalitarianism." *American Philosophical Quarterly*, 18, 2: 121–9.

Nozick, R. (1974), *Anarchy, State, and Utopia* (New York, NY: Basic Books).

Olsaretti, S., ed. (2003), *Desert and Justice* (Oxford: Oxford University Press).

Olsarettti, S. (2002a), "Desert and Luck," in D. Bell and A. de Shalit, eds., *Forms of Justice* (New York: Rowman & Littlefield).

Olsaretti, S. (2002b), "Unmasking Equality: Kagan on Equality and Desert." *Utilitas*, 14: 387–400.

Olsaretti, S. (2004), *Liberty, Desert and the Market: A Philosophical Study* (Cambridge: Cambridge University Press).

Parfit, D. (1984), *Reasons and Persons* (Oxford: Clarendon Press).

Parfit, D. (1991), "Equality or Priority? The Lindley Lectures." (Lawrence, KS: University of Kansas Press).

Parfit, D. (1997), "Equality and Priority." *Ratio*, 10, 3: 202–21.

Persson, I. (1996), "Feldman's Justicized Act Utilitarianism." *Ratio*, 9: 39–46.

Persson, I. (1997), "Ambiguities in Feldman's Desert-adjusted Values." *Utilitas*, 9, 3: 319–27.

Pojman, L. P.,and O. McLeod, eds. (1999), *What do We Deserve?: A Reader on Desert and Justice* (New York: Oxford University Press).

Pummer, Theron (unpublished), "The Priority Monster." Available at: https://sites.google.com/site/tgpummer.

Rachels, J. (1978), "What People Deserve," in J. Arthur and W. H. Shaw, eds., *Justice and Economic Distribution* (Englewood Cliffs: Prentice-Hall): 150–63.

Rawls, J. (1955), "Two Concepts of Rules." *The Philosophical Review*, 64: 3–13.

Rawls, J. (1971), *A Theory of Justice* (Cambridge, MA: Belknap Press).

Rawls, J. (1987), "Some Reasons for the Maximin Criterion." *The American Economic Review*, 64, 2, Papers and Proceedings of the Eighty-sixth Annual Meeting of the American Economic Association (May, 1974): 141–6.

Rawls, J. (1993), *Political Liberalism* (New York: Columbia University Press).

Rawls, J. (2001), *Justice as Fairness: A Restatement* (Cambridge MA: Harvard University Press).

Rendall, M. (2013), "Priority and Desert." *Ethical Theory and Moral Practice*, 16: 939–51.

Rescher, N. (1966), *Distributive Justice: A Constructive Critique of the Utilitarian Theory of Distribution* (New York: Bobbs-Merrill Co. Inc.).

Roemer, J. E. (1996), *Theories of Distributive Justice* (Cambridge: Harvard University Press).

Ross, W. D. (1930), *The Right and the Good* (Oxford: Oxford University Press).

Sadurski, W. (1985), *Giving Desert Its Due: Social Justice and Legal Theory* (Dordrecht: D. Reidel).

Sen, A. and Williams, B. eds. (1982), *Utilitarianism and Beyond* (Cambridge: Cambridge University Press).

Sher, G. (1987), *Desert* (Princeton: Princeton University Press).

Sidgwick, H. (1962), *The Methods of Ethics* (7th ed.) (London: Macmillan & Co. Ltd).

Skow, B. (2012a), "How to Adjust Utility for Desert." *Australasian Journal of Philosophy*, 90, 2: 235–57.

Skow, B. (2012b), "A Solution to the Problem of Indeterminate Desert." *Mind*, 121, 481: 37–65.

Skow, B. (2014), Review of Shelly Kagan, *The Geometry of Desert. Ethics*, 124, 2 (January 2014): 417–26.

Slote, M. A. (1973), "Desert, Consent, and Justice." *Philosophy and Public Affairs*, 2.4: 323–47.

Smilansky, S. (1996), "Responsibility and Desert: Defending the Connection." *Mind* 105: 157–63.

Sterba, J. (1974), "Justice as Desert." *Social Theory and Practice*, Special Issue of John Rawls's *A Theory of Justice* (Spring), 3, 1: 101–16.

Sverdlik, S. (1983), "The Nature of Desert". *Southern Journal of Philosophy*, 21: 585–94.

Tan, K-C. (2008), "A Defense of Luck Egalitarianism." *The Journal of Philosophy*, 105, 11: 665–90.

Temkin, L. (1993), *Inequality* (New York and Oxford: Oxford University Press).

Vallentyne, P. (1995), "Taking Justice Too Seriously." *Utilitas*. 7: 207–16.

Vallentyne, P. (2001), "Equality, Efficiency, and the Priority of the Worse-off." *Economics and Philosophy*, 16: 1–19.

Vallentyne, P. (2002), "Brute Luck, Option Luck, and Equality of Initial Opportunities." *Ethics*, 112: 529–57.

Vallentyne, P. (2011), "Nozick's Libertarian Theory of Justice," in R. M. Bader and J. Meadowcroft, eds., *The Cambridge Companion to Nozick's* Anarchy, State, and Utopia (Cambridge: Cambridge University Press): 145–67.

Van Parijs, P. (2003), "Difference Principles," in Samuel Freeman, ed., *The Cambridge Companion to Rawls* (Cambridge: Cambridge University Press): 200–40.

Woozley, A. D. (1973), "Injustice." *American Philosophical Quarterly Monograph*, 7: 109–22.

Young, R. (1992), "Egalitarianism and Personal Desert." *Ethics*, 102: 319–41.

Zaitchik, A. (1977), "On Deserving to Deserve." *Philosophy and Public Affairs*, 10: 370–88.

Index of Names

General Index

The manufacturer's authorised representative in the EU for product safety is Oxford University Press España S.A. of el Parque Empresarial San Fernando de Henares, Avenida de Castilla, 2 – 28830 Madrid (www.oup.es/en or product.safety@oup.com). OUP España S.A. also acts as importer into Spain of products made by the manufacturer.

www.ingramcontent.com/pod-product-compliance
Lightning Source LLC
LaVergne TN
LVHW011752200926
848484LV00003B/686

* 9 7 8 0 1 9 8 7 8 2 9 8 8 *